THERE GOES THE NEIGHBORHOOD

THERE GOES THE NEIGHBORHOOD

How Communities Overcome Prejudice
and Meet the Challenge
of American Immigration

Ali Noorani

Foreword by Juan Williams,
Fox News Political Analyst

With a New Preface by the Author

59 John Glenn Drive
Amherst, New York 14228

Published 2019 by Prometheus Books

Cover image © iStock Photo
Cover design by John Larson
Cover design © Prometheus Books

Inquiries should be addressed to
Prometheus Books
59 John Glenn Drive
Amherst, New York 14228
VOICE: 716–691–0133 • FAX: 716–691–0137
WWW.PROMETHEUSBOOKS.COM

23 22 21 20 19   5 4 3 2 1

The Library of Congress has cataloged the hardcover edition with:

Names: Noorani, Ali, 1973- author.
Title: There goes the neighborhood : how communities overcome prejudice and meet the
    challenge of American immigration / Ali Noorani ; foreword by Juan Williams.
Description: Amherst, New York : Prometheus Books, 2017. | Includes index. |
    Description based on print version record and CIP data provided by publisher;
    resource not viewed.
Identifiers: LCCN 2016050584 (print) | LCCN 2017012109 (ebook) |
    ISBN 9781633883086 (ebook) | ISBN 9781633883079 (hardback)
Subjects: LCSH: United States—Emigration and immigration—Social aspects. |
    Immigrants—United States—Social conditions. | United States—Ethnic relations.
    | Cultural pluralism—United States. | National characteristics, American. | BISAC:
    SOCIAL SCIENCE / Emigration & Immigration.
Classification: LCC JV6475 (ebook) | LCC JV6475 .N66 2017 (print) |
    DDC 304.8/73—dc23
LC record available at https://lccn.loc.gov/2016050584

ISBN 9781633885660 (paper) | ISBN 9781633885677 (ebook)

Printed in the United States of America

To my parents, Amjad and Najma Noorani

CONTENTS

PREFACE TO THE PAPERBACK EDITION

Since the original publication of *There Goes the Neighborhood* in 2017, President Donald Trump's "othering" of newcomers and refugees—to say nothing of his executive actions, legislative efforts, and brutal rhetoric—has permeated the nation's psyche to such an extent that it risks becoming an accepted norm. Quite frankly, President Trump's vision of an American neighborhood has no immigrants.

It doesn't have to be this way.

While darker forces have always lurked beneath the surface of our political life, three-quarters[1] of Americans still say immigration is a "good thing." They continue to believe that those who come seeking a better life ought to be able to stay, and to contribute. Dairy farmers in Twin Falls, Idaho; law-enforcement leaders in Storm Lake, Iowa; and pastors in Albertville, Alabama, still see immigrants and immigration as part and parcel of the American story.

Which is why I remain hopeful.

It's true that one does not have to look closely to see that the president wants to do more than end illegal immigration; his actions indicate a desire to severely curtail all immigration to the United States as we know it. From his comment about people coming from "shithole countries" to his claims that immigrants are stealing jobs and taking services to his administration's abhorrent treatment of migrant children along the US–Mexico border, the conversation Trump has placed in front of the American public—if not the world—is steeped in hatred and nationalism.

We have been led to believe that those fleeing violence, persecution, and hopelessness do not deserve a helping hand. That what is given to you, is what is taken from me. As a result, we are less curious about each other. Less respectful of each other. And the natural cleavages and growing tribalism in our politics only compounds the challenge.

As Adam Serwer observed in the *Atlantic*, "Once malice is embraced as a virtue, it is impossible to contain."[2] Our test, in the context of a president seeking to reshape the American identity in his own image, is to avoid falling into this trap. The angry disrespect that dominates our immigration debate and political discourse is a malice put forward as a virtue—a malice that undermines our nation's values. Instead of doing to others what we would have done to us, we separate immigrant families at the border, treat asylum seekers as criminals, and claim that our nation is being invaded.

Therefore, how communities overcome prejudice and meet the challenge of American immigration is more important to our national character than ever before. Why? Because the challenge is only going to grow.

Technological advances will continue to transform industries, the nature of work, and the livelihoods of millions of American workers. Poverty, violence, and climate change will push more people to migrate at record numbers, for generations to come. All of this will test our politics, our norms, and our role in the world. Our current crop of policymakers, from both sides of the aisle, are, for different reasons, unwilling to address these challenges. Legislative gridlock makes for a convenient relief valve that allows one side to blame the other—while compromise remains elusive and our policies continue to stagnate.

Left in the lurch is what the research-and-advocacy organization More in Common has identified as the "exhausted majority." In its comprehensive 2018 study of the American public, More in Common characterized this exhausted majority as a population "fed up by America's polarization."[3] It continued: "They know we have more in common than that which divides us: our belief in freedom, equality, and the pursuit of the American dream. They share a deep sense of gratitude that they are citizens of the United States. They want to move past our differences."

These findings from More in Common underscore what I discovered while traveling the country in recent years: Between the deeply polarized wings of the American public lies the potential to reclaim the American story.

The problem is that, when it comes to immigration, it is easier for us to look to our screens instead of our scripture, to *Fox & Friends* instead of our friends and family, to walls instead of bridges.

So, looking back and peering forward, the pastors, police chiefs, and business owners in *There Goes the Neighborhood* are more than messengers of a different conversation. Rather, they are acting in heroic ways to challenge their own assumptions, to help their communities understand a changing America, and, ultimately, to create a nation that is just and good.

And, even since publication, the heroes continue to emerge—helping us to rediscover our sense of pride in the narrative of America.

Dr. Eric Costanzo, senior pastor of South Tulsa Baptist Church, is one example. He and his son, Noah, joined me for an immigration meeting in New York City during the fall of 2018. Their post-event plans to tour the Big Apple were cut short by a bomb scare that trapped them in a holding area outside the offices of CNN. The Tulsa Fox News affiliate heard about their ordeal and later sat down with Eric and Noah for a news segment.

In describing their harrowing experience, Eric shared that the immigration event they had left before getting caught up in the bomb scare was a setting where, "We were just discussing some of the difficult topics around immigrant and refugee issues."[4]

Expanding on this theme, eleven-year-old Noah told the reporter, "At our immigration meeting, they would sit down and listen to you; but the complete opposite happened with this person [who was responsible for the bomb scare]."

"Right now that hateful, volatile, careless language . . . it's happening at every level," said Eric. "I do know that this kind of thing raises my personal awareness to choose very wisely what I say and how I say it." For Eric, whether it was in his family or in his church, he would not allow the malice driving our nation's immigration debate to define the promise of America.

Or, take the example of Tess Clark, a conservative evangelical woman in suburban Dallas. In an October 2018 interview with the *New York Times*, Tess "began to weep as she recalled visiting a migrant woman detained and separated from her daughter at the border."[5] Tess confessed that "she was 'mortified' at how she used to vote, because she had only considered abortion policy. 'We've been asleep. Now, we've woke up.'" Conservativism, for Tess, was no longer about one issue. Through her experience, and her faith, she sought a different type of leadership from policymakers.

Tess, Noah, and Eric remind us that Americans of conscience are called to take on new types of leadership during this extraordinary chapter in our national story.

They, like the individuals you will meet in *There Goes the Neighborhood*, are not working just to contain malice. Rather, by working with and within conservative communities victim to the rhetoric of anger and fear, they seek to transform it. And they do so with true virtues: compassion, empathy, and—most of all—courage.

If they are successful, if we are successful, the United States will remain a nation of laws and a nation of grace for generations to come.

FOREWORD
Juan Williams

Fox News political analyst and
author of several bestselling books, including
We the People and *Eyes on the Prize*

To a little boy, the whole idea of an immigrant becoming a citizen does not make sense.

I can tell you. I was that little boy.

In the 1960s, PS 241, my elementary school in Brooklyn, New York, drew kids from a working-class neighborhood that was a mix of Irish, Italian, and Jewish, with a steady influx of blacks moving in as the whites began to move out.

Add to that vortex of people a whole lot of immigrants, including my family. In 1958, my mother brought my brother, my sister, and me—I was four year old—from Colón, Panama, to Brooklyn.

As a family of people with roots in Panama, Jamaica, and Trinidad, we had dark skin.

But we had a different life experience than black Americans who had come to Brooklyn from the south in the fifties, with its hard rules of black-white segregation.

And our life story was different than Jewish families, many of whose parents had escaped Nazi oppression and the Holocaust in the 1940s.

In a nation with a sharp color line separating blacks and whites, we racially identified with black people. But on the street, the reality was that immigrants, black, brown, Irish, Italian, and Jewish families, often a first- or second-generation newcomer, share a common identity: newcomers striving to find success in the new land.

So at school, at the playground, and in church I knew people with different family stories, but I did not know who was a citizen. I could not tell who was born here or arrived here as a child. And I had no clue as to who was here illegally, lacking proper immigration papers. What I knew was who could run fast, who was smart, who was a bully, and who spoke a different language. Most of all, I knew who was a friend.

In *There Goes the Neighborhood* Ali Noorani sees real people inside all the political camps—advocates and opponents—surrounding the immigration issue.

This book reminds me that as a child I had no idea which day I went from "immigrant" to "naturalized citizen." It did not change my identity or my friends.

It made no difference to my teachers or the old man who sold me a fresh slice of pizza. We were all living in Brooklyn and trying to make it in America. We watched the same TV shows; rooted for the baseball team; listened to Elvis, the Beatles, and Motown; and cried together when President Kennedy was assassinated.

Noorani brings that realism to the heated debate over immigration. Told as a series of vignettes from his own work as a policy advocate, in this book Noorani discusses political, faith, and business leaders who are already harnessing their values to fight for the reform needed to get America back on track on the immigration issue on the federal, state, and local levels.

He talks to businessmen, clergy, and police—as well as immigrants and their advocates—about solutions to the fierce fights over the rising number of immigrants and the changes they bring to twenty-first-century America.

In this book, there is no sugarcoating the fearful view of immigrants as people who are taking jobs or draining the local tax base. The painful arguments are alive and very real in these pages.

But Noorani takes readers beyond the fears to the people living with the reality of immigration and looking for realistic solutions. Here are real people who are immigrants. And here are real Americans living with immigrants—some wear badges, others hold bibles, and still others run businesses that hire immigrants or serve immigrants as their customers.

What they all want to do is get beyond the rhetoric and politics dividing Americans over immigration reform.

This book does not get sidetracked by unfocused calls for compassion as well as apocalyptic visions of a nation with no borders. It is more than angry calls to build border walls, alarm over the growing number of Muslim immigrants, and pleas to let any immigrant stay. Yes, the polarizing voices are here, but so are the people seeking common ground and looking for realistic solutions that serve the nation.

It makes for an amazing journey and a fascinating book.

From personal experience, Noorani knows that US immigration involves more than partisan debates.

In 1971, two years before he was born, his parents moved from Pakistan to Livermore, California. His parents were among the many South Asians to benefit from Congress's 1965 immigration reform, the Hart-Celler Act. The new law opened the door to immigrants from places other than Western Europe.

Immigration reform is the reason Noorani was able to attend UC Berkeley and Boston University before becoming one of the nation's top immigration advocates. And it is the reason he can keep us holding on as we sweep along on the roller-coaster ride of anger and finger-pointing that often limits conversations about immigration—legal and illegal—in the United States.

Noorani finds stories of longtime residents and new arrivals treating each other as humans, not caricatures or ideologues. We see honest people finding common ground on an issue that has defeated Republicans and Democrats, the US Senate, and recently both President George W. Bush and President Barack Obama.

At one point, Noorani introduces us to a group of conservative Utah business leaders and politicians—mostly Mormons. At first they are uneasy with the idea of immigrants coming into their state. But steadily they become advocates of immigration reform as they begin to see the advantage in welcoming new arrivals who share their traditional values, such as respect for families, the free-market, and God.

Similarly, he writes about southern farmers who rely on immigrants to do planting and harvesting as a migrant labor force. As a matter of business, the farmers became opponents of a law in Alabama that required police to check a person's immigration status during any traffic stop if they seemed suspicious. The farmers had a financial interest in stopping the police from intimidating their Latino workers—too many of whom couldn't take the fear of deportation and were leaving the area, abandoning their jobs. Farmers, Noorani writes, have become "some of the most compelling politically and socially conservative spokespeople when it comes to immigrants."

He tells of the pro-life Christian Republican police sheriff of Lake County, Illinois, who initially attempted to increase enforcement of immigration policies and then, following a spiritual reawakening, lobbied for immigration reform. As he tells Noorani, "So much we share with Islam, especially evangelicals and conservative Catholics, we're both traditional marriage and pro-life and see the evils of pornography."

He tells the incredible story of a South Carolina town that is torn apart as it deals with its growing Latin American population, but suddenly comes together as longtime residents and newcomers come to know each other because someone comes up with the idea of offering language, parenting, and financial-literacy classes to these new community members.

So, for all the invective spewed over immigration in America today, Noorani finds moments of grace and miracles.

The key to creating those miracles, according to Noorani, is when advocates and opponents of immigration reform "meet people where they are" and not try to force anyone to adopt a whole new worldview.

The struggle over immigrant rights in the United States is as old as the nation itself.

In the years following the American Revolution, there were very few restrictions on who could immigrate to the country. Most of the colonists had come from Great Britain, with some from Germany, the Netherlands, France, and Sweden. As long as you were a white person, all that was required in the late 1700s was that you live in the country for two years before applying for citizenship in the new nation.

Things were different for nonwhites. Under the Naturalization Act of 1790, only "free white persons" could become citizens. According to historian Matthew Frye Jacobson, Congress debated every plank of the Naturalization Act except the "free white persons" clause.[1] It was just assumed that citizenship should be reserved for white immigrants.

The first mixing that changed the fabric of American ethnicity came in the middle of the 1800s, when more Germans as well as Irish Catholic immigrants began coming in large numbers to the young nation. While there were no federal laws barring their entry, that didn't stop discrimination at the hands of America's largely English, largely Protestant majority.

Signs on storefronts read "No Irish Need Apply." Would-be employers told them, "we want no micks here." Anti-immigrant, anti-Catholic sentiments even fueled the creation of an entire political party, the Know-Nothing Party. Among its one million members were the mayors of Boston, Chicago, Philadelphia, and San Francisco.[2]

As in the founding era, things were worse for nonwhites. When groups of Chinese immigrants who settled in California during the mid-nineteenth century allegedly caused trouble for white laborers, Congress passed an 1882 law banning Chinese laborers from immigrating to the United States.

In the early twentieth century, immigration laws were passed completely barring immigrants from China and many other Asian countries. Since immigrants who were not white could not become citizens, they could not vote and politicians had no reason to stand up for their rights.[3] In this environment, lawmakers also set up a national quota system that made it almost impossible for anyone outside Germany or the British Isles to immigrate.

The conversation shifted after World War II. With its victory, the United States became a symbol of freedom, equality, and democratic rights to the world. Discrimination against people who wanted to emigrate from eastern and southern Europe now came under attack, especially as people already in the United States asked to bring in family members from those countries.

In 1958, the Jewish Anti-Defamation League asked a young senator named John F. Kennedy to write an essay in defense of immigration reform. The Jewish group wanted reform because more Eastern European Jews could have been saved during the Holocaust if the United States had had a more liberal immigration policy.

As JFK pondered over what to write, he thought of the discrimination his nineteenth-century ancestors faced when they moved from Ireland to Boston to escape the potato famine. Even in the late 1950s, anti-Catholic prejudice among American Protestants threatened to end Kennedy's bid for president.

Kennedy's essay was published by the ADL in 1959, and then it was expanded into a book called *A Nation of Immigrants*, which was published after his death. In it, Kennedy wrote: "The Irish were the first to endure the scorn and discrimination later to be inflicted, to some degree at least, on each successive wave of immigrants by already settled 'Americans.'"[4] Thus he argued that "immigration policy should be generous; it should be fair; it should be flexible."

The Irish and Jews also found political support for their immigration-reform movement from groups of Italian, Greek, Polish, and Portuguese immigrants. While we tend to think of immigration reform as a minority issue, the fact is that 1960s immigration reform was spearheaded not by racial minorities but by white European Americans.

In July 1963, JFK sent Congress a proposal for immigration reform. Though he was assassinated before the bill could become a law, that mantle was soon taken up by his brother Senator Ted Kennedy (D-MA), and it finally passed in June 1965 as the Immigration and Nationality Act. The 1965 law replaced the old system of strict quotas with one that stressed family reunification and skilled labor.

Proponents of the bill argued that it would not alter the ethnic makeup of America. They were wrong. In 2015, the Asian population as a percentage of the total US population was six times what it was in 1965.[5] The flow of Asian immigrants was matched and exceeded by Latin American immigrants who were fleeing poverty and oppression, as well as seeking jobs in the newly vibrant American Sunbelt. Non-Hispanic whites as a percentage of the entire US population decreased from 84 to 62 percent between 1965 and 2015.[6] These shifts have sparked fear, and at points anger, in the American public.

Today, immigration is a divisive, often painful political debate. With historically high levels of immigration—both legal and illegal—President Donald Trump called for mass deportation during his 2016 campaign.

As a result of these higher levels of immigration, people born in different countries can now be found in small towns, even in rural areas. They revive some neighborhoods, bring in ethnic food, compete for jobs and space in schools, use public services, and sometimes stir resentment.

According to a poll published in July 2016 by Vox and Morning Consult, almost 40 percent of American voters feel that legal immigration should be decreased.[7] The same poll found that roughly one half of American voters believe that immigrants are a "burden on our country," with just 34 percent saying that immigrants "strengthen" it. Fourteen percent worry that it "weakens American values."

A March 2013 poll by the Public Religion Research Institute and the Brookings Institution found that as many as four in ten Americans say that immigration—legal and illegal—weakens our values.[8]

You do not need polls to gauge how many of us feel about immigrants. Donald Trump's campaign promise—to Make America Great Again— does seem to gesture toward an era back before immigration reform, back before all of these Spanish speakers came over, back when America was, well, less diverse.

Yet the facts tell a different story.

Despite talk of an immigrant "crisis," the actual number of undocumented immigrants living in the country has decreased over the last few decades, from 12.2 million in 2007 to 11.1 million in 2014.[9]

Hardly a "suck" on the US welfare state, undocumented immigrants pay $11.6 billion in local and state taxes each year.[10] Immigrants live an average of 3.4 years longer than native-born Americans, are less likely to develop obesity, alcoholism, and depression, and are less likely to die from cardiovascular diseases or cancer.[11] Young immigrant men (ages 18 to 39) are sent to jail at roughly half the rate of native-born men of the same age.[12] And immigrant communities experience significantly less crime than predominately native-born neighborhoods.[13]

Although some claim that immigrants just come here to take American jobs, a report released in September 2016 by the National Academies of Sciences, Engineering, and Medicine found that in the long run, immigrants have a very insignificant effect on the wages of native-born Americans.[14] Surprisingly, the Americans whose wages are most significantly affected by new arrivals are other, former, immigrants. While it is true that immigrants come here seeking jobs, the jobs that they "take" are replaced with the jobs they create.

Census data from 1980 through 2000 suggest that "each immigrant on average generates 1.2 local jobs for local workers, most of them going to native-born workers,"[15] according to a 2015 paper written by economists from Indiana University and the University of Virginia. Just last year, the online magazine *Politico* ran a story about Bangladeshi immigrants who are rejuvenating Detroit, Michigan, with new businesses. Journalist Dana Goldstein writes of Ehsan Taqbeem, who immigrated to Detroit in the '80s, founded an auto company that now employs seventy workers, most of whom are white.[16]

Far from saving jobs for Americans, President Donald Trump's campaign proposal to reduce free trade has the potential to start a trade war that, according to a September 2016 study released by the Peterson Institute for International Economics, could take away more than four million American private-sector jobs.[17]

Contrary to the claim that they degrade American values, immigrants are less likely to divorce and have children out of wedlock than are native-born Americans.[18] According to the Pew Research Center, a higher percentage of immigrants than native-born Americans are self-employed.[19] Sergey Brin, cofounder of Google; Pierre Omidyar, founder of eBay; and Jerry Yang, cofounder of Yahoo, are all immigrants. If strong families and entrepreneurialism are not traditional American values, I'm not sure what is.

The point is this: Today's debate focuses too much on what we lose, and too little on what we gain, from new immigrants.

But through this book, with its stories of conservatives and liberals successfully working on immigration issues, there is a window into the world of possibilities and solutions. Noorani's vision is for an America in which any foreigner who is willing to work can come here legally. He too would like to see a pathway to citizenship for the 11 million undocumented immigrants currently living in the shadows.

He sees success through political collaboration, across party lines and over the divide between conservative and liberal churches. With all the noise, all the static and fog, surrounding immigration, here is an honest book to clear the path for America to get back to celebrating its stature as a "nation of immigrants."

CHAPTER ONE

ELECTIONS MATTER . . . CULTURE MATTERS MORE

It all began with a Jew, walking to work in the snow on a Saturday.

The US Capitol is a surprisingly long, ornate building littered with lost tourists, scurrying staffers, and entourage-trailing members of Congress. Tourists, representing every walk of life from every corner of the country, lose themselves (and their guides) in the overwhelming mix of past and present.

Look closely at the paintings, the statues, and the history, and you will see that the Capitol is more than a landmark. A building built by slaves and decorated with paintings by naturalized US citizens, it is a living, breathing testament to America's identity crisis.[1] For a few hours on Saturday, December 18, 2010, that identity crisis was defined by immigrants and immigration.

It was a cold morning, with a dusting of snow on the ground, and Congress was buzzing on a rare Saturday lame-duck session. The Senate was due to take up two high-profile pieces of legislation. One, the Development, Relief, and Education for Alien Minors (DREAM) Act, granting legal status to undocumented youth. The other, the repeal of "Don't Ask, Don't Tell" (DADT), a law barring gay and lesbian members of the armed services from expressing their sexual orientation.

At around 8:00 a.m., a door to a member's entrance opened, and a blast of cold air hit our small delegation of advocates waiting for the elevator. In walked Senator Joe Lieberman (D-CT), shaking the cold off his coat. On any other day, this would not be a big deal. On a Saturday, though, it was a big deal for Lieberman, an observant Jew, to be at the Capitol.

Lieberman straightened up in the warm air and looked at us with a "no need to lobby me, I'm with you" smile we immigration-advocate types rarely receive.

Over the course of his long political career, this was by no means the first time Senator Lieberman had worked on the Sabbath, so I don't want to overstate his decision. But when he walked through the door that morning, the faith he wore on his sleeve—and what it meant to him—stuck with me.

In that moment, I realized how an individual's culture could bring him to an unlikely place at an unlikely time. Little did I know that it was going to be that feeling, and everything that created that moment, that would mark a new path for my work. Looking back, I realize Lieberman's identity as an observant Jew was central to his values. While I have no reason to believe Lieberman crossed the line separating church and state, his culture and values clearly guided his decision making—a specific cultural perspective that would not have been welcome in the US Capitol not so long ago.

Looking forward, I know that immigration will contribute to an America that continues to change—racially, ethnically, and religiously. Along the way, Americans will continue to change, prompting an important question: As a nation, do we have a common identity or set of values?

Answering this question is a struggle at the national level as much as it is at the neighborhood level. Whatever our perspective may be, our culture, our families, and our work serve as a lens for our experiences, informing our answer to this question. Some of us become more exclusive, seeking barriers to cultural change and yearning for calmer days. Others become more inclusive, shaping relationships and institutions to welcome new cultures. Some of us toggle between the two. In my thirteen years as an immigration advocate, grappling with this question through a job that has opened up a new world of relationships, I have found that my identity shapes my work, and my work shapes my identity. I too have gone back and forth.

Personally, I would much rather cajole others into telling me their stories than tell my own. In fact, I'd rather do just about anything other than tell my own story. But it turns out that writing a book about our national identity means telling my own story as well.

My parents left Pakistan in 1971 to come to the United States. After I was born in 1973 in Santa Cruz, California, they moved forty miles to the south to Salinas, an agricultural town that was primarily white or Latino. As a child of immigrants growing up in a community with very few South Asian families, I learned the importance of cultural crossover early in life. As I befriended children of farmworkers and children of farm owners, I realized that people of all walks were more similar than they seemed. These formative years taught me to be observant, keep my mouth shut, and always look for common ground. By no means was I perfect in this endeavor.

I left Salinas in 1992 to study economics and social welfare at the University of California, Berkeley. After a year of work and travel, I headed east in 1998 to earn a master of public health degree from Boston University. Public health, specifically epidemiology and environmental health, led me to become active in Boston-area community organizations, and eventually I ran public-health programs for two large community health centers in the Dorchester neighborhood of Boston. Working with communities and colleagues from countries as far flung as Kenya, Vietnam, Haiti, El Salvador, and Ireland, among others, brought to light the struggle and tension between native-born and immigrant communities—foreshadowing what lay ahead. From there, I cut my immigration teeth as executive director of the Massachusetts Immigrant and Refugee Advocacy Coalition.

Two experiences from these early years of my professional life left deep impressions. The first was while I was in Dorchester. In the 1970s, the exodus of families from Vietnam led to a large community of refugees in the Fields Corner neighborhood of Dorchester. I remember vividly an event we organized at the Dorchester House at which Sarah Ignatius, the executive director of the Political Asylum/Immigration Representation Project, met with Vietnamese youth in the neighborhood. These were good kids. But a few of them had done kid things that had gotten them into trouble with the juvenile justice system. While being processed through that system, their public defenders had recommended they plead guilty and take probation or community service. In the conversation, I realized that these kids, who had been in America since they were babies, were much more American than Vietnamese. But even though they were in the

States legally, their guilty plea was a deportable offense—something many of their defense attorneys did not even realize. For a reason I didn't fully understand, America was deporting kids who, for all intents and purposes, were American.

The second experience took place in the basement of St. James Church, in New Bedford, Massachusetts. In 2007, after I had been at the Massachusetts Immigrant and Refugee Advocacy Coalition for a few years, there was a major immigration raid in New Bedford, about sixty miles south of Boston. Over three hundred men and women, sewing backpacks for the military, were put into deportation proceedings. Working with local partners, we established a relief center in the basement of the church. It was an awful scene that rattled my senses. As I wrote for the *Boston Globe*:

> How can we look into the eyes of a young mother who has fled the repressive government and economic perils of Guatemala to stitch safety vests for our troops, and tell her to leave? How can we look into the eyes of a young father of an eight-month-old baby [who is] dehydrated because his mother has been detained, and tell him he doesn't belong here?
>
> If we allow this to continue, we will turn our backs on liberty and the American dream. Irrational fears will only drive us to the wrong side of history. Let us live up to the dreams of every immigrant of every generation that had the courage to come to this country to make a better life for their families.[2]

In both of these situations, there was a struggle between old and new. In Dorchester, families who had been in Boston for generations chafed at the influx of immigrants and refugees. And during the New Bedford immigration raid, Greater Boston's talk-radio shows lit up with callers thrilled with the idea of hundreds of immigrants being deported. The lines of the debate simplified to left versus right, communities of color versus white residents. It was hard to see how a consensus could be forged that pulled the human story of immigration out of the raging political fire.

These experiences, personal and professional, heightened how I felt on that snowy December 2010 morning. I was deeply struck by the poignancy of a Jewish senator walking to work on the Sabbath. Maybe it was the

DREAM Act that drew Lieberman to the Senate on that Saturday, maybe it was the repeal of DADT. It was probably both. Either way, the issues at hand were important enough to him, and what he believed, that he was willing to cast his vote on the Sabbath.

Remember, Lieberman was retiring from the Senate at the end of the year. With no reelection to consider, he was truly voting his conscience. The challenge we faced that day was whether or not we had changed enough hearts and minds so a majority would vote their conscience and support the DREAM Act.

Let's fast-forward a few hours.

No. Wait. First, let's go back a couple years. A lot happened in that time that set a new political and cultural stage.

ELECTIONS MATTER

On November 4, 2008, with the help of record support from Latino and Asian voters, Barack Obama was elected the forty-fourth president of the United States.[3] For the first time in history, an African American would be the leader of the free world—and he had a foreign-born father.

This was running through my head that election night as I sat in a local bar in Washington, DC, listening to Obama's speech and watching the celebration. The tears in my eyes and the lump in my throat were about more than politics and anticipation of what may lie ahead. It was great to feel that, as a nation, we could elect Barack Hussein Obama to be president. I believed it was a fundamental turning point for the nation's approach to culture and identity—a turning point that was bigger than the president. I just didn't realize the turn would be for the worse.

The diverse coalition Obama marshalled to the polls also put the House and Senate in control of the Democrats, raising liberals' expectations for legislative reforms and many to believe a golden age of progressive change was upon the country. A new electorate had flexed its muscles in 2008 and ushered in what we thought was a new age of American politics.

But underneath the electoral results, the cultural churn was surfacing an anger that had been pushed out of the mainstream for decades. Obama's Republican opponent, Senator John McCain (R-AZ), with a long history of championing immigration reform, seemed perfectly placed to ease conservatives out of their defensive posture. As a moderate Republican with a strong track record of constructively engaging in the immigration debate, he could have been a formidable general-election candidate. But the Republican primary electorate was his undoing, as McCain was forced to take increasingly anti-immigrant positions. This strategy secured him the nomination but gave oxygen to extremist forces within the party so that the outreach and engagement of Latino voters from the George W. Bush years were cast aside. Soon, the Republican brand was tarnished in the eyes of Latino voters, and McCain's share of the Latino vote dropped nine points from President Bush's 2004 historic high for Republican candidates.[4]

While victory was sweet, I didn't realize McCain's lurch to the right cut far deeper than just politics. It was cultural. A significant portion of the American electorate felt that their country had been taken away. The campaign-trail accusations that Obama was not a US-born citizen, and that he was a Muslim, led to a sense by many that he represented foreign, not American, interests. Who and what this powerful segment of Republican voters identified as American, demographically and culturally, was being challenged. And the anger they directed at, and through, McCain was a harbinger of things to come.

At the time, of course, as a card-carrying liberal, I was pretty excited. I saw the potential for incredible change. With the Democratic supermajority in control of the Senate and Speaker Nancy Pelosi in the House, we assumed it was a matter of *when*, not if, immigration reform would be passed. Which, for me, meant 11 million people living in the shadows as undocumented immigrants would get on a path to citizenship, a functioning legal immigration system that met the needs of our families and our economy, and the days of home- or workplace-invasion immigration raids like what I saw in New Bedford would come to an end. In short, it meant Congress would finally take action to value immigrants and immigration.

It was in this tumultuous period of political transition that I spent my first year in Washington, DC, as executive director of the National Immigration Forum. My predecessor was Frank Sharry; the effective and effusive leader of the Forum for sixteen years had taken the organization to national prominence. At thirty-five years old, I was a young outsider who didn't have much of an idea of how Washington, DC, worked, but I had good relationships across the country. Surrounded by great staff and generous allies who knew the town, I settled into the role and we started planning for what we hoped would be great things to come with the Obama administration.

In the first two years of the Obama administration, the Forum was the managing organization of a national campaign to execute a left-leaning strategy and mobilize the progressive base. The campaign coalition, which I chaired and my colleague, Rich Stolz, managed, Reform Immigration for America, resourced crucial immigrant rights and progressive organizations that were executing a range of strategies to advocate for immigration reform. Just as important, the campaign seeded new organizations in emerging communities and built out the first high-profile digital presence for the movement. From Arizona to New Hampshire, Alaska to Maine, we protested and pressured, we chanted and cheered. It was the best of times. Sort of.

But President Obama and congressional Democrats invested their political capital in the effort to reform the nation's healthcare system: capital that was quickly spent down through a difficult and contentious debate to pass the Affordable Care Act. Encouraged by our progressive allies to be patient, the immigrant rights community waited on the sidelines as the fight for Obamacare proceeded. But this became increasingly difficult as the administration doubled down on immigration enforcement measures, hoping to prove their "rule-of-law" mettle to skeptical Democrats and obstinate Republicans.

President George W. Bush could have told Obama he was making a tactical mistake. For example, the 2007 New Bedford, Massachusetts, raid was an instance of Bush flexing enforcement muscle to bring Republicans and business to the table. It was a failed strategy. The legislative effort that followed was still unable to get enough Republican votes to pass. All that resulted was the deportation and separation of hundreds of families. The undocumented were pushed further underground, subject to greater exploitation by unscrupulous employers who were able to push down wages and protections for immigrants and US workers alike. Employers trying to play by the rules were unable to compete with unscrupulous employers who put forward lower bids for jobs. You would be hard-pressed to find Republican members of Congress who agreed it was time to legalize 11 million undocumented people, because immigration enforcement was working too well.

While Obama did not replicate the heavy-handed deportation raids of the Bush administration, it was clear he believed an enforcement-centric approach would curry favor and trust with members whose votes he would need. Unfortunately, the Obama administration did not anticipate his opposition's ability to sow public doubt, fear, and mistrust in his actions. For our part, while we pressured the Republicans, we aimed most of our ire at the Democrats. We believed that they could do more to force the question. We believed the political power of the movement should be respected and rewarded. We failed to understand the seriousness of the nation's cultural crisis. We were having a *political* debate when the country was having a *cultural* debate.

The administration's immigration-enforcement measures exacted an enormous toll. As the Department of Homeland Security interior and border-enforcement budget grew to nearly $18 billion fiscal year 2012, deportation numbers grew well beyond what the community anticipated from the nation's first African American president—a president supported in record numbers by new American voters.[5] It seemed like every day there were news reports of detentions and deportations, along with heart-wrenching stories of families separated by immigration-enforcement actions. Over the course of 2009, as the advocacy community was locked in a case-by-case battle with Homeland Security, the excitement of Obama's election turned to disappointment and frustration, which meant there was no way to mobilize a base of support. In this moment, we didn't even think about engaging moderates and conservatives who had not yet taken a position on immigration reform. As Obama's first year in office drew to a close, our tension with the administration neared a boiling point. And on the right, an unpredictable new power emerged from the ashes of McCain's defeat: the Tea Party.

The cultural anxiety Obama's election triggered led to the radicalization of a loud minority of nativist voters and their representatives, who stridently opposed immigrants and immigration. In late 2009, this nativist anger found a new set of powerful allies in the burgeoning Tea Party movement. There were some initial attempts by Tea Party leadership to diversify their movement and begin to consider types of immigration reforms. In fact, I was invited by Tea Party Patriots president Jenny Beth Martin to coordinate a panel on immigration at their 2010 public-policy conference in Arizona. The Tea Party membership was having none of it, the panel did not go over well, and the organization soon joined forces with the nativist anti-immigrant movement.

With Democrats controlling the federal levers of power in 2009–2010, anti-immigrant extremists embarked on a state legislative strategy to further exacerbate the cultural divide that served their purposes. Of course, while the US Constitution's Article 1, section 8, clause 4 reads, "The Congress shall have Power to establish a uniform Rule of Naturalization," so was former House Speaker Tip O'Neill when he said, "All politics is local."[6]

We were about to learn this lesson in harsh terms—not only with regards to legislative change, but also with regards to culture change.

CULTURE MATTERS MORE

In January 2010, Arizona State Senator Russell Pearce (R-Mesa) introduced the "Support Our Law Enforcement and Safe Neighborhoods Act," which is commonly known as SB 1070, or more derisively as the "show me your papers" law. According to the National Council of State Legislatures, it included "provisions adding state penalties relating to immigration law-enforcement including trespassing, harboring and transporting illegal immigrants, alien registration documents, employer sanctions, and human smuggling."[7] More simply, if a pastor was giving a ride to an undocumented immigrant from their church, the pastor would face state penalties.

Arizona was simultaneously the most likely and the most unlikely place for legislation like SB 1070. Families that have lived in the Southwest for generations valued the ethnic diversity of the region and were surprised and dismayed by SB 1070. However, those who moved to the region more recently viewed their new neighbors (down the street or south of the border) with fear and anger. It seemed that retirees to Arizona from other parts of the United States (their own type of migrants) were not used to living in a racially and ethnically diverse community. And on top of these cultural concerns, the state economy had been slow to recover from the recession. The unemployment rate peaked at 11.2 percent in December 2009 and remained above 10 percent over the course of 2010; in both years, this was roughly a point higher than the national rate of unemployment.[8] Anxiety and fear stemming from the economy, race, and class created a toxic brew for Arizona.

Furthermore, Arizona's proximity to Mexico fed the perception that drugs and violence were streaming across the border. Stories of positive contributions by Latinos were drowned out by breathless media reports of the drug-trade-motivated conflicts, which were happily amplified by a national conservative media machine that drew fiery attention to the state's immigration drama. All of this is to say that under the leadership of newly appointed Republican Governor Jan Brewer, Arizona became the epicenter of America's identity crisis.

As we entered 2010, the political environment became more tense. Obamacare was on the move, special elections were underway, and the immigrant community continued to agitate for movement on legislation. At the national level, given the shrinking legislative calendar and the threat of SB 1070, we acted with a new level of urgency, laying plans to organize a rally on the National Mall on March 23, 2010, to pressure the White House and Congress. Meanwhile, four DREAMers (undocumented youth) from Florida took matters into their own hands. Felipe Matos, Gaby Pacheco, Carlos Roa, and Juan Rodriguez left their homes in Miami on January 1, 2010, to walk 1,500 miles to the US Capitol.[9]

In early 2016, journalist Jorge Ramos and I sat in his Univision office in Miami, discussing that moment back in 2010 and the emergence of the DREAMers. Jorge's short, gray hair and slight build is offset by piercing eyes and a clip to his voice. Because he has been a national nightly news anchor for decades, and one of the most trusted members of the Latino community, there is a symbiotic relationship between the power of the Latino vote and the power of the seat Ramos occupies. Over the years, he has confronted political leadership from both parties and has taken on the most aggressive of conservative cable news commentators. He has an ability to speak truth to power, and whoever holds that power—whether they are Latino, white, Democrat, or Republican. He is the Walter Cronkite of the Latino community.

Looking back on 2010, Ramos told me, "My real heroes are the DREAMers."[10] DREAMers were people who supported the DREAM (Development, Relief, and Education for Alien Minors) Act, which would provide a path to citizenship for minors. He explained, "I think they are the ones who risked everything and who gained the most in this struggle. Who would have thought that four undocumented immigrants, in 2010, walking along all the way from Miami to Washington, would create a movement that would force the president of the United States to change his position?"

Their "Trail of Dreams" took these four young people through communities across the Southeast, and they shared their story with supporters and opponents alike in a region experiencing the tensions that came with the some of the fastest growth in the foreign-born population.[11]

DREAMer Carlos Roa reflected on his walk in the *Guardian* on April 12, 2016: "Working with other courageous youth facing similar issues, I understood that education and our active involvement in politics were the main drivers that would protect us. . . . Our objective was to call attention to mass deportations nationwide and to demand an executive order halting the deportations of Dreamers—the walk served as a catalyst for the movement of that same name."[12]

It was a courageous strategy that circumvented national advocates' hand-wringing and introduced faces of people who not only were personally impacted by the broken immigration system but also represented the community in a fully bilingual, bicultural fashion—which is a key part of their story. When they spoke, they sounded like someone's neighbor or schoolmate. They were DREAMers, but they were just as "American" as anyone else. They were smart, funny, willing to listen, and genuinely empathetic to those they met along their walk, including opponents to immigrants and immigration. These four DREAMers were willing to engage people on their terms.

The Trail of Dreams was one of the first purely culture-changing strategies borne of the immigrant rights movement. These youths were not working through organizations led by non-immigrants. They were inserting their own voices and own stories into the debate. As Ramos put it, "They became proud to be undocumented. That was a huge cultural change, because they went from hiding to actual power."[13] It set in motion a level of leadership by DREAMers that began to humanize what was until then an abstract policy issue. A part of the identity question was being answered by the undocumented community themselves.

Meanwhile, the growing anger and urgency of the immigrant community mirrored the emotional climate of those working to repeal Don't Ask, Don't Tell. On March 18, 2010, Lt. Dan Choi broke away from a rally organized by national gay-rights organizations, marched to the White House, and, joined by former army infantryman Jim Pietrangelo, chained himself to the gates until he was arrested.[14] Lt. Choi's Trail of Dreams may not have covered several hundred miles, but it had just as deep an impact.

In Choi's words, "You have been told that the President has a plan. But Congressman Barney Frank confirmed to us this week that the President still is not fully committed to repealing Don't Ask, Don't Tell this year. And if we don't seize this moment it may not happen for a very long time."[15] Choi's action changed public perception of Don't Ask, Don't Tell. As an Iraq War veteran, he put forward a compelling story that Americans could understand. He didn't allow himself to be co-opted by any party or process. The gay community may have donated money to the Obama presidential campaign, but their strategy was not electoral. Choi and his allies understood the cultural context of the moment and seized their opportunity.

Three days later, on March 21, 2010, our rally took place. Over two hundred thousand immigrants and their supporters gathered on the National Mall for what we billed the "March for America." It was a show of force that exceeded our expectations, as throngs of immigrants from across the country proudly waved the American flag, and leaders jockeyed for space on the speakers list. Congressman Luis Gutierrez (D-IL), one of the most trusted and revered leaders in the Latino community, mirrored Lt. Choi's frustration with the Obama administration when he told the crowd, "We've listened quietly. We've asked politely. We've turned the other cheek so many times our heads are spinning."[16]

At the other end of the Mall, another rally took place that day. The Affordable Care Act, commonly known as Obamacare, was up for final consideration. The Tea Party, made up of people confronted by a new America they did not understand and a bill they deeply disliked, marched on the Capitol to express their opposition. At this rally there were reports of racial insults, spitting at members of Congress, and a level of anger few had ever witnessed.[17] On that day, the immigration and healthcare rallies were polar opposites in every way imaginable.

Lawrence Downes of the *New York Times* described the scene:

> Kill the bill. It throbbed in the ears, like an infection. I escaped it at the other end of the National Mall, at a rally that far eclipsed the Tea Party in size, hopefulness and decency.
>
> It's usually best to avoid depicting life in black-white contrast. Not this time. Here were two rallies: one good, one loathsome. One hopeful, one paranoid. One trying to repair how Washington works for all America, and one looking to break it so the system can go on failing.
>
> Kill the bill! Sí, se puede! Same beat, different drums. I'll take the one that rings with patience and hope. Sounds more American.[18]

The anger at the rally opposing Obamacare was the same anger blocking movement on immigration reform. We thought we could defeat this anger through political power, so we didn't try to understand it. We didn't realize how widespread it was or where it was coming from. We felt the immigration movement's electoral influence should lead to federal legislation—just like it had for healthcare reform. Whether or not we said it, we felt that if we tried to understand the anger, we were validating the anger.

We were wrong.

Because we did not understand the anger, we did not understand the country's identity crisis—much less develop a real strategy to address it.

Consequently, we left in the hands of the opposition the hearts and minds of those we could have persuaded to support reform.

Ramos told me matter-of-factly:

> There's no question that we are in the middle of a demographic revolution that is affecting everything, from the way we eat, to the way we dance, to the way we vote. So that's one of the big trends that I'm seeing. This trend has created two very different reactions. On one hand, millions of Americans embracing immigrants and embracing foreigners and embracing the changes, and a few other millions rejecting that change.
>
> . . .
>
> We didn't read the country correctly. We thought that the country was changing with us. We thought that little towns in America were being transformed, as we were being transformed. We thought that they were listening to our music and eating our food and agreeing with our arguments. But we were not paying attention. And that's what went wrong.[19]

As a result, the majority of Americans were overwhelmed by the warring talking points and dystopian data sets that made up a purely left-versus-right immigration debate. Much of this undecided middle understood the contributions and value of immigrants and immigration, but they also shared some of the economic and physical fears the nativists articulated. Today, they take part in the "full rejection"[20] Ramos described.

When Americans were looking for an answer to their question of cultural identity, we gave them a political answer instead.

UNLIKELY ALLIES IN UNLIKELY TIMES

Two days after the "March for America," President Obama signed the Affordable Care Act into law.

Thirty-three days after the "March for America," Governor Jan Brewer signed SB 1070 into law. She rationalized the law by telling the press, "Oh, our law-enforcement agencies have found bodies in the desert, either buried or just lying out there, that have been beheaded."[21]

PolitiFact found these claims to be not just false but "ridiculously false."[22] But the nativist train had already left the station.

Meanwhile, there was no sign of immigration legislation in Congress. Washington Democrats had abandoned immigrants, and Arizona Republicans had passed legislation very likely to have a disproportionate impact on brown people. In less than two years, we went from the giddy highs of electoral victory to the fear and loathing of legislative defeat. In the crossfire were 11 million undocumented immigrants fearful for their families, millions of legal immigrants wondering if this was the America they had imagined, and a political center that did not know which way to turn.

The 2009–2010 political environment had created a set of blinders; we were so focused on exerting the political power of the immigrant community that we lost sight of the broader American public. This meant that we missed not only the growth of the Tea Party movement but also the emergence of powerful new allies.

On May 12, 2010, CNN reported that a new group of conservative evangelicals were working together to craft consensus principles in favor of immigration reform.[23] And two days later, Dr. Richard Land, then president of the Ethics & Religious Liberty Commission of the Southern Baptist Convention, wrote, "Currently, the two extremes of deportation or amnesty are being played against each other, resulting in a stalemate in Congress and growing frustration and division in society."[24] He continued, "The recent passage of the new law in Arizona is a cry for help." Dr. Land laid out a conservative case for federal reform and treating the undocumented "in a manner that respects their innate dignity and humanity."

While the Convention's pro-reform position went back to a 2006 resolution, this was an important statement at a critical time.[25] As the largest non-Catholic denomination in the country, Southern Baptists are one of the biggest, most powerful conservative white constituencies. The emergence of evangelical support for immigrants—alongside consistent and growing advocacy by the Catholic Church—was an indication of things to come from white Christian America. In hindsight, the contours of a powerful coalition of secular progressives, who had long supported immigrant rights, joined by social conservatives who wielded a different sort of political power, had begun to take shape.

As important as these potential new allies were, the die had been cast for 2010, and we were not to see legislative action before the midterm election. Therefore, we turned our attention to the SB 1070 court battle and the midterm elections where Democrats hoped to retain control of the Senate. Second to Obamacare, immigrants and immigration was central to the political debate in the run-up to the election. The stakes were high. If the movement educated and mobilized a powerful base of opposition to SB 1070 and the candidates supporting it, a clear political statement would be made that neither the new Congress nor additional states should seek to replicate the Arizona law. If the movement failed, all bets were off.

With this in mind, Colorado and Nevada—two states with large numbers of Latino voters, slim margins of victory, and hotly contested races—were the points of focus. The Colorado race was between Democrat Michael Bennet, appointed to the seat in 2009, and Ken Buck, a Tea Party favorite who defeated former Lt. Governor Jane Norton in an acrimonious GOP primary. With a total price tag of over $15.5 million, the contest became the most expensive race in the country.[26]

Pressured by local immigrant activists, Bennet came out early, aggressively, and somewhat surprisingly for the DREAM Act. Surely, part of his decision was based on his history as Superintendent of the Denver Public Schools. Or perhaps he learned that there were 434,000 eligible Hispanic voters in Colorado, one in eight (13 percent of) eligible voters in Colorado are Latinos, and approximately 44 percent of Latinos in Colorado are eligible to vote.[27] Maybe it was a little of both.

Given the political environment and the insurgency of far-right Republicans, those were real numbers. Making Bennet's job easier, Buck doubled down on his approach and jumped at the opportunity to paint a stark contrast, stating his opposition to the DREAM Act and support for an enforcement-only approach. There was a clear choice between candidates, and Colorado's fast-growing Latino electorate was watching closely.[28] On election day, according to Latino Decisions exit polling, 81 percent of Latinos supported Bennet in his 28,859 vote victory.[29] Like I said, those were significant numbers.

Farther to the southwest, Republicans poured millions of dollars into Nevada, looking for a trophy in the form of a defeated Senate Majority Leader, Harry Reid. Although he told a gathering of thousands of Latinos and their allies on April 10, 2010, that "we're going to do immigration reform just like we did health care reform,"[30] Reid never greenlit legislation. But this was not his first rodeo, and he knew how to engage his Latino constituency.

Even better for Reid, his opponent, Sharron Angle, was viewed by many as a unique combination of unhinged and xenophobic. After running an ad criticizing Reid's immigration positions that featured three menacing-looking Latino men, Angle visited the Rancho High School Hispanic Union in Las Vegas. According to press reports, she said in response to a question about the ad, "You know, I don't know that all of you are Latino. Some of you look a little more Asian to me. I don't know that."[31]

I'm no political genius, but if one quarter of a state's population is Hispanic, I imagine you want to curry some amount of favor with them. Or at least not outright insult them. Ms. Angle clearly did not realize that, according to the Pew Research Center, approximately 672,000 Hispanics lived in Nevada.[32] Her sad attempt to clarify her intentions managed to trigger more than a political blowback. Over the course of her campaign, she motivated Latino voters to listen to what Jorge Ramos told me: "If you hide, you lose."[33] Her statements pushed Latinos in Nevada to assert their identities as both immigrants and Americans—through the ballot box.

Much to the surprise of pollsters who had predicted an Angle win, Reid went on to a blowout victory. He secured 90 percent of the state's Latino vote, which, according to Latino Decisions, contributed ten points to his victory.[34]

Two things happened in that 2010 midterm election. One, Republicans profoundly miscalculated the strength and tenacity of the Latino vote. They saw Republican legislative power to block reform and pass SB 1070 as a winning strategy. Second, Latinos built what Frank Sharry called a "'Latino firewall' in the West, in places like California, Colorado, and Nevada, [that] helped save the Senate for Democrats."[35]

More important, the establishment underestimated the strength of

Latino voters in nonpresidential election years. In fact, in both Colorado and Nevada, pollsters and pundits predicted Republican victories. Which led the famous *New York Times* statistical soothsayer, Nate Silver, to ask, "Did Polls Underestimate Democrats' Latino Vote?"[36] Based on the evidence, this was quite the rhetorical question.

Galvanized by this show of electoral force, there were renewed calls for legislative action when Congress returned to Washington, DC, after the election. As Edward Schumacher-Matos put it in a November 19, 2010, column "What Democrats Owe Latinos: Pass the DREAM Act," "only squeaky wheels get the oil, and the squeak among Hispanics is getting loud and angry."[37] The DREAMers demanded legislative action. They had changed the dynamics of the conversation and put their names and families in the public sphere. To the victor go the spoils.

We thought the pendulum had swung far enough in our direction this time. In our opinion, this was yet another election where Latino political power should equal legislative influence. Just as we were wrong earlier in 2010, we were wrong later in 2010. The underlying cultural challenge remained unsolved.

DECEMBER 18, 2010

All of this brings us back to the DREAM vote and that Saturday, December 18, 2010. After we saw Senator Lieberman entering the building, we sat watching from the upper galleries of the quiet US Senate chamber—no cell phones allowed. After months of organizing, and all the ups and downs that went with it, the DREAM Act was up for a vote; the legal status of millions of undocumented youth hung in the air; and we were cut off from the outside world. It made a tense situation nearly unbearable. But the movement, we thought, had secured the political upper hand, and victory was within our grasp.

Young people dressed in caps and gowns, who had worked so hard for this moment, sat listening to the speeches. Senator Richard Durbin (D-IL), one of the original sponsors of the DREAM Act, asked "for much more [than a vote on the DREAM Act]. I'm asking for what is in effect an act of political courage."[38]

Meanwhile, from the other side of the aisle, Senator Jon Kyl (R-AZ) couched his opposition in the disingenuous trope that DREAMers "would then have access to a variety of other federal programs, federal welfare programs, student loans, federal work study programs and the like."[39]

One side asked for political courage. The other stoked economic fear.

At 11:09 a.m., the DREAM Act fell five votes short of the necessary sixty-vote threshold.[40] Three Republicans supported the legislation, and five Democrats voted against it. If the five opposing Democrats (including Kay Hagan [D-NC], who had lost her reelection race and, like Senator Lieberman, had no political price to pay) had supported the DREAM Act, millions of young immigrants would now be serving in the military, going to college, or working and contributing to the economy. If Republican champions of immigration reform like Senators Lindsey Graham (R-SC) and John McCain (R-AZ) (who had just won a tough reelection battle) had supported the legislation, we would have only needed three more Democrats. The ifs, ands, and buts go on and on.

Just over four hours later, at 3:21 p.m., Don't Ask, Don't Tell was repealed with the support of sixty-five Senators (including eight Republicans) and no Democrats opposing.[41] While it wasn't legal recognition of same-sex marriage, it was one of the first legislative acknowledgements of equality for members of the LGBT community.

Immigration and LGBT issues are incredibly different. Both communities are confronted with distinctive challenges of race and class in very specific ways. But there are lessons to learn. In the face of deep societal misgivings, advocates for the repeal of Don't Ask, Don't Tell addressed policy, politics, and culture in an integrated way. They methodically built support within the Department of Defense and military hierarchy, introduced the public to compelling gay and lesbian members of the armed services, tied political donations to both parties to their agenda, and engaged both Republicans and Democrats in the development of policy proposals. They respected military culture, understood the public's appreciation for the armed services, shared stories of impacted individuals, and developed a policy and political framework that established a consensus. In short, a powerful cultural strategy led to a powerful political strategy.

We had attempted the reverse. We started with politics and backed into culture. And we lost.

After the DREAM Act vote and after the press conferences, we gathered in the Methodist Church headquarters on First Street, just across from the Supreme Court. The frustration of Senators—Democrats and Republicans who knew the vote should have gone differently—was eclipsed by the profound sadness of DREAMers, advocates, and their allies. Some of us put up a brave face. Most of us just cried. It was awful. But it was also a defining moment.

If we couldn't win a legislative fight at the height of the movement's political power, on what should have been the most compelling case we could put forward, what did that mean for the future?

We thought the immigrant rights movement had followed a similar playbook as the Don't Ask, Don't Tell community. We demanded action, we got arrested in front of the White House (including yours truly), we politically organized ourselves ahead of the election. Going into the DREAM Act vote, we knew policy wasn't the issue—there was a history of bipartisan support. We believed politics was the issue. And we had won the politics.

The political power to force a vote on sound policy got us within one mile of the finish line. What we learned is that last mile, riddled with the landmines of race and class, is not completed by politics and policy alone. That last mile is America's identity crisis. Elections matter, but culture matters more.

Moving forward, in order to answer the question of identity, we needed to prioritize culture over politics and policy. We needed a strategy to win the last, toughest mile. And the rancor and the rhetoric of 2010 (which seems so quaint these days) was shaking loose new enemies as well as new allies.

While politics is power, we learned political power does not guarantee legislative change, much less cultural change. Many will respond that in the (relatively) near future, America will become a "majority-minority" population where people of color will outnumber those who identify as white. Sure, this will make legislative change easier since the electorate will diversify. But that moment is still decades away.

Right now, too many Americans—and media—assume, "There goes the neighborhood," when immigrants become a part of their communities. Until conservative white America sees the cultural (and demographic) changes to their neighborhoods as a net positive to their lives, this will remain the assumption and the identity wars will only worsen.

What we fail to realize is that people are scared. Not necessarily in a bad way. But they are scared they will lose their jobs, then their homes. And they are scared of the new neighbors who look and sound different, who might be coming for their jobs and their homes. With fear comes a lack of trust and mutual respect. Opponents of immigrants and immigration reform prey on this fear to their benefit. Supporters ignore this fear to their peril.

In the lobby of the Methodist Church that afternoon, I remember telling a colleague, without fully understanding what I was getting at, "We are going to do things differently next time."

Which is what this story is about: a different approach to the immigration debate. This is not a story about the next legislative fight. This is a story about Americans dealing with immigration to their neighborhoods.

What America struggles with is bigger than one piece of legislation. I believe that by not understanding the fears behind America's identity crisis, we fail to provide the framework and vehicle through which we can reach Americans' hearts and minds. Solving this problem is not impossible. Liberal or conservative, we need to be willing to meet people where they are, but not leave them there.

CHAPTER TWO

UTAH'S HIT LIST

It was a cold October 2011 evening. An early-winter flurry of snow blew through the air, the ground not quite cold enough for it to stick. I could sense the mountains nearby, but it was too dark to take in the surrounding landscape. It was my first visit to Utah, and I was late for dinner.

It was the night before a regional conference the Forum had organized, in which two hundred conservative leaders from across the Mountain West would take part, after an unlikely year that saw the lily-white, ruby-red state of Utah confront and stem a tide of xenophobia sweeping the nation. We called the conference "Forging a New Consensus on Immigrants and America," and we hoped to create a new path forward on immigration. The dinner was the first time our staff had met many of the next day's speakers in person, and the first time many of the speakers had met each other.

I walked quickly to the private room we had reserved in the back of the restaurant. Working through the group of fifteen guests, I thanked people for making the trip and asked everyone to settle into a chair around the long table. One of our keynote speakers was Ruben Navarrette, a conservative Hispanic columnist based in San Diego. I remember him pulling me aside and whispering, "As you do introductions, ask people to share why they are here."

At that moment, I had no relationship with those in the room beyond e-mails, press releases, and a handful of phone calls. It felt like a tall order to connect with this group of new allies over the course of one meal.

Furthermore, as one of the most politically liberal people in the room, I didn't know what to do with a room full of conservatives in this intimate setting. We had based our invitations on our network of relationships and what someone might have said in the press. But we did not really understand the tensions these leaders faced in their own communities. We didn't appreciate the political and economic risks they took when they spoke publicly in support of immigrants and immigration. We didn't field the angry phone calls, e-mails, or faxes they received.

I didn't think we had established the trust necessary to get past rote introductions, and Ruben's idea was something I was more likely to see used in a room of progressives who loved nothing more than a good share, followed by a good cry. (My own aversion to things like having a good cry was perhaps another reason I found myself retreating to what I thought was a room of hardened conservatives.)

Turns out I wasn't the only one feeling a bit uneasy. Paul Mero, who at the time was president of a conservative Utah think tank, told me he was "uncertain about what this was all about."[1] While he had come to care deeply about the questions under discussion, he wasn't quite sure what he had gotten himself into, or why he was sitting across the table from Republican Mayor Paul Bridges of Uvalda, Georgia (population: 598).[2]

In addition to our keynote speakers, Mayor Bridges, and Ruben, the group around the table consisted of a cross section of politically and/or socially conservative faith, law enforcement, and business leaders from Idaho, Wyoming, Colorado, and Utah. I took Ruben's advice and asked everyone around the table to share why they came to speak at an immigration event in Salt Lake City. The question led to a conversation I never expected.

In their answers, no one mentioned the politics of immigration or why the Republican Party needed to recruit Hispanic voters. Few spoke to abstract policy approaches that would serve their specific needs. Rather, to a person, they shared stories about the immigrants they knew. They spoke of families who were making their congregations and communities a more vibrant place, men and women from other countries they saw not as employees or constituents but as extended family. They spoke of immigrants in their neighborhoods who faced the threat of deportation, who faced prejudice, who faced a steep climb to the American dream they sought for their children. I expected an abstract, policy-driven dinner conversation. Instead, I got a roomful of crying conservatives.

The dinner was my first glimpse at the emotional parallels between conservatives and liberals on immigration. I could see the beginning of a cultural approach to the immigration debate. As Mero put it, "I do remember, by the time [the dinner] was over, not feeling uncomfortable. Almost like even though these people were strangers to me when we sat down, there was that commonality that we shared, that humanity."[3]

The humanity discussed was one of a diverse society where a community's identity changed, social conflicts emerged, and conservative civic leaders helped their conservative communities navigate a path forward. At that point in time, 2010, Utah was the place most important and least likely for such a conversation to occur.

SHOW ME YOUR PAPERS

The story begins more than a year before that dinner, 690 miles to the south: Phoenix, Arizona, where the mountains of the Salt Lake Valley give way to the arid plains of the Southwest. Arizona and Utah are vastly different states in more ways than the landscape. With twice as many people as Utah, Arizona's urban centers are the heart of sprawling metropolitan regions teeming with energy and industry. With nearly 30 percent of the population being Hispanic, compared to Utah's 13 percent, Arizona is also a much more diverse state. This creates a set of very different political and social pressures, which we saw come to a head in early 2010.

My colleagues Rich Stolz and Nora Feely and I sat in my office on April 23, 2010. We quietly watched split-screen coverage of Phoenix. On one side, thousands of Latinos in the streets protested. On the other, an empty podium awaited Arizona Governor Jan Brewer. The scene, in my office and on the screen, was as tense as it was depressing.

After a few minutes, Governor Brewer walked to the podium to announce her intention to sign SB 1070, the "Support our Law Enforcement and Safe Neighborhoods Act." According to the National Council of State Legislatures, SB 1070 included "provisions adding state penalties relating to immigration law enforcement including trespassing, harboring and transporting illegal immigrants, alien registration documents, employer sanctions, and human smuggling."[4] In plain language, the law would have made it a state crime to be undocumented, and local officers would have to enforce federal immigration law. The law would open the door to law-enforcement personnel asking members of the public about their immigration status for no other reason than a belief that someone might be undocumented. This was a state law to prosecute undocumented immigrants under criminal trespassing, and it was the first of its kind enacted in the United States.

Let that settle in for a second. How would you identify people who are undocumented? Are they wearing a badge? A sash? Or are you just asking their immigration status based on what they sound like? The training requirements for local law enforcement were so paltry that in order to assess immigration status, enforcement would have required an unprecedented level of racial and ethnic profiling of someone who looked or sounded like an undocumented immigrant. This is to say, SB 1070 quickly became known as the "show me your papers" law.

It was not just an attack on undocumented immigrants, it was a clear effort to halt the demographic and cultural change that was taking place in Arizona, not to mention America as a whole. Although Brewer used her press conference to attempt to frame the law as a law-enforcement tool to target "the murderous greed of drug cartels,"[5] I agreed with Rich's assessment that the governor seemed incapable of viewing the world from the perspective of immigrants, the fastest growing population in the state.[6]

But the true protagonist in this story about Arizona, Utah, and culture change was not Governor Brewer. Rather, it was one State Senator Russell Pearce (R-Mesa), author and lead proponent of SB 1070. A round-faced fifth-generation Arizonan, Senator Pearce had served in the state legislature since 2001, representing the city of Mesa since 2009. Before joining the legislature, Senator Pearce served as head of the state's Motor Vehicle Division, where he led the effort to require proof of legal status in order to get a driver's license. Before that, he worked for Maricopa County's infamous Sheriff Joe Arpaio, helping him establish "Tent City" where inmates were held outside in the hot desert sun.[7] Suffice it to say, from early on in his political career, Pearce was focused on immigrants and immigration to Arizona.

Senator Pearce is also Mormon. In fact, the city he represented, Mesa, traces its roots back to the establishment of Mormon settlements in the late nineteenth century. The city is 13 percent Mormon, and in 2014, three of the seven city council seats were held by Mormons; the current and incoming mayors were Mormon as well.[8] The cultural and political influence of the Church of Jesus Christ of Latter-day Saints (or LDS Church) ran deep. Little did Senator Pearce realize that his politics and religion would collide on the issue of immigration.

Pearce introduced SB 1070 in January 2010; it quickly passed the Senate in February, was amended and passed by the House in early April, and made its way to the governor's desk for the April press conference we watched from my office.[9] While his zeal led to lightning-fast legislative movement, it also led to a fatal political mistake: Pearce claimed that the LDS Church supported the measure, which couldn't have been further from the truth.[10]

A UTAH SURPRISE

Like the rest of the country, Utah was going through major demographic changes. According to US Census data cited by the *Salt Lake Tribune*, the state's Latino population had grown by 78 percent between 2000 and 2010.[11] While the total number ranked relatively low, only 358,000 people, the community still accounted for 13 percent of the total population.[12] In Salt Lake City, the Hispanic population grew from 9.7 percent in 1990 to just over 22 percent of the city in 2010.[13] But this rate of growth did not immediately trigger the social strife and tension we saw in Arizona.

Most of us only think about Utah when we think about movie festivals, skiing, and lots of Mormons. In the last ten years, three sociopolitical events sharpened the public's understanding of the Church of Jesus Christ of Latter-day Saints. In 2008, the church played a significant role in mobilizing financial and political support of California's Proposition 8, a successful ballot measure to outlaw same-sex marriage.[14] Then, in 2012, Massachusetts Governor Mitt Romney ran for president, prompting a national conversation on the beliefs and role of the LDS Church. Neither of these were really surprising. Rather, it was the church's 2010 role on immigration that turned heads.

For most of my life, I believed all Mormons (in the world) lived in Utah, spent a couple of years abroad, and avoided coffee or alcohol. I also assumed it was an insular community wary of outsiders. Per usual, my assumptions were off.

Their worldwide membership of over 15.6 million people, and 9 million members in the United States, makes the church the second-fastest growing religion in the country.[15] And with 62 percent of its membership under the age of fifty, the growth is sure to continue.[16] Eight percent of its US membership is Latino, and 7 percent are immigrants; and some 3.9 million Mormons live across South America.[17]

The LDS Church's constructive immigration position is about more than their demographics. Yes, it is a community that sticks hard and fast to their deep religious principles. But their willingness to engage global society through their dedication to mission work allows them to move with the times and broader society. What I found is that the LDS Church's engagement on immigration is embodied throughout Mormon culture.

To learn more, I traveled to meet with Michael Otterson, managing director of public affairs for the LDS Church, and his colleague, Michael Purdy, at the Joseph Smith Memorial Building in downtown Salt Lake City. Speaking with a gentle British accent, Otterson shared that as a convert to the Mormon Church, he felt "an ownership of the church's history going back to those very early years when the church membership was being driven from place to place, into Missouri to Illinois, and then finally [to Utah]."[18] While it was a feeling shared by both converts and generational members of the church, as an immigrant to the religion and to the country, the history resonated deeply with Otterson.

Migration, in fact, was a powerful part of the church's overall narrative. To greatly oversimplify, the revelations of Joseph Smith, who founded the LDS Church, and the work by Brigham Young to seek refuge—and welcome Mormon refugees—guides the faith. Along this journey west to Utah in the mid-1800s, Mormons were ostracized, physically attacked, and forcibly removed from communities.

For a community like the LDS Church, with a relatively recent history of persecution and marginalization at the hands of the government, navigating the tense relationship between church and state was very important. Whether in states like Utah, Arizona, or Idaho, or at the national level, there is a precision to the church's communications. As Otterson and Purdy shared, what the church didn't say was often just as important as what it did say.[19] But when the church weighed in on a public policy issue, it had an impact; many attribute the passage of California's Proposition 8 ban on same-sex marriage to the political and financial capital organized by the LDS Church.[20] As SB 1070 moved northward from Arizona into Utah, the church knew a response would become necessary. The issue hit close to home, both geographically in terms of state policy, and socially in terms of impact on the community itself. Leadership knew there were certainly Mormons in favor of the Arizona law, just as the church's growing Latino membership looked to Mormon elders for comfort and protection in trying times like these. The church knew that in the context of the bitter politics of the moment, their response would be closely watched by all sides.

As Otterson and Purdy told me, three principles guided the church's engagement: love your neighbor, strengthen families, and respect the rule of law.[21] They felt these principles would determine the trajectory of the state's response to SB 1070. Fortunately, a conservative-led backlash to the law was already taking shape as leaders from Utah's religious communities (Catholic and Mormon), law enforcement, and businesses banded together to stop SB 1070's tide of nativism.

Lane Beattie, CEO of the Salt Lake Chamber, and Natalie Gochnour, their chief economist, broke the mold of profit-obsessed business leaders as they described the process that led to the announcement of the Utah Compact (to be described shortly) on November 11, 2010. Natalie recalled, "It was very much an unusual day here in the sense that there was this peace and calm and beautiful weather. It was like the heavens opened in a weird way."[22]

Indeed. What happened in Utah was that a group of new and unlikely allies worked together to move heaven and earth to remind Utahans of their culture and values. Along the way, they got the country's immigration debate back on track. It was an effort whose foundation was religious, and its practicalities were rooted in the reality faced by law enforcement and business leaders. It was an effort that culminated on November 11 with the announcement of the Utah Compact, a platform endorsed by the widest possible range of conservative faith, law enforcement, and business leadership in the state. It also aligned with the principles of the LDS Church—a powerful silent partner in the early efforts to correct the course of the state's immigration debate.

How Utah reached this point is important. As with all good ideas, Utah's response was the child of many parents, but two players popped up as unique and crucial: Paul Mero, then president of the Sutherland Institute, a conservative think tank in Utah, and Jason Mathis, executive vice president of the Salt Lake Chamber (and National Immigration Forum board member). They came to the issue from drastically different political perspectives.

Like Otterson, Mero was a convert to the LDS Church. Long-winded in a likeable way, Paul is a true-believer conservative: ideological, but not necessarily political. I have seen Mero agree with President Obama on immigration-related executive actions just as strongly as I've seen him disagree with the administration on same-sex-marriage. As I have gotten to know him over the years, he has become incredibly self-aware (incredible only because I avoid self-awareness at all costs).

Looking back on that year after SB 1070, we sat on matching couches, facing each other across the expanse of his living room, about thirty minutes south of downtown Salt Lake. It was a formal setting but an informal and rolling conversation. In his baritone voice, Mero told me, "So this compassion for the weak is part of my temperament. I have never liked bullies. It makes my blood boil."[23] Then his voice got a little quieter, "Yet my wife says, you know, that's kind of one of these ironies of my life, that I hate bullies but I'm actually one of the biggest bullies around, right. But mostly in defense, I hope it is, in defense of the weak."[24]

Like I said, his self-awareness was scary. Which only made me feel more awkward.

Meanwhile, Jason Mathis is a card-carrying member of the small progressive business establishment in Salt Lake City. His dry sense of humor, slightly mischievous eyes, and unwillingness to suffer fools makes Jason the perfect strategic partner. A lifelong resident of Utah, Jason grew up in a Mormon family. While his family remains very active in the LDS Church, he stopped participating early in adulthood when he "decided that God was bigger than just one church."[25] But, he says, "I still have a ton of respect and affection for the religion of my childhood, but it's not a major part of my daily life anymore."

While their politics were different, their teamwork as the wranglers of Utah's civic leadership on this issue wasn't really all that surprising. Paul Mero approached the process as a way to draw on the values he found important and to confront those intent on bullying the poor and disenfranchised. Jason Mathis saw the compact as a way for leaders across the political spectrum to speak with one voice and not get "shouted down by a small but mean-spirited, vehement group of anti-immigration activists."[26]

Soon after SB 1070 was signed into law by Governor Brewer, rumors started to spread of a similar legislative effort in Utah. Paul, Jason, and friends started to plant seeds of an opposition movement. After several sidebar conversations, Carter Livingston, a consultant based in Utah and on contract with the Forum, teamed up with Mero's Sutherland Institute and others to organize a late spring 2010 public panel, "Our Undocumented Neighbors: What the Conversation Should Be About."

Among the speakers were the Most Reverend John C. Wester, Bishop of the Catholic Diocese of Salt Lake City, and Brett Tolman, former US attorney for the state of Utah and a George W. Bush appointee. Press, policymakers, and civic leaders in the audience were introduced to the conservative reasons why immigrants should be welcomed to the state. Strategically, there was no official representative of the LDS Church on the panel. But it was understood by participants that the panel was an important first step in terms of gauging the reaction of church members. The event was successful in terms of planting the seeds of a constructive immigration debate.

In the months following the event, quiet conversations led to quiet meetings, which led to a quiet campaign to organize opposition to the replication of SB 1070 in Utah. The central players included, but were not limited to, the Catholic Diocese, Utah Attorney General Mark Shurtleff (R), Salt Lake City Police Chief Chris Burbank, the Sutherland Institute, the Salt Lake Chamber, and Democratic State Senator Luz Robles. Various back-channel conversations took place with the church, among other key players in the community. To the outside observer, it was a motley crew who decided to work together to make sure Utah didn't follow in the footsteps of Arizona. But it wasn't quite as motley as one would expect. As Jason explained, "We basically looked for community leaders who were willing to speak out publicly against Utah adopting Arizona's approach. We didn't really care if they were liberal or conservative, just that they were respected and reasonable."[27]

Then came an opportunity generated by a crisis. On July 13, 2010, as reported by the *Deseret News*, "An anonymous group says it quietly watched Hispanics in their neighborhoods, schools, churches and 'public welfare buildings' to compile a list of 1,300 people it says are illegal immigrants living in Utah. The group sent the list to law-enforcement agencies and news media demanding that those named 'be deported immediately.'"[28] The list, it turned out, was compiled by a small number of state workers who had taken it upon themselves to investigate the immigration status of Latinos in Utah. It even included pregnant women and their due dates, presumably to prevent birthright citizenship. The majority of the names proved to be only one thing: Hispanic. The bureaucratic vigilantism had a chilling effect on the Latino community in Utah and across the United States.

Sadly, on the heels of SB 1070, the list was not surprising. It was an ugly time for the immigration debate, and it felt like the country was lashing out against immigrants and immigration. The immigrant community and their allies were on edge. Calling from Utah a few days after the initial news, Carter Livingston warned me that the story about the list was gaining traction among press and policymakers on either side of the issue. He thought it was big enough for a national audience. Since I am a press hound—um, public-policy advocate—I remember saying, "Okay, let's do a press conference. Think you can get a conservative leader on the phone?"

Carter was confident he could get a handful of leaders, including Republican Attorney General Mark Shurtleff to participate.

Over the next forty-eight hours, the story grew and national reporters took notice of our July 21, 2010, telephonic press conference (less than ten days after the news broke). About an hour ahead of the press conference, which I was moderating, I got organized enough to poke around the Internet and get a sense of who we were about to put into the national limelight. For the most part, the speakers were pretty standard. No real surprises. Clarissa Martinez de Castro, director of Immigration and National Campaigns for the National Council of Lá Raza; State Senator Luz Robles (D); Paul Mero, president of the Sutherland Institute; and Bishop John Wester of the Salt Lake City Catholic Diocese. So far, a strong, bipartisan group able to cogently advance the issue, free of unpredictable bomb-throwers.

Then I did a Google search for Attorney General Mark Shurtleff. Near the top of the search results I found a June 18, 2010, article (only a month earlier) from the *Guardian*, "Utah Firing Squad Executes Death Row Inmate."[29] In the article, a Shurtleff tweet is quoted, "I just gave the go ahead to Corrections Director to proceed with Gardner's execution. May God grant him the mercy he denied his victims."[30]

Alright-y, then, I thought to myself, *Shurtleff is a real-deal conservative.*

Shurtleff called in to the press conference from a local high school where he had just spoken to a room full of students. As we waited for the teleconference to start, I immediately noticed the easy cadence to his speech; he knew his way around a press call, and his excitement was infectious. More than that, I was struck by how comfortably this set of Utah leadership, from different political and social corners, was ready and willing to wade into one of the most contentious cultural debates of the day. They fully understood the tension roiling their state but were exceedingly confident in their position and power to calm that tension.

About halfway through the press conference, a journalist asked Shurtleff if he would prosecute the individuals who released the list. As reported by CNN, Mark responded, "Clearly, it's not even meant as a blacklist. It's more like a hit list. It is, I think, to put people at fear, to terrorize, to get people mobilized to do things."[31]

Let me restate this: The Attorney General of the State of Utah referred to this list of 1,300 individuals as a "hit list." He was not going to let the bullies win.

What Paul told me about bullies rang true. Utahans didn't like bullies. And in his office that morning several years later, Lane Beattie, CEO of the Salt Lake Chamber, recalled the flash point created by the list as the "crescendo."[32]

The political environment grew more polarized in the ensuing months. While the group held its ultimate plan close to the vest, they vigorously engaged in the public debate. Mero, in his typically subtle fashion, challenged the enforcement-only approach head-on. He described to me a debate Sutherland Institute had organized just south of Salt Lake City that drew an especially raucous audience. In his closing comments, Mero told me he went as far as to "compare the enforcement-only heavy-handedness to Jim Crow."[33] He chuckled as he continued, "Oh my gosh, they went crazy." Even though he and his wife needed a police escort out of the event, Mero was taking on the opposition with verbal two-by-fours.

Keep in mind that the broader 2010 political debate at this point was dominated by the emergence of the Tea Party. A harsh narrative was being set as fiscal conservatives surged to the front of the news; Democrats were on the defensive and establishment Republicans were in a state of confusion as they tried to understand how to navigate these new waters. (A precursor of the chaos of the 2016 presidential election, one could argue.) In Utah, the Tea Party proved a particularly powerful force when three-term Republican US Senator Bob Bennett lost his re-election primary bid to a Tea Party favorite in a bitterly fought battle at the state's GOP convention. Across Utah and the country, unless you were a no-holds-barred fiscal conservative willing to confront the status quo, you stood a slim chance of winning a Republican primary.

Recognizing the ferocity of the political headwinds blowing against the interests of pro-immigration forces, the motley band of pro-immigrant Utahans ready to challenge SB 1070 worked behind the scenes, waiting for the election to pass. This was a smart approach, since on November 2, 2010, those headwinds reached electoral ground and swept the Tea Party to power.

Nine days later, on November 11, the date in 1620 that the pilgrims signed the Mayflower Compact, a dozen faith leaders, former governors, business leaders, and law-enforcement officials gathered in Salt Lake City. As Utah's KSL.com reported, "Representatives from corporations and businesses, state and city governments, community organizations and faiths stepped forward to lend support to" the Utah Compact.[34]

The compact itself is a remarkably simple document—concise, principled, something for everyone. It reads:

THE UTAH COMPACT

A DECLARATION OF FIVE PRINCIPLES TO GUIDE UTAH'S IMMIGRATION DISCUSSION

FEDERAL SOLUTIONS: Immigration is a federal policy issue between the U.S. government and other countries—not Utah and other countries. We urge Utah's congressional delegation, and others, to lead efforts to strengthen federal laws and protect our national borders. We urge state leaders to adopt reasonable policies addressing immigrants in Utah.

LAW ENFORCEMENT: We respect the rule of law and support law enforcement's professional judgment and discretion. Local law enforcement resources should focus on criminal activities, not civil violations of federal code.

FAMILIES: Strong families are the foundation of successful communities. We oppose policies that unnecessarily separate families. We champion policies that support families and improve the health, education and well-being of all Utah children.

ECONOMY: Utah is best served by a free-market philosophy that maximizes individual freedom and opportunity. We acknowledge the economic role immigrants play as workers and taxpayers. Utah's immigration policies must reaffirm our global reputation as a welcoming and business-friendly state.

A FREE SOCIETY: Immigrants are integrated into communities across Utah. We must adopt a humane approach to this reality, reflecting our unique culture, history and spirit of inclusion. The way we treat immigrants will say more about us as a free society and less about our immigrant neighbors. Utah should always be a place that welcomes people of goodwill.[35]

At the compact's public announcement, Bishop John Wester voiced the Catholic community's strong opposition to SB 1070: "I'm hoping that we can speak loudly and clearly that we do not want oppressive and Draconian legislation."[36]

Chris Burbank, the Salt Lake City chief of police at the time, reflected on the moment over lunch one day, "The interesting thing about the compact is it didn't solve the problem. The compact did not give you the answer. The compact gave you an avenue to work towards the answer."[37]

This was the elegance of the compact. It was not intended to provide a legislative solution. It was designed to stop harmful legislation with a set of principles based on values fundamental to the broader community. Put another way, culture and values defeated politics and policy.

At the local and national level, press and policymakers quickly recognized the significance of the Utah Compact. In the months ahead, elected officials from Georgia to Indiana to Washington called leaders in Utah to seek advice. They all saw the compact as a way to craft a constructive conversation on immigration and avoid the rancor of Arizona's ugly approach.

It truly was a special moment. Utah is one of the most conservative states in the nation, and an anti-immigrant tide was sweeping across the country. If there was any state in the nation sure to follow Arizona, it should have been Utah. Yet, in short order, this state, white as white can be, conservative as conservative can get, turned things around.

Utah's response to changing demographics, and the racial and ethnic tension that came with it, was based on the culture and values of the dominant community. And the response came with a political savvy that used all the levers of power at their disposal. Yes, church and state are separate. But the politics of immigration changed in Utah because the politics were informed by religious values. This may not be transferable to other states, but in a conservative, monolithic place like Utah, it worked.

Why did this happen? What was unique about Utah?

As Burbank put it, "I think why it transcended is . . . [that] you had the human factor that this collective group bought into."[38] He continued, "So from a faith community, they saw their parishioners, their people that were participating with them. From a business community, it was employees that were participating with them. From a law-enforcement perspective, it was the people that you dealt with every day and the stories that you heard."

This human factor Burbank mentions brings us back to the church. In addition to putting the immigration question in the hands of the federal government, the compact addressed the LDS Church's guiding principles: love your neighbor, strengthen families, and respect the rule of law. While there was no official church representative at the announcement, the church statement released minutes after the event made its position clear: "The Church regards the declaration of the *Utah Compact* as a responsible approach to the urgent challenge of immigration reform."[39] The endorsement by the LDS Church continued, and it went further than people expected: "Public officials should create and administer laws that reflect the best of our aspirations as a just and caring society. Such laws will properly balance love for neighbors, family cohesion, and the observance of just and enforceable laws."[40]

As Otterson and Purdy, leadership of the church's external communications, shared with me, the LDS Church's public response had been careful to position the compact for what it was: a vehicle designed and driven by the wide range of stakeholders in order to have maximum impact.[41] They wanted to make sure the compact stood independent of the church but also send a clear signal of support.

This was not a quiet thumb on the scale. This was the most powerful institution in the state, and one of the most powerful in the region and the country, urging lawmakers to create a legal framework that welcomed, protected, and valued immigrants and refugees. This was not only a statement of principle for the church but also a clear message to its membership that Arizona's anti-immigrant legislation was not representative of church doctrine.

Mike Otterson told me, "I think in a way [Pearce and SB 1070] was a catalyst to drive the church's very public position in supporting the Utah Compact. We could not ever be seen to be bigoted against Hispanic immigrants of our membership. So we had to be extremely clear."[42]

The church's clear stance, as I mentioned earlier, led to a very complicated 2011 for Russell Pearce, who had just been elected state senate president in Arizona. (More on this in a minute.)

Throughout all of this, I was learning to work with people who had very different politics and beliefs than I did. My fellow (progressive, non-religious) immigration advocates thought we were crazy for working with Mormons. Yet I came to realize that our common ground was greater than I could have imagined. This became the core of our approach—find your common ground, hold on tight, and learn all that you can about people you think are different from you.

In December 2010, I was on an evening flight from Dallas–Fort Worth to Washington, DC. On this particular flight, much to my surprise, I found myself sitting next to Secretary of Health and Human Services Kathy Sebelius (D). Less than a year after passing the Affordable Care Act, I am sure Secretary Sebelius expected to be the recipient of various and sundry healthcare opinions. Luckily for her, I didn't have a dog in the healthcare fight. But the advocate in me wasn't going to pass up the opportunity to chat with the former governor of Kansas.

So I struck up a conversation and we exchanged pleasantries. Our conversation hadn't turned to immigration for more than a couple minutes before the secretary reached into her seat pocket, rummaged through a small stack of newspapers, and whipped out the December 4, 2010, *New York Times*. She quarter-folded to the editorial page and pointed to the lead editorial, "The Utah Compact."[43] I recall her saying, rather excitedly, something along the lines of, "Have you heard about what they are doing in Utah? It's incredible."

Why, yes, Madame Secretary, I have heard about the Utah Compact.

COMING HOME TO ROOST

A few months later, on January 27, 2011, Arizonans for a Better Government announced a campaign to recall Senate President Pearce.[44] Led by the whip-smart and ready-to-rumble community activist DeeDee Blase, the coalition to take down Pearce included Republicans, Democrats, and Libertarians. Forecasting the determining factor, Blase told the *Phoenix New Times*, "And what's going to help us with the Mormon community is the Utah Compact. . . . We believe there is a change in the Mormon attitude over immigration. We're going to remind Mormons of that as well."[45] DeeDee was spot-on.

In early 2011, parts of SB 1070 were enjoined by the federal courts while other parts were implemented. Outside of the legal machinations, immigration continued to dominate Arizona as local and national organizations ran various campaigns to build public opposition. Caught in the middle, per usual, was the immigrant community.

By the end of May 2011, the campaign had gathered enough signatures to force a recall election. By the time of the first (and only) public debate, the race was whittled down to two: Pearce and charter-school executive, Jerry Lewis—who, incidentally, was very active in the LDS community and opposed SB 1070.

Then an interesting year got more interesting. Brahm Resnik, a local television reporter for Phoenix's Channel 12 News filed a bombshell of a story on October 14, 2011, just under a year after the Utah Compact and less than a month before the recall election.[46] Resnik had video footage of a town hall where Pearce said, "I got a hold of [LDS] Church headquarters in Salt Lake too and they said they absolutely do not oppose what Arizona is doing and none of their statements should reflect that."[47] For Arizona politics and the LDS Church, that a Mormon politician would directly contradict church statements was TMZ-level drama.

In his report, Resnik shared the footage of Pearce's comments with church officials and received this response from Michael Purdy, "While the Church of Jesus Christ of Latter-day Saints has not taken a position on any specific Arizona legislation, we have made our immigration position clear. The Church believes an enforcement-only approach is inadequate."[48]

In case you weren't following along, SB 1070 was the epitome of an enforcement-only approach. Purdy's statement to Resnik continued with the point that such an approach did nothing to meet the church's principles of "love thy neighbor," family, and the rule of law.[49]

Based on the press coverage of the conflict, the number of Mormon voters in Mesa, Arizona, and the way conservative leaders pounced on Pearce's misstep, it is not difficult to argue that the church's response to Pearce's claims contributed to a blowout twelve-point victory on November 8, 2011, for Jerry Lewis.[50]

Lewis, in fact, credited the Utah Compact for his win. Days after his victory, I moderated a telephonic press conference to mark the one-year anniversary of the Utah Compact. (I told you, I am a press hound.) During the press conference, Senator-elect Lewis said, "The Utah Compact has had a tremendous influence on the state of Arizona and more particularly this recent election."[51] He continued, "What it did was give a set of guiding principles that would help people realize that there is hope on the way. We don't need to have knee-jerk reactions to the real issues. We need to focus on principles to guide that discussion, and the Utah Compact did just that."[52]

The culture and values represented in the Utah Compact stopped SB 1070 from infecting Utah. And along the way, the compact defeated SB 1070's author.

What made it all the more remarkable was Utah's white Republican population whose personal experiences and faith, defined by a culture steeped in the refugee story, made the ultimate difference. At the beginning of this journey, I perceived Mormons to be isolated and unwelcoming. In reality, it was one of the worldliest and most welcoming communities I had ever met.

GENERAL CONFERENCE

On a sunny Sunday afternoon in April 2016, I was in Salt Lake for the final session of the Church of Jesus Christ of Latter-day Saints' 186th General Conference. Twice a year, over twenty-one thousand church members gather in Salt Lake, and millions watch online, to receive guidance and encouragement from church leaders. As I walked through the church gardens, Hispanic, Asian, and African families made up a large number of the throngs. Regardless of skin color, the crowd felt young. There were kids skipping about, young or middle-aged parents watching them, and older youth chattering in small groups. Everyone took pictures of the ornate church buildings and the blooming flowers. The afternoon felt like a massive family picnic.

I wandered through the grounds, taking in the scene, and ventured across West North Street to the Conference Center. Lines snaked around the building as members made their way to the afternoon session. I began to wonder how all these people were going to fit in a building that wasn't a sports stadium. I made my way to the media entrance; we went through security and quickly made our way through a vast lobby. I still couldn't get a sense of the gathering's scale. That soon changed.

The auditorium was unlike anything I had ever seen. Reports claim the Conference Center is the largest theater-style auditorium ever built.[53] There were at least three levels of auditorium seating, and red chairs as far as the eye could see, quickly filling with church members and guests. On the massive stage, majestically looming behind the Mormon Tabernacle Choir, were the golden pipes of the Tabernacle organ. Some 11,623 individual pipes strong, the organ filled the cavernous auditorium with a warm, gentle sound as we found our seats.[54]

The choir itself consisted of 360 members—men in black robes on the right, and women in red on the left. Just below the choir sat members of the General Presidency. On the first row of the stage sat a line of men, the Quorum of the Twelve Apostles and the First Presidency. The auditorium seemed to lack edges, physical or emotional, which created a massive gathering that was quiet, was peaceful, and simply put you at ease. It was an imposing setting.

Just over five years after the Utah Compact, immigrants and immigration were back in the spotlight. Since the summer of 2015, a year earlier, an international refugee crisis had dominated the news. On a daily basis, the American public was inundated by stories of families fleeing Syria and streaming into Europe, as well as women and children presenting themselves at the US–Mexico border, afraid for their lives in Central America. New stories surfaced daily of Syrian refugees drowning in the Mediterranean Sea as their rickety human-smuggler boats capsized. Meanwhile, a backlash bubbled across Europe as their outdated immigration systems buckled under the weight of the crisis. In the United States, Donald Trump's campaign for president stoked the fires of nativism and prejudice.

In the United States as well as Europe, there was a growing sense that governments had lost control of their borders, and that nations' identities and culture were being lost in the wave of migrants. Often ignored in this hand-wringing was the fact that millions of Syrians were fleeing war to find themselves in the hands of smugglers, huddling in refugee camps, or the target of attacks in the media. Utah as a state, and the Mormon community as a church, understood and met this challenge.

In late 2015, when Trump trumpeted his call to ban Muslim immigration,[55] the LDS Church issued their first statement of the electoral season. The short statement began with, "The Church of Jesus Christ of Latter-day Saints is neutral in regard to party politics and election campaigns. However, it is not neutral in relation to religious freedom."[56] The statement closed with a quote from Joseph Smith from 1841: "Be it ordained by the City Council of the City of Nauvoo, that the Catholics, Presbyterians, Methodists, Baptists, Latter-day Saints, Quakers, Episcopal[ian]s, Universalists, Unitarians, Mohammedans [Muslims], and all other religious sects and denominations whatever, shall have free toleration, and equal privileges in this city. . . ."[57]

Reminded of the church's founding principles, Utah's Republican elected officials followed suit with near-unanimous opposition to Trump. That morning in the offices of the Salt Lake Chamber of Commerce, Natalie Gochnour, chief economist for the Salt Lake Chamber, told me, "When I hear Donald Trump talk about building a wall or when I just hear him slamming Mexicans, I'm infuriated because my son is serving those people and he loves those people and I love those people. I just compound that over generations of Utahans who have interacted or have that cultural experience. I think that changes our hearts."[58] She went on, "If you are a mean bully, particularly with vulnerable people, that will not fly here."

Again, the word *bully*. And this time from Natalie, who is always smiling—I can even hear her smile on the phone. I couldn't imagine her being infuriated by anything. But Trump bullying immigrants triggered a fury that was not economic but moral. Her emotion, and the church's strategic response to Trump, resembled the Mormon community's reaction to SB 1070 and the Utah Compact.

When the European refugee crisis first emerged in the summer of 2015, with the news stories and tragic photos, the church made a $5 million commitment on September 28, 2015, to support Syrian refugees and families in Europe.[59] Elder Patrick Kearon, a General Authority Seventy of the LDS Church and President of the Europe Area said at the time of this commitment, "We continue to be moved, like so many others, by the stories and images of those struggling for basic necessities of food, water, and temporary shelter," he said.[60] "They have lost so much."

One month later, the church mobilized at an international level when the First Presidency sent a letter to church membership that was scheduled to be read during the church's Sunday worship services around the globe.[61] Signed by three members of the First Presidency, including President Dieter F. Uchtdorf, the letter offered guidance on how members could assist in the humanitarian effort, "Members may contribute to the Church Humanitarian Fund using the Tithing and Other Offerings donations slip. We also invite Church units, families, and individuals to participate in local refugee relief projects, where practical."[62]

Each communication linked the historical experience of the Mormon community and scripture to the plight immigrants and refugees faced in modern time. Just as important, leadership provided a way for the community to take action, all of which created a foundation of support and understanding for the April 2016 sessions.

A few months after this letter and a week before the General Conference, thousands of women and girls gathered for the General Women's Session. In her talk, Linda K. Burton, Relief Society General President, began with the story of President Brigham Young's October 1865 call for assistance to "handcart pioneers" struggling on the winter trail to Salt Lake:

> Sister [Lucy Meserve] Smith recorded . . . that after President Young's exhortation, those in attendance took action. . . . Women "[removed] their petticoats [large underskirts that were part of the fashion of the day and that also provided warmth], stockings, and everything they could spare, right there in the [old] Tabernacle, and piled [them] into the wagons to send to the Saints in the mountains."[63]

Based on this shared understanding of their culture and values, Burton used her sermon to illustrate the plight of the 60 million refugees displaced from their homes with stories of women and children she had met. And she linked the church's contemporary approach to this communal experience as she continued, "My beloved sisters, this account might be likened to our day and those who are suffering throughout the world. Another 'extraordinary occasion' touches our hearts."[64]

A week later, as I sat in the Conference Center on that Sunday afternoon with thousands of others, Elder Patrick Kearon came to the podium. He began with scripture: "'For I was an hungred, and ye gave me meat: I was thirsty, and ye gave me drink: I was a stranger, and ye took me in. . . . Verily I say unto you, Inasmuch as ye have done it unto one of the least of these my brethren, ye have done it unto me.'"[65]

Again, Kearon couched his call to action in the community's understanding of their own history:

> As members of the Church, as a people, we don't have to look back far in our history to reflect on times when we were refugees, violently driven from homes and farms over and over again. Last weekend in speaking of refugees, Sister Linda Burton asked the women of the Church to consider, "What if *their* story were *my* story?" Their story *is* our story, not that many years ago.[66]

Kearon's was one of several sermons that afternoon. On topics of family, faith, and community, the audience was attentive throughout. But when Elder Kearon spoke, a stillness settled over the gathering as we sensed the emotion in his voice. Around me, men and women dabbed their eyes with tissues as Elder Kearon's words settled over the massive auditorium.

As he spoke, Elder Kearon's voice remained calm, and his hands moved ever so slightly, making the sermon feel as big and warm as the auditorium. His closing words served as a spiritual confrontation of the global audience he spoke to:

> Being a refugee may be a defining moment in the lives of those who are refugees, but being a refugee does not define them. Like countless thousands before them, this will be a period—we hope a short period— in their lives. Some of them will go on to be Nobel laureates, public servants, physicians, scientists, musicians, artists, religious leaders, and contributors in other fields. Indeed, many of them were these things before they lost everything. This moment does not define them, but our response will help define us.[67]

President Uchtdorf, who was moderating the afternoon session, walked to the podium to introduce the next speaker. Uchtdorf was a crowd favorite, and his gentle humor and relaxed demeanor had kept the gathering light and serious. A German refugee himself, Uchtdorf earlier in the session had shared his story of fleeing bomb raids as a four-year-old. As his family had run up the hill, in the pitch-black night, to the bomb shelter, he described the green flares dropping from the skies to mark targets. Poignantly, he shared with the community that they called these flares "Christmas trees."

Before he began to speak, I noticed that President Uchtdorf's body language was different when he approached the podium than it had been earlier in the afternoon. A deep, emotional sigh prefaced, "Thank you brethren," as he looked seriously and intently at his notes. He seemed to gather himself. When he looked up, I noticed his eyes were puffy. As he moved through the program, introducing the upcoming speakers, his voice cracked multiple times.[68] Following Kearon's personal challenge to their community, Uchtdorf too was crying.[69]

The next day, as we discussed Elder Kearon's sermon, Michael Otterson told me, "That was unusual, by the way. That was an unusual address, because it was about a specific contemporary issue rather than about how you live the principles of the church, the gospel. But it was obviously done with approval and permission from the highest authorities of the church."[70]

Approximately three months after General Conference, the LDS Church presented $3 million to the World Food Programme to help refugees. In a visit to refugee camps in Greece after making the award, President Uchtdorf said, "The gratitude we saw in the eyes of these refugees for the generosity and kindness of our church members will never be forgotten. I could deeply feel the bond of love and compassion with these stranded families."[71]

ACTING ON YOUR BELIEFS

To a large extent, the 2010 Utah Compact and the LDS Church's 2015 reaction to the refugee crisis completed a circle. Because, in between those points, in March 2013 and April 2014, Uchtdorf joined interfaith leadership delegations to meet with President Obama as Congress debated reform legislation.[72] In news reports of both meetings, Uchtdorf articulated the church's support for immigration reform, based on both scripture and the principles outlined in the Utah Compact.[73] And, with the refugee crisis, the principles that guided the compact led the LDS Church to play a leadership role at the international level. Utah's response to SB 1070 stopped hateful legislation, influenced the national debate, and, over the course of five years, played a role in catapulting the Mormon community to a leadership role in domestic immigration reform and an international migration crisis.

In chapter 24 of the LDS Church's *Teachings of Presidents of the Church*, John Taylor, the third president of the church, reported on a conversation with Joseph Smith regarding governance. In the teachings, Taylor shares that Smith said, "'I teach them correct principles, and they govern themselves.'"[74] It isn't fair to say this approach is unique to Mormons. Most religions, societies, and organizations govern themselves by an agreed-upon set of principles. Of course, those who do not ascribe to a particular faith are value-driven people as well. But in the case of the LDS Church, how their members act on these principles is a testament to how Americans can find common ground on unlikely issues. Michael Purdy put it well when he said, "The church is famous for its political neutrality, but we don't want our members to be politically neutral. We hope that we can teach correct principles, and they make decisions."[75]

The *Economist* wrote that Utah had created something new, something that could be called a "model of constructive Republicanism."[76] In this case, that model moved beyond state lines to impact the politics of states across the country—as we will see.

Utah's unique culture and values imbued the state with a sense that it is part of a global society. To a certain degree, the self-confidence is easier in an ethnically and religiously homogenous state. But there are cities, towns, and states across the country just as homogenous that have not handled these challenges constructively. In the case of Utah, their culture and values mitigated this identity crisis and allowed the racial and ethnic evolution of Utah to proceed in a positive way. Thinking back to that dinner with crying conservatives, and the role Utah has come to play, I think it is fair to say that America could use some more constructive Republicanism.

CHAPTER THREE

SOUL FREEDOM

I n June of 2016, thousands of evangelical Protestants gathered in St. Louis, Missouri, for what Ed Stetzer, then executive director of Lifeway Research, a research organization studying evangelical culture in America, called, "the human equivalent of a potluck dinner."[1] That potluck was the two-day Southern Baptist Convention annual meeting that convened thousands of church pastors, deacons, and others from all walks of Southern Baptist life.

The meeting serves as an opportunity for elected messengers of Southern Baptist churches and organizations to weigh in on much of the denomination's business and offer resolutions that define the positions of its public-policy arm, the Ethics & Religious Liberty Commission. The meeting is a remarkably open and transparent space where debate is substantive, votes are binding, and direct questions are posed to convention leadership from the meeting floor. Closely followed by Christian media and conservative policymakers, the annual meeting is an assertion of Southern Baptist culture and identity. Exuding the confidence that comes with growth, news reports ahead of the 2016 annual meeting pointed to a 51 percent pre-registration increase over 2015.[2]

As the largest non-Catholic denomination in the nation, and representing some 15 million people, the annual meeting solidifies the convention's reputation as a grassroots-driven organization with its finger on the pulse of social conservatives in America. Controversial and difficult issues are often openly addressed; and, this year, the country was rife with difficult issues. In the months preceding the 2016 meeting, ISIS-inspired terrorism, refugees to the United States, and the perceived spread of Islam dominated the conversation.

A debate raged within Southern Baptist life. On one side, this fear and anger manifested itself in what can only be called anti-Islam efforts to end immigration of Muslims or block the establishment of mosques. On the other side was a call for religious liberty and the engagement of Muslims as fellow humans. It was a clash of cultures.

A week before the meeting, Gerald Harris, the influential editor of the *Christian Index*, wrote a searing column, "Do Muslims Really Qualify for Religious Freedom Benefits?"[3] In addition to arguing Islam was more of a geopolitical movement than a religion, Harris took Dr. Russell Moore, president of the Ethics & Religious and Liberty Commission of the Southern Baptist Convention, to task for signing an amicus brief in support of a New Jersey Muslim community's effort to build a mosque. In his third year as president, Moore had taken significant, and often controversial, steps to broaden the commission's approach to social-justice issues while remaining focused on conservative flash points such as life or traditional marriage. When it came to issues of race and social justice, Moore put his leadership role on the line as he challenged the old guard of Southern Baptist life—also known as America's Religious Right. The Harris post was a direct challenge to Moore's leadership, as well as a legitimate representation of the fear and resentment bubbling within the socially conservative evangelical community.

The tension came to a head on the second day of the annual meeting as Moore took questions from the thousands of church messengers in the audience.[4] At stage right stood Dr. Ronnie Floyd, president of the Southern Baptist Convention, and senior pastor of Cross Church in Northwest Arkansas. Wearing a fashionable, trimly cut seersucker suit, pastel tie, and a matching pocket square, he presided over the session behind a Plexiglas podium. Stage left, behind a similar podium, stood Moore with his carefully combed dark hair, conservatively cut dark-blue suit, with a jacket about a half-size too big and a broad-striped tie. No pocket square to be seen. Where Floyd leaned into the podium, arms straight, exerting a presence over the dialogue, Moore's body language was relaxed, arms resting on the podium.

Floyd motioned to the audience to ask for the next question. John Wofford of Armorel Baptist Church, in Armorel, Arkansas, was at the microphone in the cavernous hall. Armorel is an unincorporated community in Mississippi County in the northeast corner of Arkansas. According to a 2016 compliance report, the Armorel School District reported a total enrollment of 404 students.[5] Of the 215 students enrolled in Armorel High School, just 2 percent were Asian and 4 percent were Hispanic.[6] I do not want to stereotype Armorel or dismiss Wofford's concerns, but according to the data, the region was the textbook definition of a culturally isolated American community.

Wofford had cropped, gray hair, was slightly overweight, was wearing a brown polo shirt, and had his credential hanging around his neck. He spoke with what I have to call a slow southern drawl. After introducing himself, Wofford's question to Moore started with, "How in the world would someone within the Southern Baptist Convention support the defending of rights for Muslims to construct mosques in the United States?"[7]

Wofford continued, "[Muslims] are murdering Christians, beheading Christians, imprisoning Christians all over the world." He closed with a thinly veiled allegation that Islam engages in idolatry and blasphemy, "Do you actually believe that if Jesus Christ were here today that he would support this and he would stand up and say, 'Well, let us protect the rights of those Baal worshippers to erect Temples to Baal?' Do you believe that . . . Dr. Moore?"[8]

Behind the forty-four-year-old Moore sat his senior staff. Based on their average age, the team sent a clear message to the younger evangelicals in the audience that they were represented. Just over Moore's left shoulder, in the bottom right corner of the screen, was Daniel Patterson, Moore's longtime assistant and chief of staff. With his short, blond hair and exacting gaze, Patterson seemed to be literally watching every word Moore spoke.

Standing stock-still, Moore began his response to Wofford, "You know, sometimes we have to deal with questions that are really complicated." Patterson looked worried.

Moore continued, "We have to spend a lot of time thinking them through . . . and . . . and, not sure what the final result is going to be." Patterson's eyes widened with concern.

Moore's pace and volume started to pick up, "Sometimes we have really hard decisions to make." (At this point, Patterson really needed to take a breath.)

His Mississippi accent sharpened as Moore drove his point home, "This isn't one of those things."

Patterson exhaled, smiled, and started to applaud.

"What it means to be a Baptist," Moore continued as he raised his right hand and gently, but energetically, pointed to the growing applause from the crowd, "is to support soul freedom for everybody."

He kept his right hand moving in the air and seemed to look in Wofford's direction. Moore went on, "And brothers and sisters, when we have a government [that] says we can decide whether or not a house of worship can be constructed based upon the theological beliefs of that house of worship" (insert nodding and smiling from Patterson here), "then there are going to be Southern Baptist churches in San Francisco and New York and throughout this country [that we] are not going to be able to build."

Moore's right hand came down. His left hand rose as he defined the bigger issue, "A government that has the power to outlaw people from assembling together and saying what they believe, that does not turn people into Christians."

Closing to resounding applause, Moore straightened up as he reached a crescendo, "That turns people into pretend Christians, and it sends them straight to hell."

On that note, Moore looked over at Floyd, calmly stepped back from the podium, and closed his leather portfolio.[9]

Mic drop.

Moore out.

When I watching video footage of this Q&A session for the first time, I felt like Patterson. I knew it was a tense situation and Moore was under pressure from his membership. I, too, wondered in which direction Moore would take his answer.

At a time when calls to ban Muslim immigration ricocheted through conservative media, for the president of the Ethics & Religious Liberty Commission to stand up for the right of Muslims to build houses of worship was no rhetorical flourish. It was a moment of moral courage that summarized the question facing conservative white Christian America: In a racially, ethnically, and culturally diversifying society, where do white Christians fit?

As deep as the impact of this declaration was within Southern Baptist life, it was also a surprising crossover moment into broader American culture with a position more commonly identified with the political left. Up to this point in time, the religious and secular left were the ones standing up for and defending the rights of Muslims. For the left, this was an issue of human and civil rights—just as the right to same-sex marriage was a civil and human right. But for conservative white evangelicals, this was as an issue of religious liberty, the same argument they made in opposition to same-sex marriage. This moment of powerful consensus was found on the contentious issue of Muslims' right to worship.

Whether it was civil rights or religious liberty, it was a specific values framework that allowed the left or the right to understand the ways their neighborhoods were changing.

LESS CURSING, MORE PRAYING

For years, we assumed a fact-based economic case would increase public support for immigrants and immigration. But time after time, an economics-only, business-led strategy to fix the immigration system fell short. This was true when America's economy was doing well (2007) and not so well (2013). We thought reform was a question of changing someone's mind through data, not their heart through a cultural approach. We were happier to call opponents racist if they questioned the value of diversity. What we learned, very late in the game, is that in order to address the questions of identity and culture change that come with immigration, we must engage people's hearts and minds. Through conversations with conservative faith leaders at the local and national level, I realized the country wasn't worried about the policy or the politics of immigrants and immigration. People were worried that their nation was changing, their culture was changing, and their values were changing. For conservatives, immigration wasn't about the economy. It was a social issue and needed to be addressed as such. The question was, How could a liberal Muslim(ish) guy from California engage some of the most conservative faith leaders in the country on cultural issues?

I have made a career of being relatively quiet about my cultural identity. I have never liked talking about myself or telling my story. (Just ignore the fact I am writing a book about my story for a minute.) I have always been more comfortable asking questions than answering them. As a result, I can move across political and social lines fairly easily. I've also developed the useful ability to smile and nod in a number of languages.

When pressed, I identify as culturally Muslim, but I am not necessarily religious. Truth be told, for most of my life I have been deeply skeptical of religion and am now only scraping the outer surface of questions of my faith. Therefore, I have no intention of getting into a theological discussion of faith in America. But I have developed a much greater appreciation and respect for the role religion plays in our culture. Without the diversity of faiths in America, we would not be such an exceptional nation.

Early in this process of engaging unlikely allies, I realized that the liberal left—particularly those of us advocating for civil and human rights—have an oversimplified understanding of social conservatives. Our assumptions, which are often incorrect, limit our understanding of America and create barriers where we could build bridges. In a political age dominated by sharply worded tweets and twenty-four-hour news cycles, it is hard to look past our respective trenches. To overcome this deficiency, advocates turn to liberal faith leaders with whom we agree on social issues such as marriage in order to "check the faith box." Liberal faith leaders are good people, but they live in an entirely separate reality from social conservatives and have no influence over conservative congregants. In fact, I have driven through the south listening to Christian radio stations, with significant audiences, pillory those they see as liberal-left evangelical leaders. At the national level, there is certainly collaboration between conservative and liberal faith leaders. But those are collaborations that make political pundits and advocates feel good; at this point in time, they do not necessarily translate to change at the local level.

As I started to engage with conservative faith leaders, I realized that my discomfort with religion had led to an impressive level of hypocrisy. For years, I enjoyed pontificating about the need for conservatives to develop relationships with immigrant communities and those on the political left who were leading the push for immigration reform. I felt the right needed to meet the left where they are, not the other way around. I quickly realized this could not be a one-way street. So I tried to develop the relationships and understanding that allowed me to break through my own boundaries.

In the years since I began working with social conservatives, I have never felt pressure to change who I am or what I believe politically or socially. But in order to develop the trust necessary to get work done, there was an unspoken requirement to listen, to respect perspectives, and to move forward even if there is disagreement. Maybe this was easier since I am not Catholic, Mormon, or evangelical. Maybe it was easier because the parameters of our partnership are clearly limited to immigrants and immigration.

I admit that it wasn't easy to suppress the sanctimoniousness that comes with being a liberal know-it-all. (Which is why I decided to write a book about how I know it all.) I worked to get past policy and political differences and tried to understand personal motivations and principles. I challenged my own assumptions. I was not always successful, but I found a surprising number of willing and gracious partners from across the aisle of political and social beliefs.

My initial outreach to evangelical and Catholic leaders was transactional. I viewed the faith community as our latest tactic to wedge Republicans. I saw these leaders and their congregations as a political opportunity; they were fault lines that would help us divide conservative politics. Somewhere in late 2011, my colleague Nora Feely challenged this mind-set. She made the case that if we were going to truly build the level of trust we knew culture change (and ultimately legislative change) would require, we could no longer be the stereotypical liberals dismissive of conservative religious leaders. Quite simply, we could no longer say, "crazy evangelicals." Nora was right.

So instead of rushing to a transactional outcome, we took a more incremental approach. We got to know the people we were working with and learned to ask questions about their lives, politics, and faith. Authenticity took the place of talking points. Our team had countless conversations with people, like author Matt Soerens of World Relief, along the lines of:

"Matt, should we capitalize evangelical in this press release?"

"No, it should be lowercase because 'evangelical' is not a monolithic religion."

"It's not?"

Then Matt would patiently, kindly explain the intricacies of whichever denomination we happened to be speaking with while we furiously scribbled notes to keep up. We took the time to listen to conservative faith leaders' language, their interests, and what they wanted for the immigrants they served. Even when it was uncomfortable, we learned to use language that didn't alienate our new partners. For example, we learned social conservatives saw the abortion debate as an issue of "life," while the left framed it as a question of "choice." Whether or not we personally agreed with their position, in order to develop the necessary level of trust, we had to respect their beliefs and their values framework.

Soon, I took on a role of not only communicating with conservative faith leaders and developing collaborative strategies but also translating strategies, tactics, and language between the left and right. Of course, my organization's motivations were questioned from both sides. I was attacked by some on the left for working with social conservatives opposed to gay marriage. Others thought the legislative debate would skew too conservative because we would grant conservatives disproportionate power in the debate. And from the right, there were regular attacks that I was not a "real conservative." Both attacks were correct. We were looking to empower conservatives so that they could play a constructive role in the nation's immigration debate as full partners. And, true, I am not a real conservative. But our vantage point allowed us to understand that real bipartisanship was necessary. We explained to conservatives why the left cared so passionately about the rights of immigrants. And we explained to the left the steps conservatives needed to take in order to engage on the issue. Success required support and commitment from both sides of the aisle.

As stakeholders came to understand the strategy and our role, the most consistent question I got was, "What is the difference between working with liberals and working with conservatives?"

With conservatives, there's a lot less cursing and a lot more praying.

HEARTS AND MINDS

To the credit of DREAMers and the broader undocumented community, issues of race and humanity were raised when they publicly declared their unauthorized immigration status. Their stories opened the eyes of millions of Americans who did not realize their friends, their students, their neighbors were undocumented. These men, women, and children introduced themselves to the American public as economic contributors, not cases of charity and goodwill.

The activism from liberal educators, labor leaders, civil rights organizations, advocates, and others created tension and conflict with the right. Over time, however, the sheer force of demographic change ensured urban areas were culturally and ethnically diverse. As a result, the organizing and activism of liberal organizations created multiple ways one could change a person's heart and mind. Simply put, the diversity of schools, churches, and other anchor institutions in cities created openings for organizations to create relationships between ethnic communities. As a result, elected officials were pressured to support policies that integrated and welcomed immigrants into these culturally diverse urban areas.

Step outside the urban core, however, and the political environment changes quickly: cultural and racial diversity decreases; the values framework becomes more religious, more conservative; the environment is less welcoming of immigrants and immigration. Educational institutions continue to play a powerful role in the integration of immigrants, as we will see below. But with lower union penetration in conservative states and outside of urban areas, organized labor does not have the same power. And there just isn't the organizational capacity within the immigrant community to provide a base of activist support, social or economic.

In 2010, while the country struggled to recover from the 2008 recession, our allies in the business community were ineffective. We realized the economic case for immigrants and immigration was difficult, if not impossible, to make in suburban or rural areas with struggling economies. Immigrants and immigration were convenient to blame for a fast-changing world.

In these communities, we realized churches play the role of social convener around a common set of values. Figuratively speaking, we went to church to understand how to reach people's hearts.

As Matthew Soerens and Jenny Yang pointed out in their extraordinary book, *Welcoming the Stranger*, the Latin word *ger* embodied these voices in the Bible. *Ger*, which scholars believe refers to "'a person not native to the local area,' and thus often without family or land," appears ninety-two times in the Old Testament.[10] Soerens and Yang's book provided the information and tools for evangelicals to understand and engage in the immigration debate. Of many biblical citations offered, Soerens and Yang point out that in Leviticus 19:33–34, God commands the Israelites, "When an alien lives with you in your land, do not mistreat him. The alien living with you must be treated as one of your native born. Love him as yourself, for you were aliens in Egypt. I am the LORD your God." *Welcoming the Stranger* was more than a window into the immigration debate; for many white pastors, the book provided scriptural guidance in the context of a diversifying country and their diversifying congregations.

Without a doubt, Hispanic and Asian evangelical leaders at the local and national level play a crucial role in presenting these stories to their Anglo peers. This leadership includes Hyepin Im of the Korean Churches for Community Development; Noel Castellanos of the Christian Community Development Association; Luis Cortes of Esperanza; Samuel Rodriguez of the National Hispanic Christian Leadership Conference; and Gabriel Salguero of the National Latino Evangelical Coalition. Each has played a different role in the broader faith community to powerfully advance the interests of the community they and their membership serve. Importantly, whether it was through their own relationships or within broader organizations such as the National Association of Evangelicals, their influence serves as a clear reminder that much of the growth in the evangelical community depends on immigrants.

A 2015 survey of 35,000 Americans by the Pew Research Center found that the percentage of adults (ages eighteen and older) who describe themselves as Christians dropped by nearly eight percentage points in just seven years, from 78.4 percent in 2007 to 70.6 percent in 2014.[11] In the same time period, the religiously unaffiliated grew more than six points, from 16.1 percent to 22.8 percent.[12] (A note to secular liberals who rejoice in these falling numbers and hope for a nation freed from religion: 70 percent is still a lot of Americans.)

Robert P. Jones's recent book, *The End of White Christian America*, digs deep into the past, present, and future of the Christian community. Jones found that in 1974, nearly two-thirds of Americans identified as Protestant and approximately one-quarter identified as Catholic.[13] Only 7 percent claimed no religious affiliation. "These numbers remained mostly steady until the 1990s, when something unusual happened," wrote Jones.[14] "The numbers of Americans who identified as Protestant began to slip." Specifically, the percentage of Americans who identified as white Protestants slipped from 51 percent in 1993 to 32 percent in 2014. The number of black Protestants held steady; the only growth came from Hispanic Protestants.

Like American society writ large, American Christianity diversified. Pew Research found that "racial and ethnic minorities now make up 41% of Catholics (up from 35% in 2007), 24% of evangelical Protestants (up from 19%) and 14% of mainline Protestants (up from 9%)."[15] The community is also aging. In 2014, the median age of all Christians in the United States was 49, up from 46 in 2007.[16]

As microcosms of a larger society that is diversifying, evangelical churches face the questions of identity and culture that come with American immigration. These changes present an opportunity and a challenge for church leadership. On one hand, there's an opportunity to expand their congregations and spread the Gospel. On the other hand, there's a challenge to confront the anxiety and fear that comes with demographic change. In this hyperpolarized media environment, congregants are just as likely, if not more likely, to seek guidance from Fox News as from their pastor. The church may be a sanctuary, but it is not a bubble.

So America is changing, as are churches across the country. Is the evangelical community changing with it? Yes and no.

Over the course of the 2016 presidential election, a cultural and demographic fissure emerged among evangelicals. On one side, old guard evangelical leaders such as Ralph Reed, Pat Robertson, or James C. Dobson endorsed Donald Trump for president.[17] Their support remained steadfast in the face of race-baiting, fearmongering, and rampant misogynistic statements by Trump on the campaign trail.[18] Reed, Robertson, Dobson, and others—the Moral Majority faction, if you will, put issues of life and marriage above all others, ready and willing for their leadership and influence to be turned over to the Republican Party, regardless of the candidate. Polls showed that a plurality of evangelicals, 45 percent, agreed with them and were ready to vote for Trump.[19] On the other side, white evangelical leaders such as Russell Moore and Jen Hatmaker opposed Trump for these very same statements.[20] This camp included 62 percent of African Americans, Hispanic Americans, and Asian Americans with evangelical beliefs who supported Hillary Clinton, versus the 15 percent who supported Trump.[21]

The intense debate carried through the election and the fissure grew. While the number of evangelicals who ultimately voted for President Trump is the subject of yet another intense debate, given the demographic changes within evangelical life, the battle for political influence will continue for years. Healing this fracture in the context of local churches presents a different type of challenge. How do churches attract younger, more diverse churchgoers supportive of immigration reform, racial justice, or climate issues without turning away older populations who are worried about the cultural changes that come with these issues and, for the most part, remain singularly focused on issues of life and marriage? In a hyperpolarized environment where evangelical voters are assumed to be rock-ribbed Republicans and the left oozes sarcastic glee with news of shrinking numbers of Christians, this is no easy task for pastoral leadership. As much as they may want to grow their congregations with immigrants and young people, losing congregants comes with its own risks. It takes a special type of leadership to navigate these tensions in congregations, much less the evangelical community writ large.

This brings us to Dr. Barrett Duke. At first blush, Barrett can be intimidating. He has combed-back white hair, careful, methodical speech, and introspective eyes. Certainly one of the most politically and socially conservative people I know, for twenty years Barrett served as vice president for public policy and research for the Ethics & Religious Liberty Commission of the Southern Baptist Convention. I have come to appreciate Barrett as one of the warmest, funniest people I have ever met. He also embodies the cultural conflict facing white evangelicals, and how it is overcome.

Barrett's story began when he grew up in New Orleans and fell into the city's drug culture. He told me, "I basically came to the end of myself at twenty-one years of age and just didn't see any purpose for life. It was just meaningless."[22] His life changed when "God used that to break through the hardness of my heart, and I found the Lord and understood the path toward peace of God and trusted Jesus as my savior."[23] This path took him to a small bible college in Dallas and then Denver for seminary. About thirteen years later, in 1997, he left the church he built in Denver to join the Christian Life Commission, an early name for the Ethics & Religious Liberty Commission. During the Bush administration, the organization was drawn into immigration with high-profile legislative debates in 2001, 2006, and 2007. These debates, long before the first time I met Barrett in 2009, challenged his understanding of immigration, legality, and demographic change.

As a church man for forty years, Barrett's perspective on the cultural challenges that come with immigration did not hinge on a personal experience with immigrants. Growing up in New Orleans, Barrett lived in a white community and went to a racially integrated school. In Denver, his church served a middle-class white suburb. But in neither case did he come into contact with an immigrant community of any significant size.

Barrett told me, "It was really through reading my Bible that God began to give me a different understanding for the vulnerable, the stranger, the alien in the land."[24] His studies and reflection helped him gain a deeper understanding of the choice immigrants made to migrate, legally or illegally. But the rule of law weighed heavy and Barrett struggled to get past the fact that undocumented immigrants knowingly broke the law. He knew it was a tension between the law of the land and an immigrant family's deeply personal decision to survive. For most people navigating this tension, a personal experience with an immigrant softened the hardness of their heart. For Barrett, it was his faith.

Over time, instead of blaming the immigrants for their decision to illegally immigrate to the United States to increase the chances of their family's survival, Barrett held the government accountable for failing to establish an immigration system that provided a sense of justice for the American or the immigrant. As he put it, "Why should I blame the immigrant for some of my own country's failings?"[25]

While his heart was changed by his faith, his mind continued to waiver. "Now, I have to say, at any moment I can jump back into the other, into the other place, because it still bothers me that [undocumented immigrants] seem quite willing to use fraudulent documentation."[26] But, he continued, "They deserve to be treated as human beings regardless. So I need for God to continue to remind me of that. As long as God reminds me of that, I stay in this place where I relate to the undocumented from a different perspective."[27]

His own struggle with this tension is what makes Barrett such a powerful messenger to Southern Baptist pastors as they struggle with the very same questions—personally or with members of their congregations. Sometimes, these are pastors whose communities are quickly diversifying, who seek to grow their churches by serving immigrants' spiritual needs. Other times, they are pastors quick to blame immigrants for the economic struggles of their congregations.

Barrett has been in that place. He has confronted his own assumptions. He allowed his faith to change his heart, which led him to change his mind.

RECOVERING THE AMERICAN SOUL

"I grew up in Oklahoma, in a segregated society," Dr. Jo Anne Lyon told me.[28]

I was about a half hour outside of downtown Indianapolis, visiting the headquarters of the Wesleyan Church; at the time, Lyon served as its general superintendent. What strikes me every time I speak with Jo Anne is that she could have just traveled halfway around the world, but she will greet you with a warm smile and her full attention. She is a person who legitimately enjoys people.

We started our conversation with a recollection of her life as a five-year-old. Jo Anne remembered an African American woman who came to pick up the household's trash every Wednesday. She never saw this woman any other day of the week. So one day she asked her father where she went the rest of the days. Lyon's father took her to the neighborhood where the woman lived, and she recalled, "Where the paved road ended and the dirt roads began, I saw this whole world I didn't even know existed."

Jo Anne asked her father, who was a pastor, "Why don't they come to our church?"

He told her, "Well, they have their own church."

"Why don't they go to my school, kindergarten?"

"Well, they have their own school."

She concluded, "In my five-year-old mind, that never equated."[29] A life committed to justice was born.

The Wesleyan Church was the perfect home for Lyon. Named after John Wesley, it was organized in 1843; it split from the Methodist Episcopal Church, a predecessor body of the United Methodist Church, primarily over objections to slavery.[30] Taking their social-justice mission further than others, the Wesleyan Church was also one of the first to advocate equal rights and opportunities for women within the denomination.

Lyon's career began in 1980 at the Grand Rapids, Michigan, Center for Ecumenism. There, she lived through formative experiences with the, "migrant camps, the deplorable conditions for migrants at that time."[31] These camps reminded her of that childhood visit to the African American neighborhood in segregated Oklahoma.

After a trip to Ethiopia with the Grand Rapids ABC affiliate to film a documentary on the famine there, Lyon founded World Hope International in 1996, a Christian relief and development organization now operating in fifteen countries. She stepped down from World Hope International in 2008 when she was elected general superintendent of the Wesleyan Church. In close collaboration with her amiable and thoughtful chief of staff, David Drury, Lyon engaged Wesleyan leadership and congregants across the country to help members grapple with the demographic and cultural changes that came with immigration. Methodically, she brought the denomination's conversation back to a vision of "loving your neighbor as yourself, loving your neighbor as your equal."[32]

Given her personal and professional experience, a natural outgrowth of this work was a strategic focus on multiethnic churches—a strategy to culturally and ethnically diversify congregations. According to Jo Anne, the majority of the Wesleyan Church's membership is in the Midwest, where there are communities experiencing some of the fastest growth in the foreign-born population. Her focus on multiethnic churches took advantage of an opportunity to grow the denomination and confronted the challenge of community-wide culture change. Lyon's efforts were successful: Up from 8 percent when she started, Jo Anne told me that 20 percent of Wesleyan churches are now multiethnic.[33] Getting to this point took innovative local leadership.

Lyon was eager to tell me about Logansport, Indiana, population 18,034. A conservative, working-class area that is over 73 percent white, the region supported Donald Trump in the 2015 Republican primary and is represented in Congress by Republican Todd Rokita.[34] Lyon told me, "So we put a person there to pastor this church, which was probably going to close, [because there were] just a few little old ladies there."[35] She realized the community around what was then called Riverview Church was changing, but the church was not changing with it.

Reverend Zach Szmara, who was tasked with leading the church, urged leadership in Indianapolis to see the changes as an opportunity. Soon, Zach was one of the first to participate in the Wesleyan Church's new trainings to establish immigration centers. As Szmara puts it in a video, "We changed our name to the Bridge Community and began to try to mirror what our community looked like."[36]

Bridge Community Church was on track to becoming a multicultural, multilingual, and ethnic church. The video includes testimonials from congregants and pictures of longtime white church members in the pews, praying with immigrant families. Szmara captured the spiritual connection between communities when he said, "And the more we got to know people who were different than us, the more we realized it was God's heart."[37] Bridge Community Church also provided an important service for its immigrant community as the only immigration legal clinic for fifty miles. For a growing immigrant community in Logansport, Zach was both a spiritual and legal guide.

What struck me about the video isn't the diversity of the congregation, nor the scenes of immigrant families with the "little old ladies" Jo Anne fondly referred to. Rather, it was the brief glimpse of the church's back wall. On it, hung side by side above the door, were the American, Mexican, and Guatemalan flags. It was a scene I had seen in secular community centers across the country. In this case, it was the spiritual meeting the political.

In some ways, every pastor is a politician. Their mission is to spread the gospel and grow their congregation. In this day and age, to accomplish this goal, pastors need to serve the needs of increasingly diverse communities. In Logansport, Zach Szmara developed a model that relied on scripture to keep long-term members in the pews and build membership by providing services that were important to new congregants. Instead of closing doors, Bridge Community Church was hanging new flags.

While the evangelical community is decentralized and relational, the rigorous hierarchy of the Catholic community creates a different footprint. The scale and structure of the Catholic community also creates a level of diversity that other faiths haven't seen. In 2014, 20.8 percent of Americans identified themselves as Catholics. Sixty-five percent of Catholics are white, and a startling 29 percent are Hispanic.[38]

Florida's Archbishop Thomas Wenski has fully ensconced himself in the diversity and energy of a changing church in a changing state. Appointed the fourth archbishop of Miami and metropolitan of the province of Miami (which includes the seven dioceses of the state of Florida) by Pope Benedict XVI on April 20, 2010, Wenski is more than a fixture in Florida politics and religion.[39] He is a local kid who did good.

A native of West Palm Beach, Florida, and a linguistic quick study, when Wenski was ordained in 1976, "the priest said I was almost like the poster boy for bilingualism, because I was an Anglo who learned Spanish."[40] Along these lines, his first assignment was at a mainly Hispanic congregation at Corpus Christi Church in Celebration, Florida, just south of Orlando. As Wenski put it, "The pastor spoke English, but not very well. His associate didn't speak any English. So I did the English mass, and once a month they let me do the Spanish mass because that was the big mass."[41] This was also the church where Wenski got to know the Haitian community and learned Creole. Archbishop McCarthy, then leading the Diocese, learned of Wenski's new language and assigned him full time to work with the Haitian community. "So I did, for eighteen years," said Wenski.[42]

For decades, Miami has been the entry point for Cubans and Haitians fleeing oppressive regimes. These influxes caused legitimate stresses on the receiving community of Miami. In 1985, after having received approximately 100,000 Cubans as part of the Mariel boatlift, south Florida braced for another influx as the new Cuban Adjustment Act allowed Cuban refugees to apply for legal permanent residence—allowing them to sponsor relatives' trips to the United States. A May 1985 report released by Dade County Manager Merritt Stierheim catalogued $45,645,000 in refugee expenditures that were not reimbursed by the federal government.[43] On top of the economic stress, there was social stress. A prominent Cuban community leader told the *Chicago Tribune*, "It got the local rednecks a little scared that perhaps the nature of the community is being changed forever. It is."[44]

As Wenski put it, "In the early 1980s, Miami was really ground zero for a lot of anti-immigrant sentiment, because of not only the Haitians coming in, but also the Cuban Mariel exodus . . . So there was bad feelings towards the Cubans, and of course a lot of that towards the Haitians."[45] Today, there are at least 1.2 million Cubans in Miami; 400,000 arrived after 1980 in a third migration wave begun by the Mariel boatlift.[46] Approximately 197,000 Haitians call south Florida home; most arrived after the collapse of the Duvalier administration in 1980, others since the 2010 earthquake.[47] When Archbishop Wenski came onto the scene, at the height of this demographic change, he told me the saying was, "Last American to leave Miami, please take the flag." This wasn't intended as a compliment. This was not the Miami of Gloria Estefan, Dwayne Wade, or South Beach. This was Miami in the midst of massive cultural and demographic changes.

Wenski immersed himself in his work with the Haitian and Cuban communities. He offered mass at detention centers, visited Haiti, and quickly put himself on a unique career path within the US Catholic Church. But it was more than language. Archbishop Wenski understood early on that religion is inextricably linked to the immigration of Cubans and Haitians to the region—islands just 94 and 707 miles off the Florida coast, respectively.

Personal experiences with the immigrant community defined Wenski's leadership. He had seen the fears of the immigrant and refugee community, prayed with Haitian detainees pondering their fate, and sat with Cuban refugees worried about their families. Revered in the Haitian community, sought after by Cubans, and just edgy enough to enjoy a ride on his beloved Harley-Davidson (often for charity), Wenski is where the community goes when tragedy strikes Cuba, Haiti, or a local neighborhood.[48]

As we talked in his office, I gained a greater appreciation for the human condition—whether immigrant or native-born. Wenski spoke of the difference between natural and positive law, explaining the difference between what is wrong because it violates natural, moral, or public principles (*malum in se*), and what is wrong because it has been deemed so in statute (*malum prohibitum*). In our conversation, Wenski summed up this paradox with, "Americans will think abortion is legal, so there can't be anything wrong with it." But, he continued, "A Mexican is illegal, so there must be something wrong with him." In my liberal secular world, this difference was boiled down to the slogan, "No human being is illegal." Although it's a catchy slogan, it lacks the context of the laws we make versus the laws we believe. It is up to society to determine a legal structure to determine what action is illegal or not. It does not mean the person is illegal (e.g., I got a speeding ticket—does that make me illegal?), but the rule of law is the bedrock of America.

A few weeks after we spoke, Archbishop Wenski delivered the homily at Red Mass at the Basilica of St. Mary Star of the Sea in Key West. A tradition of the Catholic Church since the thirteenth century, the Red Mass is celebrated to recognize the work performed by the judiciary and members of the bar.[49] In his homily Wenski confronted the fear sweeping across the American politic: "We sense that our country and our culture is indeed undergoing a transformation that is as unprecedented as it is unpredictable. Implicit in this change of an age is a crisis of values and a crisis of leadership. And behind the anger and frustration of many people is simply fear."[50]

To his audience of policymakers and lawyers, Wenski put the fear coursing through the nation in the context of our immigration debate:

> "Illegal" immigrants are "criminals" only because government policy declares them to be or treats them as such—in the same way that persons openly practicing Christianity or Judaism in Soviet Russia were "criminals" only because government policy declared them to be. And conversely if government policy determines that something is "legal" like abortion, then the current conventional wisdom is "if it's legal it can't be wrong."[51]

To move is one of the most natural things we do as human beings. Whether it is moving to another neighborhood, city, or country, moving is a choice we make to seek a better life. The 65 million people worldwide currently forcibly displaced from their homes act on a very natural desire to stay alive.[52] The homes they leave are torn apart by war, economic crises, and/or natural disasters. They don't always want to migrate, but they have to. And this essentially human action creates stress and tension within receiving communities. Competition for resources (e.g., jobs, food, etc.) can be fierce, and those in receiving communities often make equally natural decisions to protect their own well-being.

To address this tension through a case built solely on data and policy ignores the human emotion behind migration. We are left with a framework of positive law, rules and regulations that seek to control a natural act. If there is no understanding of the natural acts, and their emotions, anxieties, and realities, our immigration system (much less debate) positions a natural action as something inherently illegal.

Yes, this is an abstract approach. And the natural-versus-positive-law framework is applied across a range controversial social issues (e.g., marriage, life/abortion, etc.) that crop up in society. I may or may not agree the application of natural law to other questions, but I now think about those issues differently. I also have a greater level of respect for those who arrive at different answers.

In this case, the idea of open and unregulated borders is neither pragmatic nor welcome. I believe the nation-state is absolutely necessary and Americans' concerns regarding border security are legitimate. But how do we strike a balance between this natural act of migration and national sovereignty? The struggle between the emotions of the heart and the realities of the mind may require, as Wenski put it, "a little bit of recovery of the American soul."[53]

KEEPING THE KEYS

Stephan Bauman grew up in a small town in Wisconsin. It was mostly Catholic, with a few Lutherans. In his professional life, he rarely traveled and was on the path to a well-compensated business consulting career. Stephan's wife, Belinda, his "chief mentor in life," talked him into taking a six-month leave in 1994 to volunteer in West Africa with a faith-based relief agency that did hospital care.[54]

"My whole world just flipped upside down," Bauman told me, and they stayed for six years.[55] Before he knew it, Bauman had tendered his resignation via fax machine from Africa and was barreling down a path to resettle refugees and engage evangelicals around the world. In 1994 there was no Internet, no Facebook, no Twitter. Refugee displacement was far removed from the thoughts of most Americans. These days, the stories of millions of refugees are beamed to the phones of millions of Americans. The stories can be unsettling, inspiring, and terrifying. Stephan's experiences provide a unique vantage point on both the refugee story and the way Americans understand it.

The US refugee resettlement program has, for many years, been a point of pride for the nation. Founded in 1948, the program was established to deal with an influx of displaced Europeans after WWII and the

Soviet invasions of Eastern Europe. Later, the 1980 Refugee Act provided the basis for the current resettlement programs, whereby the president decides that year's ceiling of accepted refugees. While the largest annual number of refugees, 207,000, were resettled in 1980 when the bill was passed, three million refugees have been resettled since.[56]

For many years, refugee resettlement was one of the few federal programs that enjoyed bipartisan support. The program was protected across the political spectrum, even if it was not always well funded. On April 15, 2013, just as millions of refugees began to flee Syria, that began to change.

On the third Monday of each April, Boston celebrates Patriots' Day. As far as I could tell from the ten years I spent in Boston, this was an opportunity to get in an early Red Sox home game and watch the Boston Marathon from the comfort of the local pub. In other words, participate in some serious day-drinking. Patriots' Day 2013 took a dark turn when the Tsarnaev brothers conducted a terrorist attack at the finish line that killed three, injured 260, and set off a days-long manhunt that brought the city to a standstill.

The Tsarnaev brothers were ethnic Chechens who had lived in Kyrgyzstan due to their inability to return to Chechnya. Their parents came to the country on a tourist visa and then applied for asylum status. As asylees, they were never subject to the security review the UN High Commission for Refugees conducts for refugees.[57] Regardless, the media began to link the brothers and their family to refugee resettlement efforts after Senator Rand Paul (R-KY) stated that the Tsarnaevs were refugees who were "coddled" by the United States.[58] The anti-refugee sentiment stoked in reaction to the Boston bombing was a turning point.

As the Middle East spiraled into disarray, millions of refugees began to flee Syria by boat and land. We saw pictures of Syrian men, women, and children streaming through eastern Europe or brimming boats landing on the shores of Greece. Public opinion hardened and European Union countries, along with the United States, slow-walked their search for a solution.

On July 17, 2015, German Chancellor Angela Merkel was speaking at a forum for young people. As reported by the BBC, a young Palestinian girl shared, in fluent German, that she would like to go to university.

Merkel told the young girl that "some [migrants] will have to go home" and gently stroked the young girl as she broke down into tears, an exchange captured by the cameras and broadcasted around the world.[59] It was clear neither Germany, nor Europe more broadly, was ready to welcome the mass migration of people.

All that changed in less than two months. On September 2, 2015, a photo of a young boy, face down on the beach, drowned, ricocheted across the Internet. The boy was Aylan. He was a three-year-old Syrian who was fleeing war and violence, a tragic victim of a capsized smuggler's boat going from Turkey to Greece. His father, Abdullah, was the sole surviving family member.[60] The international outcry was enormous. By the end of that month, Chancellor Merkel was leading the efforts to provide refugees safe haven.[61] While the European countries were working to manage the settlement of tens of thousands of people, the Obama administration grudgingly committed to settling an additional 10,000 Syrian refugees in America.

Public opinion was split. A December 2015 poll by the Public Religion Research Institute reported that four in ten Americans (41 percent) opposed admitting Syrian refugees in the country, and only 35 percent of Republicans supported allowing Syrian refugees into the United States.[62] By religious affiliation, 43 percent of white evangelical Protestants supported Syrian refugee resettlement in the country, compared with 57 percent of Catholics. Meanwhile, nearly half (47 percent) of all Americans said they are very or somewhat worried that they or someone in their family will be a victim of terrorism. Less than two years removed from the high-profile Boston bombing that conflated terrorism and refugees, people were scared, and all they saw were Syrian refugees teeming across borders all over the world.

The *Atlantic*'s Molly Ball captured the impact of fear on the public psyche: "It makes people hold more tightly to what they have and regard the unfamiliar more warily. It makes them want to be protected. The fear reaction is a universal one to which everyone is susceptible."[63]

In this environment, Stephan Bauman and his team at World Relief sought to provide refugees from around the world, and the Middle East in particular, a safe haven. Along the way, Bauman realized, "In many ways, my journey is often to sit with people like me, Anglo evangelicals, to share my story and help people step out of their own [lives]."[64]

It is a role that is more important and more difficult than ever before. Inspired by public opinion swinging against refugee programs, over the course of the 114th Congress (2015–2016), at least thirty-seven anti-refugee bills were filed in Congress and forty-two in state legislatures. And in December 2015, Donald Trump bellowed his support for a ban on Muslim immigration to the United States.[65]

Looking back at this period of time, Bauman felt that a sense of identity was lost in the fear and anxiety. Not the sense of American identity, but the loss of identity for refugees forcibly displaced. Just like some Americans did not want refugees to come to their communities, refugees themselves didn't want to leave their homes.

"The mothers and fathers [I meet] all have their house keys," Bauman told me as he drove to work one morning.[66] "Why do they do that? That's because, just like you or me, if you had a choice, you know, if you spent your whole life in a community, the first thing you would want to do is go back home and make a life there."[67] Very few of the refugees left their homes by choice. They left to save their lives. As Bauman pointed out, they lose their identity in this grueling journey. "The Syrian father, he's terrified to let go of their way of life, their culture, their house, their home, their land."[68]

This made the tension between policy choices and scripture all the more clear. "We're first meant to respond to the values of God before we subscribe to the values of our political nation-state," said Bauman.[69] Which is "where religion or faith can't just cave into politics. Sometimes it needs to, in the best sense of this word, be prophetic or challenge the political system."[70]

Unlike traditional immigration work, there is a decidedly international approach to refugee resettlement. Organizations urge the US government to work with international partners to address the root causes of economic and political instability, and advocate that the State Department establish regional processing centers so families can begin the vetting process before their harrowing journeys, often in the hands of smugglers.

After a bruising 2016 election where President Trump sowed deep currents of isolationism and xenophobia, how America's understanding of the world changes remains to be seen. But the engagement of faith communities overseas, amplified by the modern ease of communication, breaks down this myopia and serves as a small, important step toward understanding why people migrate.

When the highly respected Lynne Hybels, wife of Willow Creek Church Senior Pastor Bill Hybels, writes, "I believe the American Church has an extraordinary opportunity to remake the Middle East through the only power strong enough to stand against the hatred, violence, and fear that currently dominate the region: the power of God's love manifested and enfleshed by God's people," it is more than a call to mission.[71] It is a call to engage in the world.

MY BROTHERS AND SISTERS

Bridging the cultural divide that comes with demographic change requires politics to be driven by values, not ideology. Voters are disenchanted with both parties, and people are exhausted by endless recriminations. Of course, as Trump's election demonstrated, there remains a significant number of rural and suburban voters so ideological, so fearful and angry, that they were willing to vote for a radical change agent in 2016. Liberals cannot ignore these voters just as conservatives cannot ignore urban voters.

There is an opportunity to break out of our political ideologies to create new alliances that advance a range of issues, including immigration. Just as many liberals sought to support candidates other than Hillary Clinton, many social conservatives distanced themselves from Trump. Post-election, both communities, liberal and conservative, are in the midst of a dramatic realignment. Immigration, and the cultural change that comes with it, is one of the issues challenging conservatives to find a political center.

I met Russ Moore, whom you read about at the beginning of this chapter, for dinner on a Saturday in Washington, DC. Growing up in Biloxi, Mississippi, Russ experienced the influx of Vietnamese refugees who fled Saigon and settled along the Gulf Coast to become a part of the seafood industry. It was an insular community, and early on Russ didn't get to know many Vietnamese people. But he told me, "[what] I would notice as a kid was the reaction of white people to the Vietnamese immigrants that didn't make sense to me."[72] People claimed the Vietnamese were coming to America for welfare benefits. But the same people said the Vietnamese were taking all the jobs in the shrimping industry. "Well," Russ said, "I knew even as a kid both of those things couldn't be true. It was evident to me that the problem wasn't with anything that the Vietnamese immigrants were doing. It was just a reflexive fear of them."[73]

To be effective agents of culture change, faith institutions have an opportunity to serve as points of social integration for immigrants. The Catholic community's history, hierarchy, and inherent diversity makes this easier. For older white evangelicals who grew up in homogenous communities in decentralized denominations, when their neighborhoods start to change, this is harder (and more important).

This is where global missions help churches engage and understand changing neighborhoods. As Russ put it, "[in] churches that are really committed to global missions, . . . the identity of the congregation has had a sense of international solidarity."[74] While mission work has long been a part evangelical life, "carrying the gospel to the end of the earth," as Russ described it, the increased means of communication have changed the way congregations relate to missionaries. The ability of congregations to maintain a personal connection to those who travel overseas, or with the communities they commit to help, expands the worldviews of the community. This makes it a little easier for churches to welcome the stranger into their midst. Russ summed it up, "So, as communities start to diversify, the churches that are evangelistic are the churches that survive. So [it's] kind of a Darwinian principle for non-Darwinian people."[75]

This is where my advocate side comes out. I shared my impatience with Russ, wishing pastors were more aggressive in their policy positions when it comes to immigration. Or at least that pastors speak explicitly about immigrants and immigration from the pulpit. "To be fair, I think their pastor has talked about it," Russ said. "What he hasn't talked about is policy as it relates to immigration."[76] Russ described the approach in the context of poverty. "A typical evangelical pastor is going to say 'I can tell you that you have a mandate to care for the poor, and I can tell you here [are] the things we're doing as a congregation to care for the poor around us.'" He continued, "What I can't adjudicate is the dispute between the guy who says 'Let's raise the minimum wage to a living wage,' and the guy who says 'If you do that, you are going to cause businesses to lay people off and you are going to have greater unemployment.'"[77]

Russ's example supports my hypothesis that the immigration debate, if not our national identity crisis, is more about culture and values than it is about politics and policy. Taking a pastor, our best player, off the field to jabber about policy details is a strategic failure. When we are talking about immigration policy, not immigrants as people, we are losing the debate.

In their book about "believing and voting," *Faith in the Voting Booth*, Leith Anderson and Galen Carey, the president and vice president of the National Association of Evangelicals, respectively, offer scriptural guidance on the range of public-policy issues that voters confront these days.[78] It is an important book at an important time. Overwhelmed by the partisanship of our politics and our media, evangelicals of all stripes are looking for such guidance. In the case of the culture change that comes with immigration, the raw emotions trigger a particularly raw set of politics. Anderson and Carey delve into the immigration debate in a chapter asking, "What Would the Statue of Liberty Say Today?"

An important subtext to this is the audience that evangelical pastors face. In February 2015, Lifeway Research, one of the most respected organizations when it comes to understanding evangelicals in America, polled one thousand evangelicals for their views on immigration. Interestingly, Lifeway found that when it came to immigration, a greater percentage of evangelicals are more influenced by media than they are by the Bible.[79] In this context, Anderson and Carey cited scripture to make the point that it commands us to love God, our neighbors, and immigrants.[80] In today's media environment, where powerful conservative outlets such as *Breitbart News* exceed the hyperbole of Fox News, sharing this message requires a level of moral courage and risk-taking that is hard to appreciate from outside the world of social conservatives.

In the summer of 2014, alongside a constant stream of news of Syrian refugees, stories of large numbers of unaccompanied minors fleeing gang violence in Central America and presenting themselves to US Customs and Border Patrol officers began to emerge. These children were not sneaking across the border. They were not hiding. They were fleeing the Northern Triangle countries of Guatemala, El Salvador, and Honduras, where 80 percent of drugs coming to the United States flowed and cartels dominated their neighborhoods. They put their lives in the hands of human smugglers to then turn themselves over to US officials. To the general public, the world was on the move, borders around the world were out of control, and Fox News was telling citizens that America was being invaded by five-year-old Central Americans.

Soon, pictures of Latino boys and girls huddled in cold cement cells and draped in emergency blankets were leaked to conservative press. Instead of a debate about the safety and security of children, conservative news outlets shrieked about the threat of invasion from south of the border. As evidenced by the photos, federal agencies responsible for the processing and protection of these young people were overwhelmed. Stories of Central American women and children unceremoniously dropped at bus stations by the government ran rampant through conservative media.[81] A fierce political debate overshadowed the very human tragedy underway along the southwestern border.

The first four days of July 2014 clarified the situation. In order to manage scarce shelter and processing resources, Customs and Border Patrol began to transfer women and children to facilities beyond the border region. One of these facilities was in Murrieta, California, a small city of approximately 103,000 about an hour and a half north of the US–Mexico border.

According to July 1 news reports, three buses transporting women and children detainees were greeted by two hundred to three hundred protesters. Breaking through a small contingent of Murrieta police officers, the protesters waved American flags and held signs that read, "Stop Illegal Immigration," "Send Them Back with Birth Control," or "Return to Sender."[82] The images of sun-drenched activists—white on one side of the road, brown on the other—while buses full of children and mothers idled in the background, led the news. Although the bus's shades were pulled down, it didn't take much to imagine the young passengers' fear as they watched the scene outside.

A few days later, at a special Fourth of July ceremony in the East Room of the White House, President Obama welcomed twenty-five new American citizens.[83] The new citizens were service members or their families and came from a wide range of countries around the world. As I sat in the East Room that day, I listened to the president say, "The basic idea of welcoming immigrants to our shores is central to our way of life, it is in our DNA."[84] As he spoke, I couldn't help but think about the women and children on those buses, scared behind the window shades. I found it hard to believe that the idea of welcoming immigrants was any longer in our national DNA.

About a week afterward, Russ reached out to me. The Southern Baptist community was divided on the issue, and Russ wanted to send a message that these were children to be cared for, not shunned or scapegoated. So I urged the relevant federal agencies to create a process through which outside stakeholders could visit facilities and meet the young people fleeing Central America. Soon, a trip to the Rio Grande Valley came together for the end of July.

On July 13, Moore wrote in a powerful blog post called "The Road to Jericho and the Border Crisis," "Our answer to the border crisis cannot be quick and easy. But, for the people of God, our consciences must be informed by a kingdom more ancient and more permanent than the United States. Our response cannot be to say, in Spanish: 'And who is my neighbor?' (Luke 10:29)."[85]

In the hot morning air of Brownsville, Texas, we pulled up to the Customs and Border Protection facility, a nondescript building that looked like any other low-slung warehouse in the area. The powerful delegation of social conservative leaders consisted of Moore, president of the Ethics & Religious Liberty Commission of the Southern Baptist Convention; Ronnie Floyd, president of the Southern Baptist Convention; Bishop Daniel Flores of Brownsville, Texas; Jim Richards, executive director of the Southern Baptists of Texas Convention; and Pastor Tim Moore with the Evangelical Immigration Table, along with a few of their colleagues—and me, clearly not a powerful social conservative leader.

The facility's waiting room was more of a holding room—no chairs or windows, and a vinyl tile floor. We received our instructions, met our Border Patrol guide, and walked down a narrow hallway to a gray metal door that opened to a sprawling warehouse space. The gleaming chain-link-fence holding pens were jarring. There were thirty-foot by thirty-foot enclosures that were clean, orderly, and arranged for reasons ranging from age to gender to recreation. In a handful of them were groups of fifteen to twenty children, separated by age and gender. The children were safe, fed, and warm. But it was a sterile, imposing space where no parent would want to see their child.

As we walked through the facility, I watched the faces of the white men in the delegation. (Bishop Flores was the only faith leader of color.) Other than an occasional question for Border Patrol or to ask Bishop Flores to translate a conversation with one of the youth, not much was said. Just deep breaths, teary eyes, and clenched jaws. From the mouths of these babes came stories of violence, long journeys, and lost families. There was no media filter for the delegation. This was reality.

That day in Texas, Russ Moore and Floyd stood together as leaders of Southern Baptist life in America. They spoke to the dignity of the young people they met. Floyd told the *Christian Post*, "I think what touring the facilities did for me, is it basically crystalized this incredible national issue right before my eyes."[86] He added, "I saw children and I saw young people face-to-face. They weren't [in] someone's newspaper or [on] someone's website, but they were real people, real lives—someone's children, someone's grandchildren."

Moore went further and told the *New York Times*, "the anger directed to vulnerable children is deplorable and disgusting. . . . These children are made in the image of God, and we ought to respond to them with compassion, not fear."[87] This took place on July 22, 2014, about two years before Moore and Floyd stood together on the Southern Baptist Annual Convention stage in St. Louis, challenging calls to scapegoat Muslims.

With the exception of Bishop Flores, none of the evangelical leaders had any reason to relate to the young people they met that day. They were not Central American. They were not Latino. To my knowledge, none had fled violence at a young age. These were white men with very little in common with these young people. They knew a lot of their followers weren't standing behind them; in fact, a significant number of Southern Baptists thought the children were breaking the law, that they should be forced to return to Central America. But these leaders had been touched by their visit, so they decided to lead.

Over that dinner in Washington, DC, in 2016, Moore and I talked about the ugly electoral cycle in which Mexicans, Muslims, and other immigrant communities were attacked by politicians. Bucking the trend within conservative circles, Moore led what could be called the opposition movement. But he didn't see himself as a Republican working to save the party from itself. He understood the political risks he was taking; particularly when a number of conservative Hispanic evangelicals had endorsed Trump. Russ told me, "As a Christian, my primary identity is not white southerner. My primary identity is in Christ. So when I'm standing up for Hispanic immigrant communities or vulnerable Asian first-generation Americans, I'm not kind of crossing a boundary here. These are my people because these are brothers and sisters in Christ."[88]

CHAPTER FOUR

AS SOUTH CAROLINA GOES, SO GOES AMERICA

T he drive to North Greenville University winds through upstate South Carolina's country roads. Rolling hills, pastures greening in the late winter, shallow wooded valleys, and small homes dot the landscape. It is the idyllic Carolina countryside of postcards and prints.

The North Greenville University campus of dark-red-brick buildings sits on a small hill where Highways 414 and 253 intersect. In the cold morning air, I wandered the campus looking for the right building. Of course, as a student kindly pointed out, it was right in front of me. Affiliated with the South Carolina Baptist Convention, in 2016 North Greenville University ranked in the top 5 percent in terms of gender diversity, but number 1,522 nationally in terms of ethnic diversity.[1]

Associate professor in linguistics and Spanish Victor Prieto met me at the door of the Averyt/Wood Learning Center. We walked down what could have been a hallway on any college campus in America, as it smelled of freshly mopped vinyl floors and the bulletin boards were covered with event flyers. Victor had an office typical of an associate professor at the beginning of his academic career: enough room for a desk, crammed bookshelves, and a chair or two for inquiring minds. No windows. Just fluorescent lights.

He wore a dark sweater and, like the linguist he is, spoke clearly with a subtle Latino accent. There was never any anger or frustration in his voice, but there was a seriousness of purpose. As we talked, I realized that Victor embodied the steady demographic and political changes altering the identity of South Carolina.

Victor was born and raised in Venezuela in a very religious family. His father was a policeman; his mother, a nurse. After earning an undergraduate degree in theology and church ministry, he went on to get a second degree in English. Victor met his wife, a Colombian immigrant to Venezuela, at a church where he used to minister.

In 1998, Victor left Venezuela (with his wife) to begin his master's studies in linguistics at the University of Florida (which explained the Gators football paraphernalia taking up valuable bookshelf space in his office). As he put it, "Because my last bachelor degree was [in Venezuela] in English education, I wanted to go to an English-speaking country to better my English, and then go back to Venezuela to be a teacher at the university level."[2]

Prieto never intended to stay in the United States, but life intervened when his son was born in Florida in 1999. Since his wife's family was already in Florida and the political and economic situation in Venezuela was worsening due to a military coup and low oil prices, among other issues, Victor "decided to stay, mostly for him—for our son."[3] Years later, as he finished his doctorate in linguistics, Victor started the job search.

What took him to South Carolina in 2005 was a prayer answered: "I prayed to God [that] whoever offers me the job first, I'm going to say yes. Because I didn't want to be worried about that. I just wanted to write a dissertation and finish up. So that's what I did. This was the first solid offer that I had, so I said yes to the first one. That's how I ended up [in South Carolina]."[4] Victor didn't come to South Carolina to sweep floors, mow lawns, or install roofs. He was a "Baptist from Venezuela," and he was there to teach young Baptists.[5]

Just as Victor never thought he would end up in the Palmetto State, the Palmetto State never expected Victor. As a Latino immigrant teaching at a predominantly white Southern Baptist university, Prieto's situation was also the opposite of the experience of white teachers in South Carolina, who found themselves teaching increasingly diverse classrooms in a rapidly changing state. For the state's fast-growing Hispanic community, life was not easy.

As the number of Hispanic churches in the state began to grow, Victor stepped into the role of liaison between these new churches and the

Baptist churches in the region. He described how the community felt after Arizona's anti-immigrant law was passed in 2010. It created a wave of anti-immigrant sentiment across the country and filled the lives of South Carolina's immigrants with a new fear. "Then we lost people. The local churches lost people," Victor told me.[6] "We have people who are living in the shadows. They are afraid of doing things publicly."

The situation was so tense that even acts of kindness by white churches caused fear and anxiety. As one of the Hispanic churches began to grow, Victor told me they approached a large, white, evangelical church, asking for space to accommodate more people. The church kindly agreed, and the group began to meet there on Sunday mornings. Since these larger evangelical churches caused quite a bit of traffic, local police sent cruisers with flashing lights to help manage flow and keep cars moving. These officers caused alarm within the immigrant community, many of whom lacked access to a driver's license due to their immigration status. "So it is our feeling that a lot of the invitations we gave to people or a lot of the outreach efforts we did might have not worked because the people were afraid of going to the church because of the cops, who were terrifying to them," Victor said. "[The immigrant community] thought it was a checkpoint or something. We didn't grow much on that site, so we moved."[7]

Much of the Hispanic community members for whom Victor sought a place of worship were undocumented or just afraid of interacting with the police. As they sought to improve the lives of their families, they lived a life of fear. Victor went on, "So we see our people in this unstable situation and it hurts. It hurts because in a sense they are part of our families, not only because we're Hispanics, but, first of all, they are humans. Second, they are part of our churches also."

Ultimately, only a policy change that allowed access to driver's licenses would quell the fear of police checkpoints and driving. Instead, in a deeply religious state like South Carolina, people were afraid to go to church.

THE WINDS OF CHANGE

South Carolina is the south's racial and cultural petri dish. As the first state to secede from the Union and one of the last to surrender, the state seems to face an eternal identity crisis. In fact, only after the tragic murder of nine African Americans at Charleston's Emanuel African Methodist Episcopal Church sparked a national outcry did the state lower the Confederate flag from the state capitol grounds. While many conservative leaders celebrated the flag's removal, the move was not without opposition from entrenched extremists in the state.

But South Carolina is no longer only defined by the relationship between its black and white communities. As of 2016, the state is home to one of the nation's two South Asian American governors, Nikki Haley. The black community has reached new heights with Tim Scott, the first African American Republican senator to represent South Carolina since Reconstruction (1865–1877). While the lone Democratic congressional representative for the state, Jim Clyburn, has served as the dean of the delegation since 1993, South Carolina is a reliably red Republican state.

The dynamics of South Carolina's "first in the south" presidential primary best describes the historically binary politics of the state. Republicans lean far to the right in order to garner increasingly conservative slices of the electorate. Meanwhile, Democrats speak directly to the interests of black voters in order to secure the state's important early primary delegates. Once the hard-fought primary is over, the dominance of Republican voters makes the general election contest, for all intents and purposes, moot. There is no margin of victory to analyze, just a resounding win for the Republican candidate.

While the political identity of the state will take generations to change, South Carolina is at the cusp of a demographic revolution. In 1990, a mere 1.1 percent of South Carolina's population was Latino.[8] Over the course of the 1990s, the "browning" of South Carolina began. The state's Latino population tripled from 30,551 in 1990 to 95,076 in 2000. The trend continued in the first decade of the new century, when the Latino population increased 148 percent, to 235,682.[9] By 2011, 5 percent of South Carolina's population was Hispanic, encompassing a total of 241,000 people. Most important, at that point, 56 percent of Latinos in South Carolina were born in the United States.[10]

In fact, according to the National Council of La Raza, between 2000 and 2010 in South Carolina, the Latino child population (under age eighteen) more than doubled, with a 192 percent increase.[11] And between 2008 and 2010 in South Carolina, 88 percent of Latino children were citizens by birth; of these children, 65 percent lived in immigrant families and 33 percent lived in linguistically isolated households where no member over the age of fourteen spoke English very well. The bottom line is that between 2000 and 2010, South Carolina experienced the fastest increase in the Hispanic population in the nation, followed by North Carolina, which saw a 111 percent increase. The winds of change had blown into South Carolina Hispanic seeds that were taking root and would have a long-term impact on what it means (and looks like) to be a South Carolinian. Latinos did not come to South Carolina for the barbeque. They came to fill plentiful jobs in a fast-changing, growing economy.

As Dr. Donald Schunk and Dr. Douglas Woodward of the Darla Moore School of Business at the University of South Carolina wrote back in February 2000, "The South Carolina economy is currently in the midst of a historic shift away from manufacturing towards the service and trade sectors. However, this fundamental change is just the most recent in a history of significant economic transitions in South Carolina."[12] As Schunk and Woodward shared in their paper, "A Profile of the Diversified South Carolina Economy," South Carolina mill owners took advantage of the state's access to cheap power (rivers) to grow from 14 mills with 2,100 workers in 1880 to 239 mills with 94,800 workers in 1930, thereby representing roughly 75 percent of all industrial workers in the state. The authors found that in 1970, manufacturing industries accounted for 28.9 percent of all full- and part-time jobs in South Carolina. But, "driven by the sharp decline in the textile and apparel industries, manufacturing jobs made up just 17.3 percent of total employment in 1997."

As textile manufacturing moved out of the country, the region's leadership made an aggressive play for auto manufacturing. On June 24, 1992, the state announced that BMW was going to open a new manufacturing plant in Spartanburg.[13] More than twenty years later, it is clear that the plant has been an economic boon to the region. A University of South Carolina report found "the production of BMW automobiles support 30,777 jobs in South Carolina. . . . For every direct job created at the BMW plant, an additional three jobs are created elsewhere in South Carolina through the economic multiplier effect."[14]

Just as important, Betty Joyce Nash wrote for the Federal Reserve Bank of Richmond, "BMW's arrival accelerated the Upstate's nascent culture change."[15] German workers, families, and restaurants began to pop up; the economic change spurred a cultural change.

Like most of the nation and certainly helped by the arrival of BMW, South Carolina's economy prospered through the last decade of the century. In December 1990, the state's unemployment rate hovered at 5.4 percent. Seven years later, the rate clocked in at a much lower 3.6 percent.[16]

But the impact of BMW's successful plant and the overall boom of the 1990s went well beyond a handful of engineers. As textile mills moved out, Latinos moved in. Demographically and culturally, a third factor had been introduced to the historically black-white state. It was the beginning of a new South Carolina and a new set of dynamics for the state's schools, churches, and politics. Dynamics uniquely explained by people who lived through the change.

Harold Smith, a lifelong resident of Spartanburg County, is a white southerner who grew up during segregation, experienced integration, and described the changes that led to a new South Carolina as a place where "the world came to us."[17]

In what was clearly *his* recliner, Smith fidgeted as we watched the returns of the 2016 Super Tuesday primaries on March 1. The steady click of the rocking recliner was the metronome to his southern accent. We had just finished an informal family dinner where grandparents doted, parents talked, and grandkids cried and played. Smith's mother sat on the couch nearby, and his son, Derrick, sat on another recliner across the room.

Smith told me stories of his childhood in South Carolina and life through desegregation. He didn't sugarcoat the tension and tragedies of the time, nor did he delve deeply into what was underneath those experiences. "I do remember going to the water fountain and seeing 'white' and 'colored,'" Harold told me.[18] "I remember that as a little kid. I must have been eight or nine years old. . . . As a kid you don't know. You kind of learn, it's like, oh, maybe they've got something that we don't need to get rubbed off on us. It was not spoken, though. It wasn't spoken like we hate them or [we're] against them. It was just like, oh, you stay away from those folks."

His was a "simple life—really simple. We were sort of protected, but I do remember watching the news and seeing [the violence of the civil rights movement], thinking what is going on? Why are [the police] beating people up with sticks? Just didn't make much sense to me as a kid." These days, Smith lives in a gated subdivision where he fishes on a small lake just off his backyard deck. But over time he realized how the changes around him impacted the way he saw the world. The bubble he grew up in was not impenetrable. "That's why I say, one of my sayings is, too, my dad was less prejudiced than his dad. I'm less prejudiced than my dad and my children are less prejudiced than me, and their children will be less prejudiced than them."[19]

Smith grew up in a South Carolina that was black and white, and governed by whites. Now, the Palmetto State is black, white, and brown, and, until very recently, it was governed by a South Asian. All things considered, South Carolina's economy has been stable, but the identity of the state has not been. While Americans of Harold's generation have seen a lot, today's changes are coming fast, and they are coming loudly. So in his living room, with CNN flickering in the background, I asked Harold where he thought today's racial and cultural tension was coming from.

He rocked in his recliner for an extra beat and said, "I think it's the political correctness. I knew my grandpa, he didn't own any slaves. My daddy didn't own any slaves. I didn't own any slaves. Somehow I owe somebody something. Nobody in my family ever owned a slave, but somehow I feel like I'm blamed for it. . . . What are your needs? Your needs are the same as mine. Let's get up and go to work. I don't quite understand. I don't know."[20]

There wasn't any anger in Harold's voice. There was confusion, frustration, and pain, but not anger. Just like how he hoped his grandchildren would be better people, less prejudiced, than him, Harold also wanted to make sure his family prospered. Demographic change and racial equality weren't necessarily a threat to him, but they were points of confusion. And to help him address this question, he felt the best choice for president was Donald Trump.

SCHOOLS ARE THE TOUCHPOINT

About a three-hour drive northwest of Charleston, Spartanburg is a town of just over 37,000 people, within an overall Spartanburg County population of approximately 284,000 (in 2016).[21] In general, the homes are modest and low-slung with a modern small-town feel. Downtown Spartanburg, known as Morgan Square, has undergone a revitalization. Hipster coffee shops, a Marriott hotel, and restaurants inhabit the three-block radius. Just a block or two outside downtown is Spartanburg's first micro-distillery, Motte and Sons. It is a town trying to change with the times.

On my visit to Spartanburg, I parked myself at the Beacon, a required restaurant for all presidential candidates. The parking lot is huge (for your campaign bus), the seating is plenty (for your voters), and the smell of fried food is glorious (but terrible for your arteries). Once you walk up to the counter, you must be ready to place your order.

Looking like a Yankee leftover from the previous week's presidential primary (button-down shirt, slacks, computer bag), I asked the counter clerk if the Beacon did a grilled cheese sandwich.

"Yes. With bacon," was the unimpressed response.

"Umm," I paused, much to his chagrin, "Could I sub tomatoes for the bacon?"

With a sigh, he bellowed my tomato-substituted grilled cheese order to the line cooks sweating over massive griddles. Sensing I was losing the room, I made a desperate attempt to save face and added an order of fries and onion rings.

"Large or small?"

I noticed the largeness of the large fries and meekly responded, "Small."

With that, my campaign for president came crashing to an end.

On the other hand, the Chuck Bagwell presidential campaign was ready to go, as Bagwell sat down with the lunch of future commanders in chief: double cheeseburger, large fries, and sweet tea.

A former basketball player, Chuck squeezed into our booth and sat diagonally in order to ease the creakiness of bum knees. Raised in Spartanburg since age four, Chuck had recently retired from serving as principal of Arcadia Elementary School for over thirteen years. He had a big smile and a gentle voice that immediately put me at ease but would surely have terrified me as a third grader.

Chuck graduated from Spartanburg's Dorman High School and attended West Point Academy for a year before moving back home to attend Wofford College, where he studied biology and played varsity basketball. He went on to earn a doctorate in education administration from South Carolina State University, a historically black college and university (HBCU). Or as Chuck—a white man who attended a South Carolina HBCU—put it in the first few minutes of our conversation, "a minority school. But I thought it was very important for me to do that because of my job. We all need to get a perspective on life."[22]

Yes indeed, we all need to get a perspective on life.

Chuck made a conscious decision to gain a new perspective with his choice of college. South Carolina youth, whether they were new to the country or their parents had been there for generations, had no such option. During Chuck's career, it was (and still is) incumbent upon primary schools to introduce these different perspectives in thoughtful ways—particularly since the pace of change in the school system, and the communities they serve, was so rapid.

Another leader in Spartanburg education, Dr. Laura Barbas, moved to the town in the summer of 2000 to teach Spanish at Wofford College. Long active in the community's growing Hispanic community, Dr. Barbas saw "schools that became the first touchpoint for the preexisting community," as native-born South Carolinians got to know their new neighbors through their children's experiences.[23] More important, Dr. Barbas "found a predisposition on the part of school teachers and leaders to want to do something on the human side without asking a lot of questions about politics."

Arcadia Elementary is a prime example of schools as touchpoints: it has the highest percentage of ESOL (English for speakers of other languages) students in the district, more than 57 percent. When Chuck arrived as principal of Arcadia in 2003, he said the students were "24 percent [English language learners], and within seven or eight years we went to 66 percent ESOL."[24] From his perspective, this provided "a greater opportunity to learn from each other and to help each other." It was the challenge and opportunity of these changes that motivated Chuck, and his Arcadia team, to turn the school into not just an elementary school but a place for families of all nationalities to come together and learn.

The story of Arcadia Elementary has several lead characters in addition to Chuck. We'll start with Jana White. At the Adult Learning Center in downtown Spartanburg, Jana's office doubled as a classroom, and her Nebraska accent didn't slow anything down; at one point in the interview she told me, "You have to get your questions in edge-wise."[25]

Beginning in 1994, Jana taught English literature to students at a local junior high for thirteen years. Since she came into the job with a master's degree in English, the principal asked her to teach English as a second language (ESL). "I object to [the term] ESL, because it's not their second language, but for most it's their third or fourth," Jana told me.[26] "Only [native-born] Americans learn second languages."

In 2007, Jana White retired from "the bureaucracy,"[27] as she called it, to find herself teaching adult immigrants how to speak English at the Learning Center.

Her desk and computer were at the far end of the narrow room. It held two banquet tables, placed end to end, with flags hanging on the walls and, as Jana pointed out, "There is a map with the United States on one side and the world on the other. It is not there for the international students, except for the international students to show the Americans where they came from."[28]

The downtown evening classes she taught early in the 2000s clearly met a need, but Jana knew there were more adult students in the community who would take advantage of the program if they had the opportunity and the programs were easier to access.

So Jana partnered with Norma Blanton, a teacher at Arcadia Elementary School, to start an English-language-learning program for adults. As she described it, "Norma was going to take the first group and I was going to test them. We figured twenty-five [students], and then we'll get sorted

out. We'll know how many teachers we need. We had fifty the first night.
. . . They came back. Usually they check out a program, [and] if you don't
cut the mustard, they don't come back. That [first night] was a Tuesday.
Thursday night we had seventy-five."[29]

In the conversation, I noticed White referred to her immigrant or refugee
students as "internationals." While at first I flinched at this homogenous
term, I came to understand that this generalization of identity helped ease
the anxiety of culture change within the school and allowed teachers and
students to respect diversity but not delve into nationality. Jana understood
the power and importance of relationship building and the power of shared
experiences to break down barriers. Free from the shackles of a bureaucracy,
Jana put into motion some guerilla tactics to mix advanced literacy classes
with English-language-learning classes in order to build relationships. "After
we had done the advanced [English-learning] class, basic literacy was across
the hall."[30] She continued, "So I started growing basic literacy and beginning
English speakers together. We had the United Nations in there every day."

Jana wasn't waiting for a church, much less a school administrator,
to sign off on what she felt was right. She saw that if relationships were
built between adult students, new understanding could be shaped and good
things could happen outside the classroom. The benefits were both cultural
and educational for the students. "So now we have evolved to where we
have Americans and internationals. They are learning from each other. The
Americans have heard the word in English and can help the international
say the word if the international starts to say it wrong."

The next evening, I visited Norma Blanton at Arcadia Elementary,
which is home to a student body of about five hundred. It was almost 5:00
p.m., and the parking lot was almost half full and the building bustled
with activity. Around a makeshift registration desk/security checkpoint,
children, teenagers, and adults milled about, waiting for classes to start
or questions to be answered. A young Hispanic woman asked me to wait
while she spoke into her walkie-talkie to find Norma.

I leaned against the white-cinder-block walls and watched the scene as
Norma walked up carrying her own walkie-talkie. She was short in height
and hair but, as I learned, tall in vision. We walked to the other side of the

school and stepped into a small classroom/office, where we sat in child-sized chairs and I reintroduced myself to my kneecaps.

Norma arrived in Spartanburg in 1999 after spending several years overseas on missions with her husband, David, who was a Southern Baptist pastor. "They were starting a program of foreign language," Norma told me.[31] "Just having come back from Ecuador, they thought I knew Spanish. The funny thing was nobody asked me to speak Spanish or say anything. They just said, 'We'll hire you.'"

After five years of teaching Spanish, Norma transitioned to teach ESOL just as Arcadia's Hispanic population began to increase. Word of mouth spread quickly in the community. As the school's Hispanic population more than tripled, Norma told me that the word on the street was, "Just get on [Highway] 26 and get off at our exit, and they'll take care of you at Arcadia Elementary School."[32]

Keep in mind that during this time, the state's undocumented immigrant population also grew dramatically.[33] So, in addition to language, transportation, and poverty, the lack of legal status deepened the community's isolation. Whether it was going to church, as we heard earlier from Victor Prieto, or integrating into broader society, the immigrant community faced obstacles and fears at every turn.

Norma told me, "They put a stop sign right out here [in front of the school]. There didn't used to be."[34] It was a trap, she said, "[The city] put it there with the expectation to catch people from the community to check their papers. And we lost several families [as a result]. Dad is here one day, gone the next." In spite of this kind of pressure, Norma, Jana, Chuck, and others forged ahead.

They soon realized that to involve the parents of their new Hispanic students would take a different approach. Norma told me, "So I would say, and some of the rest of us would say, 'Well, have you sent that home in Spanish? Do they know what you want? Do they understand what you need from them?' Of course, the answer was no."[35] The programs at Arcadia Elementary weren't meeting the parents where they were.

As Bagwell had shared with me, "As your community changes, I think those in the community have to change. If you want to help people who are different than you, you need to learn where they're coming from and you need to learn their story."[36] So from Chuck Bagwell to Norma Blanton to the institution's commitment to hire a Hispanic receptionist, the school fully embraced the new population.

From this commitment came the first parenting classes for the Latino community at Arcadia. Norma reached beyond the language barrier. "I don't think before [parents] had felt valued, because of their lack of [English]. So we've tried to say it doesn't matter if you don't really speak English. Here are things you can do to be part of your child's education. It doesn't matter what language you speak."[37] The partnership with Jana from the Adult Learning Center downtown quickly grew to "six classes, four levels, basically just learning English, and then two classes that feed into the GED program."[38]

And, soon, Arcadia Elementary School became a touchstone for the parents as much as it was for their children. These Latino families saw this building as a place where they could be with each other and learn how to integrate into American life. More important, they knew they could trust the staff of Arcadia Elementary.

Later that evening, we stood outside the second meeting of a new class helping families understand how to manage their finances. As women walked out, everyone who walked by knew Norma. More than one, she pointed out, had already "graduated" from a particular class but kept coming back in order to learn more and be a part of an extended family.

Our conversation sobered as Norma and I discussed the tension in the city around immigrants and refugee resettlement, as well as the awful political rhetoric that dominated the national news. Norma told me, "We talk a lot about it in my class, because they're just fascinated with the politics. We talk about Trump, and a little guy who is a brick mason said, 'Why does he hate me and he doesn't even know me?' I said, 'Jose, if he knew you, he'd like you because you're a hard worker.'"[39]

THE CHANGING CHURCH

Chuck Bagwell understood the importance of the church in his life. As he put it, "Don't just talk about faith, live your faith. Don't talk about going to church, be the church."[40] In a state that is 78 percent Christian and where 74 percent of adults' belief in God is, "absolutely certain," it is fair to assume the state's identity is wrapped in the moral compass and social tension provided by Christianity.[41]

South Carolina's political establishment acts accordingly. Some, like Governor Niki Haley (R) and Senator Lindsey Graham (R), tend to be more private about their faith, while Representatives Mick Mulvaney (R-SC) and Trey Gowdy (R-SC) are more outspoken. For all, issues of life, marriage, contraception, and morality are woven into political speeches. On these issues, political statements link back to scripture and "family values."

It is too simplistic to accuse politicians of blurring the line between church and state. South Carolina politicians know their constituents identify as deeply religious people, so they speak to that common set of values. They see life, marriage, and contraception as color-blind. They are framed as questions of values, not politics or policy. But immigration is not color-blind. Which, on one hand, is a challenge in a conservative state with a long, contentious history on race relations. On the other hand, the changing demographics of the state's faith community provides an opportunity (and a safe space) for elected officials to engage social conservatives.

According to the Public Religion Research Institute, 36 percent of South Carolina identified as white evangelical Protestant in 2007.[42] While that number dropped ten points by 2015, the nonwhite Christian population grew six percentage points to 29 percent. Put it this way: For a pastor grappling with demographic changes, a congregation is small enough to talk to and understand, yet big enough to test approaches on various issues.

First Baptist Spartanburg is one of the largest Southern Baptist Churches in South Carolina. In fact, in 2014, it was one of the seventy-five largest in the nation.[43] Dr. Steve Wise, minister of missions for First Baptist Spartanburg, put it best: "I think you'd be surprised for us being a small southern town, and a big Baptist church in a small southern town, at how many different colors you might see in our [congregation]."[44]

With sandy-blond hair, a firm handshake, and kind enough temperament to address me as "Mr. Noorani," Kimmy LaMee works for Steve at First Baptist Spartanburg as the director of Local MPACT, a church program whose acronym is derived from its mission statement: to lead First Baptist to be "Mobilized in missions by Partnering with other organizations to Alleviate suffering, Communicate the Gospel, and Train disciple makers here in Spartanburg, in South Carolina, in the USA, and across the world."[45]

Kimmy grew up in Inman, South Carolina, on the Belcher Brothers Farm, a family farm that grew peaches. According to the *South Carolina Farmer Magazine*, the state is the second largest peach-producing state in the nation, and peaches are a $90 million sales crop for South Carolina, with a $300 million impact on its economy.[46] Growing up on a farm was far from an isolating experience. Kimmy "loved growing up on a farm— as a little girl, there were people around and I got to be with my family pretty much all the time."[47] It was also an opportunity to get to know the migrant farmworkers who were the economic backbone of the operation. "I remember my dad and mom helping many of them either with a sandwich when they didn't have one or giving them a ride home after a long day of work. As a little girl, the guys that worked on my daddy's farm were my friends and family. I don't ever remember my parents uttering a bad word about these guys and their families."[48]

It is certainly fair to ask about the wages and protections Kimmy's parents offered these workers. Across the country, low-wage workers are too often exploited by their employers. Perhaps I should have steered the conversation in that direction. But I have come across more than enough growers who would never create the environment Kimmy described from her childhood—an environment that led to a values framework for her that extended well beyond the peach farm.

In fact, the farm was not her only point of contact with the immigrant community. As Kimmy shared, "When my church, Holston Creek Baptist in Inman, began a Hispanic church in our gym, it was just natural for me to be involved. I began playing keyboards. As a teenager, I started helping with English tutoring. . . . Growing up, seeing the example from my parents and my church, I was taught that all people matter and how I serve and love and treat them matters."[49]

Kimmy went on to attend North Greenville University. From there, she moved to New Orleans to attend seminary. Hurricane Katrina brought her back home. She finished seminary remotely and served as an associate at First Baptist, as she "began to sense God calling me to move overseas."[50]

While in North Africa for two years, Kimmy "heard a little girl, five years old, talking in English. I was desperate at that time for English. I turned around and I said, 'Are you speaking English?' And the mom looked at me like *yeah*, kind of like *duh*." Kimmy became close friends with the family. "So through our relationship, I was to share Jesus. She finally looked at me one day, and she was like, 'Please don't. I hate Christians.'

"I was like, 'I'm a Christian. What are you talking about?'

"She said, 'Well, I lived for twelve years in a city in Texas, and not one Christian befriended me or welcomed me into their home.'"[51]

This was a challenge Kimmy confronted every day. She told me, "Internationals say all the time here in Spartanburg, we'll come here for four years in college and never be invited into an American home for a holiday, for spring break, for anything."[52]

Kimmy grew up in an environment where immigrants were part of her daily life, whether on the farm or at church. The belief that she, as a Christian, should "welcome the stranger" was ingrained early on in her life. For other Christians, though, with deep cultural or economic fears, this was incredibly difficult. Taking this step requires a leap of faith, a willingness to establish a new relationship with a new person, to open oneself to a set of experiences that will be completely foreign (in more ways than one). The pressure on immigrants and refugees to integrate into society, learn English, become "American," is great. But if native-born Americans don't meet them halfway, the cultural isolation only deepens.

In this way LaMee bears the responsibility of being the new version of the old South Carolina. With a two-year-old daughter, two young boys adopted from the Congo, and another child on the way, what LaMee and her husband teach their children determines the cultural trajectory of the state.

I asked Kimmy if she saw her family as the future of South Carolina and Southern Baptists. "Oh how I hope that my sweet children will be that voice. I pray that they see and love refugees, just as God commanded us to and as their daddy and I taught them."[53]

She continued, "We have to teach them (even as two-year-olds) that we will not live in fear, we will serve and love and welcome [refugees] in our homes. We have to model to our children even when it's inconvenient and hard."[54] For LaMee, the process started with her parents, growing up with immigrants on the family farm. Now, working to resettle refugees through faith institutions, she passes those values on as a parent herself. She was fortunate to have multiple experiences with immigrants and refugees that brought her to this place. Most white Americans living in suburban or rural areas do not have the same life experiences.

While schools, community organizations, and other institutions provide opportunities for native-born Americans to get to know immigrants (and vice versa), in states like South Carolina with large faith communities, the church is the most effective platform to help facilitate these conversations and relationships. Particularly when, as in South Carolina, the faith community itself is diversifying.

To greatly oversimplify, there are two strategies within the evangelical community to help congregations understand demographic changes or diversify themselves. One is to introduce experiences to the congregation that build relationships with the foreign-born community. The other is to start, or "plant," new churches with the intention to build a diverse congregation that was not separated by race or ethnicity from its inception.

Encouraged by First Baptist Spartanburg's senior pastor, Dr. Don Wilton, who is an immigrant from South Africa himself, Kimmy had worked with her supervisor, Steve Wise, to build an effective missionary program. Through these programs, refugees were welcomed into the community and congregants traveled overseas to volunteer their services and time. Through meetings and activities, Wise and Kimmy could introduce congregants to the issues and ease the community's cultural transition through an organized set of experiences that allowed for questions and reflection.

When I visited them in the spring of 2016, they had just announced a mission trip to a Syrian refugee camp. As Wise told me, "Our thought was we want some of our people to go and see how [Syrian refugees] are living while they are waiting to come here."[55] To his pleasant surprise, their initial information session was packed with interested church members. "Of all ages," Kimmy added.[56]

"[There] was a psychologist, psychiatrist that wants to go; the retired couple we mentioned earlier, retired educators; an engineer who has worked in international settings, mostly in the Middle East; [a] retired army [member] who has served multiple times in the Middle East; and then two students [who] are high school students. So it was pretty amazing to look around the table. There were more in there, and I didn't know what they did."[57]

Neither Wise nor Kimmy claimed their work was done. But they understood its importance. As Kimmy shared, "So those conversations [about refugees], they can't happen on a national level. It's got to be around a table like this with—in our minds in faith-based communities, in faith-based conversations, which is a big task because there's [a] lot of communities."[58] The focus of Kimmy and Steve's work was the First Baptist Spartanburg congregation. But it was remarkably similar to what Jana White was doing with her mix of "international" and American students just down the road at the Adult Learning Center. Same goal, different institutions.

With regard to the idea of creating more diverse congregations altogether, the families of Harold Smith and Norma Blanton were a bridge. In September 2009, Derrick Smith and his wife, Meghan (who were son and daughter of Harold and Norma, respectively), planted their own multiethnic church in Spartanburg and called it Kaleidoscope. As Derrick told me, "So a lot of American Christians grow up sort of thinking when you die everybody turns white and gets blond hair. . . . Everybody gets a white robe and everybody turns white. But that isn't true. . . . Kaleidoscope was an effort to do it the right way, to taste unity across ethnic lines now."[59] The thesis of Derrick's first sermon was "that we're already unified because of our Creator. We're already one."[60] He went on, "Out of our unity in Christ, God blesses our cultural and ethnic and linguistic diversity. In fact, that's what he always wanted in the original covenant with Adam and Eve [. . .] to be fruitful, multiply, and fill the earth and subdue it or steward it well."

Through her mother's work and her personal advocacy for immigration reform, Meghan, Derrick's wife, saw what was happening in the broader community. She saw the difference between schools facing the changes within their student body and the churches' decision to step beyond their threshold and engage a diversifying community. "But the churches, I see a much more growing movement of, by choice, people reaching out to people who are different than them and inviting them in. Whereas the schools kind of have been given this opportunity and have had to learn and adapt to it, but the churches, some of them have seen the opportunity and have learned to adapt and kind of, by choice, try to become more diverse."[61]

Whether it was starting a new church, like Meghan had attempted with her husband, or the work her mother did to help families at Arcadia Elementary, the largest and most stable institutions—one secular, the other religious—schools and churches, were the place to try new approaches to managing culture change.

ROOTED IN BIBLICAL VALUES

Unsurprisingly, the fast-changing demographics of South Carolina made the state a flashpoint in the nation's immigration debate. Up until 2013, the response from immigrant advocates was primarily political: We will register more voters or organize larger protests. In the south, even in a state like South Carolina where the Latino community was growing rapidly, this approach would not work. There just weren't enough Latino voters to change the politics of the state. Therefore, a strategy steeped in the culture and values of the region was necessary.

In February 2013, Numbers USA, an organization committed to "lower immigration levels," ran a television ad attacking Senator Lindsey Graham as "Senator Graham-nesty" ready to let "the illegals" in to take American jobs.[62] The ad campaign was designed to weaken support for the immigration-reform legislation Graham was preparing to introduce in the US Senate later that year. This was by no means the first time Numbers USA had mounted this type of attack on immigrants and immigration, much less on Senator Graham. The good senator had been dealing with this sort of thing since at least 2006. He had never backed down from his position, nor, for that matter, had he ever lost an election.

The initial response by proponents of the immigration-reform legislation Senator Graham championed was from the Charleston Metro Chamber of Commerce. The legislation would have provided legal status and citizenship for the majority of undocumented immigrants in the United States, created a new legal immigration system, and established a more humane and effective enforcement system.[63] The Charleston chamber partnered with Republicans for Immigration Reform on a $60,000 ad buy to show support for immigration reform and Senator Graham. Bryan Derreberry, president of the Charleston chamber, was featured in the ad:

> Today's immigration laws are not written for today. South Carolina businesses will not be able to continue to grow without real immigration solutions. Senator Graham is right on target in fighting for immigration reform. He knows how important it is for South Carolina businesses, he knows for South Carolina to compete in the 21st century we have to be able to update our immigration laws; a modern economy needs modern immigration laws. Senator Graham gets that.[64]

As important as this counter-ad was, it wasn't what changed the conversation. It was another business voice in the debate, making a policy argument that, to the skeptic, merely increased the number of low-skill workers competing for jobs.

To take a quick step back, the National Immigration Forum had been working with the Evangelical Immigration Table for a couple of years at this point. The Evangelical Immigration Table was a coalition of the nation's leading evangelical associations and denominations working together to advocate for immigration reform consistent with biblical values.[65] On the ground in South Carolina, for the Evangelical Immigration Table, was yet another member of the Blanton family, Matthew Blanton. (It's unclear if any of the Blantons ever sleep.)

Based on the intel and relationships gathered by Matthew, the Evangelical Immigration Table put into motion a cultural strategy to engage the hundreds of thousands of evangelicals in the state. Rev. Jim Goodroe, director of missions for the Spartanburg County Baptist Network, recorded a radio ad that ran in March 2013 with the following script:

Christians should be known by our love. I'm Reverend Jim Goodroe. Many of our neighbors came here seeking opportunity, but our dysfunctional immigration system breaks up families across the US. Christ calls evangelicals to compassion and justice, so please join a growing movement of Christians asking our political leaders for immigration solutions rooted in biblical values, which reflect each person's God-given dignity, respect the rule of law, protect family unity, guarantee secure borders, ensure fairness to taxpayers, and establish a path to citizenship. Our South Carolina elected officials need your prayers and to hear your voice. Speak out today for commonsense, just immigration laws by texting "immigration" to [phone number].

The powerful Ethics & Religious Liberty Commission of the Southern Baptist Convention, which we met in the last chapter, amplified the ad through its own press work. The commission's president at the time, Dr. Richard Land, said, "This is an issue of conviction; it's an issue of values; it's an issue of bringing our biblical values to bear on an issue that's rending the social fabric of the nation."[66]

Reverend Goodroe then joined forces with the business community to coauthor with Hal Stevenson, president of Grace Outdoor, a high-profile family-owned business operating across South Carolina, an op-ed that ran in the *Post and Courier*. They wrote, "At a unique moment in our nation's history—a time when our political leaders are considering reforms to our immigration system—we, a business leader from Columbia and a pastor from Spartanburg, are joining together to urge our neighbors to look at our immigrant neighbors with fresh eyes."[67] It was a moment that framed issues of identity and what it meant to be a South Carolinian in deeply personal terms.

From that moment on, Senator Graham rarely talked about immigration reform in the state without Rev. Goodroe by his side. On Capitol Hill, Senator Graham was the loudest proponent of evangelical engagement in the immigration debate. As Reverend Goodroe told the *State*, "One of the things we're trying to do is trying to get Christians to first of all think about anything from a Christian perspective, including immigration . . . and realize that any immigrant is a person first. Immigration is an issue, a subject, but immigrants are people like you and me. At bottom, we need to treat everybody with respect."[68] At that moment, the church could help the community navigate the tension that came with immigration. The anti-immigrant attack launched against Graham by Numbers USA proved ineffective. A powerful new coalition of conservative faith and business interests had coalesced, and the South Carolina strategy emboldened local and national evangelical leadership.

Later that summer, the Evangelical Immigration Table ran radio ads with the same script as Rev. Goodroe's ad. Coinciding with a legislative debate that had moved to the House of Representatives, the Table spent $400,000 in fifty-six congressional districts across fourteen states. The majority of ads featured a local pastor. Barrett Duke, vice president of the Southern Baptist Ethics & Religious Liberty Commission, told the *Washington Post*, "The combination of this ad buy and our continued prayer for reform gatherings send one clear message: Evangelicals support action by the House of Representatives on immigration."[69]

About a year after Rev. Goodroe's radio ad, the House began to seriously consider immigration legislation. And Congressman Mick Mulvaney, a Tea Party Republican who represented the 5th district of South Carolina, convened the state's first congressional town hall for Latino evangelical pastors. The *New York Times* reported, "The politics of immigration are gradually shifting in South Carolina and some other Southern states, where not long ago most conservatives passionately rejected legalization as amnesty that rewarded lawbreakers. Like Mr. Mulvaney, a number of Republicans are moving toward the view that the immigration system needs fixing, and that 11.7 million illegal immigrants will not be deported and need a path to legal status."[70]

For Congressman Mulvaney, who wore his faith on his sleeve, to sit with a room of Latino pastors and lay out a vision for immigration reform that met the needs of their community was a clear indication that the ground was beginning to shift in conservative South Carolina. For the first time, the question of identity and immigration was being constructively addressed through a campaign based on culture and values, not just politics and policy. The message may not resonate with secular voters, but they were neither the audience nor the challenge—for the most part, they overwhelmingly supported immigrants and immigration.

Social scientists documented the success. Michele Margolis, an assistant professor of political science at the University of Pennsylvania, examined public opinion among evangelicals where the radio ads ran. The *Christian Post* reported her presentation to the American Political Science Association Annual Meeting: "Opposition to immigration reform among white Evangelicals decreased 15 percentage points, 62 to 47 percent, in the states that had the EIT radio ads—Arizona, California, Colorado, Florida, Georgia, Idaho, Illinois, Kentucky, Montana, North Carolina, Ohio, Oklahoma, South Carolina, Tennessee, Texas and Wisconsin. In states without the ads, however, white Evangelical opposition to immigration reform remained the same at 50 percent."[71]

Wherever the Evangelical Immigration Table's radio campaign ran, it made use of the same elements we saw in South Carolina. Local pastors (in most cases) narrated the ad, organized events to coincide with their broadcast, and authored op-eds in local publications. This meant that as Republican members of Congress were debating immigration-reform legislation, district staff whose job was to monitor local conservative media (such as Christian radio stations) heard some of their most influential constituents, pastors, making the biblical case for immigrants and immigration. This was the micro-targeting of a legislative campaign to a very specific audience, based on their culture and values.

There is a very short list of advocacy campaigns that can lay claim to a fifteen-point swing in opinion of such a tough audience. It is all the more remarkable because it occurred in such a short period of time, on a difficult issue, and in a volatile political environment.

The progress we made could not withstand the fear that came with terrorism.

THE FEAR OF FEAR

Days before the introduction of the 2013 Senate immigration reform bill that Senator Graham and others had led, the nation was shocked by the Boston Marathon bombings. As we learned from Stephen Bauman, CEO of

World Relief, the Tsarnaev brothers' immigration story had a chilling effect on refugee policies in the United States when politicians used the attack to misleadingly conflate immigrants, refugees, and terrorism. When the Syrian civil war led millions of refugees into Europe, America once again faced a public debate on refugees that soon spilled into South Carolina.

In the spring of 2015, Bauman's international refugee resettlement organization, World Relief, opened a South Carolina office in order to help refugees resettle in the region. Operating in twenty-seven US cities and fourteen countries, World Relief works closely with faith leaders in local communities to resettle refugees from around the world. According to Bauman, the organization underwent an exhaustive process to determine the willingness of the local elected and faith community to help welcome and resettle refugees. But the environment changed, and over the summer of 2015, one year after the radio ads and work mentioned above, their new office was greeted with great controversy.

What was a local issue quickly became national. The *New York Times* reported on a town-hall meeting that included members of the John Birch Society, one of the nation's oldest and most influential far-right organizations that "advocates ending government assistance to illegal immigrants and not granting amnesty."[72] The *Times* stated "State Representative Mike Burns, a Republican from Greenville County, spoke more broadly of immigration policies that were threatening traditional American culture. [He said:] 'This immigration fiasco that we're in the middle of is going to take away the very things that we're dear about.'"[73] Burns was sending a clear signal that immigrants and refugees were going to change South Carolina's culture and that voters should rise up in opposition to World Relief.

Jason Lee, the director of World Relief's new Spartanburg office, found himself in the middle of a maelstrom he did not entirely expect. He spent years resettling refugees in Tennessee, but told the *Times* about the South Carolina environment, "The fearmongering seems really different."[74]

Then, two months later, the Paris attacks shocked the world.

On Friday evening, November 13, 2015, a string of coordinated terrorist attacks took place across Paris, killing 130 people and injuring 368. The Islamic State of Iraq and the Levant (ISIL) claimed responsibility, and the Syrian refugee crisis in Europe was quickly blamed. Days later, South Carolina governor Nikki Haley joined over two dozen Republican governors across the country to ask the US State Department not to resettle Syrian refugees in their states.[75]

For a state that had begun to turn the corner and welcome immigrants and refugees, this was a dramatic change for South Carolina. Fear had trumped religion. What was underneath this outcry was not a political fight per se. Rather, it was a fear of the unknown congregant, of a changing church, of a changing community. It was a question of identity exacerbated by fears of terrorism. What had started as a debate about the role of World Relief became a question of whether or not refugees should even be admitted.

In January 2016, Republican state senators Lee Bright and Kevin Bryant introduced separate legislation on the issue of refugee resettlement in the state. According to *USA Today*, Bright's bill would require that all refugees register with the state, would hold private resettlement agencies civilly liable for any action by a refugee, and would ban any state or local funds being spent on refugees without additional legislative authorization.[76] After several fits and starts, the legislation passed the Senate on March 23, 2016, just one day after yet another terrorist attack in Europe.[77]

But similar to the 2013 faith-led response to immigration-reform legislation, a unique coalition of stakeholders of religions organizations, the ACLU (American Civil Liberties Union), immigrant rights organizations, and others took shape. Surprisingly, the binding element was the same: scripture.

As Alan Cross, Southern Baptist pastor and organizer working with the National Immigration Forum, wrote, "The ministry to refugees and the sojourner is an explicit Christian command found in both the Old and New Testaments. How much authority does the government have to infringe upon that command or to create a climate of fear where anyone ministering to a refugee in need in the name of Jesus will be held liable for anything that that refugee might one day do?"[78]

Over a matter of months, the broad coalition organized itself to urge lawmakers to protect religious liberty and allow refugee resettlement organizations to do their work. It was an argument not only similar to the radio ads but remarkably close to arguments made by social conservatives on the topics of marriage, sexual identity, or contraception. This was not a business argument. Nor was it political. Instead, it framed the issue in terms of a shared culture and a common set of values. And, this time, secular organizations were supporting a social conservative argument. Their common goal led these unlikely allies to find common ground.

NOBODY SHOULD BE AFRAID

Where South Carolina goes on identity, so goes the South. If South Carolina can devise ways to manage such rapid demographic change by marrying liberal and conservative strategies, across a range of institutions, the approach can be replicated across the region. To a certain extent, that path will be determined by demographics. Eventually, the size of the Hispanic population will lead to important leadership roles across civic society. But more than that, it will be the negotiation of culture and values between communities. Families like those of the Blantons, Smiths, LaMees, or Prietos are just a few examples of how immigrants and immigration will change South Carolina and South Carolinians.

After we visited the financial literacy class at Arcadia Elementary School, Norma Blanton and I returned to her office. The ugly politics of the 2016 presidential race reentered the conversation. Norma knew immigrant families were afraid to come to school and were afraid to go shopping. She told me of a father who was afraid to drive to the Walmart down the road to get food for his children. "I thought, this is the United States of America, for heaven's sakes. Nobody should be afraid to drive to Walmart to buy food for their children."[79]

It was my last interview in South Carolina. I met incredible people, ate great food, and learned more than I ever imagined. "Norma," I asked. "What gives you hope?"

Norma paused, looked down at the table. Her eyes teared up, and she replied, "They [the immigrants] keep coming back."[80]

CHAPTER FIVE

WE ARE ALL AFRAID

W hether or not Americans have a reason to be afraid, we are. Since September 11, 2001, it has been increasingly difficult to separate immigration and national security. At our worst moments, press and policymakers are quick to link potential terrorist events to Muslims. At our best moments, few and far between, we take a breath and get the facts before we react.

The fear is both well-founded and irrational. We are led by too many politicians and pundits to feel that all terrorist attacks are perpetrated by "radical Islam." Whether they are disenchanted with society or claim allegiance to terrorist organizations, we assume they all have a deep hatred of the West. Meanwhile, attacks by terrorists in Muslim countries, killing hundreds of Muslims, are seen as political, not human, stories in US media.

In this brutally partisan political environment, conservative lawmakers who advocate a calm approach are a rare breed. National-security concerns, plus the sense that an international migration crisis has challenged governments' abilities to control their borders have changed the Western world's politics. The *Economist* cover on August 5, 2016, artfully depicted the new political divide as a chasm: on one side, there were walls around people who were standing near a "Keep Out" sign; on the other side of the chasm, there was a rainbow and a group of people holding hands around a "Welcome" sign.[1]

This divide was put into stark terms on December 2, 2015. In San Bernardino, California, Tashfeen Malik and her husband, Syed Rizwan Farook, carried out one of the deadliest terrorist assaults in the country since the September 11 attacks.[2] The shooting took place at a social-service agency's holiday party. Fourteen Americans were killed, and Malik and Farook were killed by police in a chase afterward.

To greatly oversimplify, Democrats framed the terrorist attack as another reason to limit access to automatic weapons. Republicans, meanwhile, focused on the term "radical Islamic terrorism" and the need to wage a more aggressive war against the Islamic State.[3] Days after the shooting, the FBI learned of the attackers' support of Islamic State ideology, which heightened fear and unease in American society.

In an effort to calm the nation, President Obama addressed the country from the Oval Office on Sunday, December 6. In his remarks, Obama said, "It is clear that the two [attackers] had gone down the dark path of radicalization, embracing a perverted interpretation of Islam that calls for war against America and the West. They had stockpiled assault weapons, ammunition, and pipe bombs. So this was an act of terrorism, designed to kill innocent people."[4]

While Obama acknowledged that the majority of victims of terrorism around the world were Muslim, he also placed responsibility on Muslim leaders to "speak out against not just acts of violence, but also those interpretations of Islam that are incompatible with the values of religious tolerance, mutual respect, and human dignity."[5] Importantly, Obama said, "It is our responsibility to reject religious tests on who we admit into this country."

Donald Trump responded to the attack quite differently. Early in the morning on Monday, December 7, 2015, I landed in Los Angeles after a few days of meetings in Mexico City. I went through US Customs, grabbed my rental car, and skimmed through my Twitter feed. The San Bernardino attack and the president's speech led the coverage. That is, until the Trump campaign released a statement "calling for a total and complete shutdown of Muslims entering the United States."[6] This wasn't a fringe candidate at the bottom of the polls. At that time, Trump was just ahead of a surging Senator Ted Cruz for the Republican nomination for president.[7]

Even for Trump, it was a dramatic statement: bar an entire religious group from entering the United States of America. Of course, this was not the first time he had scapegoated an entire ethnic community. For instance, he had launched his campaign with a claim that Mexico was sending "rapists" to the United States.[8] Throughout his presidential campaign,

Trump fertilized America's seeds of fear and division with his own brand of verbal fertilizer. His followers loved it. They wanted a strongman. The rest of America was repulsed or confused.

For me personally, Trump's statement triggered a set of emotions I didn't expect. Up to that point, my job as executive director of the National Immigration Forum was easy. I could make it through the day with the knowledge that I am not an immigrant. I am not Latino. Rarely did I feel that I was advocating for myself. At most, I am a South Asian American. But rarely did I have to speak or think about issues that uniquely impact South Asians, much less Muslims. It's not that these issues weren't important or part of the Forum's broad mission; they were part of the larger mix of issues we addressed as an organization.

I relished this arm's-length space. It made things easier. I felt I could maintain my objectivity and move between communities and groups more easily. I also knew that I occupied a luxurious space in the advocacy community. The courage immigrants, documented or not, showed when they spoke of the need for policy changes that directly impacted their lives was beyond my job description. The poise that immigrant women and men displayed when they engaged policymakers, from the president to a state legislator, never ceased to inspire me.

With Trump's latest statement, my emotional detachment disappeared. Trump's call to ban Muslim immigration, and the ugly debate that ensued, conflated immigrants, refugees, and Islam. And there I was, an American Muslim advocating for immigrants and refugees, both documented and undocumented. On that Monday in Los Angeles, I was a Trump trifecta: a Muslim who'd just arrived from a trip to Mexico and advocated for immigrants.

Over the course of the day in Los Angeles, I went from meeting to meeting, tracking the news along the way. Countless questions came to my head. If I identified as part of the broader Muslim community, should I feel responsible for the San Bernardino terrorist attacks? If I don't practice the religion, am I even Muslim? Am I American enough? Finally, how do I speak to what is personal without it seeming personal?

Jet-lagged and exhausted, I woke up early the next morning in my sister's guest bedroom. The house was quiet as I got ready for my day. I scanned the morning news clips, saw that Trump's statements continued to dominate, and sent e-mails to staff as we planned out the day. As I packed for my afternoon flight back to Washington, DC, I saw my US passport on the dresser near the bedroom door.

Up to that point, both personally and organizationally, I had been silent regarding Trump's statement. Our strategy was to let the story play out. Which for such a high-impact statement by a leading candidate for president was out of the norm for us. We didn't want to get caught up in what was an increasingly ugly debate. And, truthfully, I was grappling with my own emotions. I didn't want to drag the organization into what some might see as a personal debate.

But seeing my passport on the table, it hit home. I am an American Muslim. I advocate for the rights and opportunities of immigrants, documented or not, and, yes, I was scared too. But I wasn't going to be scared of Donald Trump.

I realized that if the work was going to be more personal, I needed to be more personal—which was out of character for me. I grabbed my passport and posted a picture to Facebook, "On a day like this, I am proud my #Muslim parents immigrated to the #USA from #Pakistan and I have one of these."[9]

THE ISLAMIFICATION OF THE DEBATE

In our rapidly diversifying nation, terrorist stereotypes are colored by immigration but not limited to immigrants. There is a steady flow of stories across the media conflating immigrants, refugees, and terrorism, including baseless stories of terrorists crossing the United States–Mexico border, adding to the cumulative burden on the American psyche.[10] The pressure manifests itself in unfortunate ways. Individuals who look like Muslims are taken off airline flights because passengers are worried, or a fourteen-year-old Ahmed Mohamed is arrested for bringing a clock he built to school because it had been mistaken for a bomb.[11] All of this emboldens racist elements of society.

In this chaotic environment, it was difficult for the public to separate national security and terrorism from immigration. The Public Religion Research Institute's 2015 "American Values Survey" of 2,695 adults from all fifty states and Washington, DC, found terrorism (62 percent) to be among the top three issues that Americans say are critical to them personally.[12] For Republicans, the concerns were particularly acute. Nearly eight in ten (79 percent) of them cited terrorism as a critical issue; 59 percent found immigration to be a critical issue to them personally.

This was the foundation from which many Republican candidates sought to grow their support. They connected immigration and terrorism in voters' minds to create a high-intensity issue and differentiate a crowded electoral field. When it came to the modern-day Republican primary electorate, I'm not sure they were wrong.

Of course, from the press coverage Muslims receive in the States, you would think my people were everywhere. In reality, our numbers are tiny. According to the Pew Research Center there were about 3.3 million Muslims of all ages living in the United States in 2015.[13] That is approximately one percent of the nation's total population. Pew went on to project the Muslim community would grow to 8.1 million by 2050. The anti-immigrant news outlet *Breitbart News*, framed this as, "Muslim Population in U.S. to Double by 2050, Study Says," and claimed that Muslims will become "the country's second-largest religious group after Christianity."[14] This may be true, but it is more a comment on the lack of religious diversity in the country than anything else.

While America will remain by far a majority-Christian society for the foreseeable future, the world will continue to religiously diversify.[15] By 2050 the number of Muslims in the world will nearly equal the number of Christians. These changes feed into the anxiety and fear within America that the world is being taken over by Muslims. A fear, as we will see, that needs to be calmly and compassionately addressed by political and civic leadership .

Six months after he announced his proposal to halt Muslim immigration, Trump emerged as the Republican Party's presumptive nominee for president. His campaign gave voice to the fear and anxiety coursing through the Republican electorate. A June 2016 survey of 2,607 adults by

Public Religion Research Institute and the Brookings Institution found that more than three-quarters of Trump supporters and 64 percent of Republicans supported a temporary ban on Muslims who are not US citizens entering the country; only 40 percent of the general public supported such a ban.[16] A similar split was found in Syrian-refugee resettlement in the United States: 78 percent of Trump supporters and 66 percent of Republicans favored barring Syrian refugees from the country, but less than half (44 percent) of the larger public shared that sentiment.[17]

The political nerve Trump tapped went beyond Muslim immigration to the United States. Eight in ten (82 percent of) Trump supporters and about two-thirds (66 percent) of Republicans supported Trump's "beautiful wall" along the US–Mexico border. Again, only 41 percent of the public supported this proposal. Independents tended to mirror the American public on these issues (only in the 40 percent support range), while Democrats were overwhelmingly opposed to Trump's proposals.[18]

Online news magazine *Vox* partnered with Morning Consult, a nonpartisan media and technology company, to conduct an online poll of 2,001 registered voters between June 3, 2016, and July 4, 2016.[19] When asked "What's your biggest concern, if any, about immigration?" 39 percent of respondents chose "hurts national security" or "increases crime." These responses scored 20 points higher than "weakens the economy." The poll also underscored the perception of immigrants from different countries; respondents viewed immigrants from Europe and Asia much more positively than immigrants from Africa and Latin America. Meanwhile, immigrants from the Middle East were viewed least positively of all.[20] Trump had successfully conflated national security, terrorism, and immigration. He Islamified the debate. No longer was the challenge just to present Latino immigrants as net contributors to American society. Anxiety about immigrants competing for jobs was overshadowed by the fear associated with Muslim immigration. Together, these ideas created a combination of cultural and economic fears that cannot be addressed through policy alone. In his article, Matthew Yglesias of *Vox* summed up the present-day immigration debate perfectly, "Talking about the economy is neither here nor there."[21]

An Islamified debate cut a number of ways—which reminds me of a conversation on that fateful Monday in Los Angeles. Cathleen Farrell, the National Immigration Forum's communications director, and I were in Santa Monica meeting with Gregory Rodriguez, founder and publisher of Zócalo Public Square, an influential digital publication. As one of the leading Latino intellectuals in the country, he followed the immigration debate very closely. We sat in his office, catching up and discussing the impact of Trump's campaign and what the debate meant for US politics.

In his big, gregarious voice, Gregory said, "You know, Latinos aren't the biggest scapegoats in this election."[22] To which I replied, as the only Muslim in the room, "You're welcome."

Obviously, the issue at hand is much larger than who is the bigger victim. Islam has been positioned as an existential threat to the United States, and over the course of the 2016 presidential campaign, we saw a spike in attacks on Muslim Americans.[23] In big, diverse, politically liberal cities, the response to these attacks has been forceful. In the days after the election, both Eric Garcetti and Bill de Blasio, the mayors of Los Angeles and New York, respectively, committed to protecting their immigrant residents.[24] In taking these important steps, they rely on principles of justice and equality in their communications to the public.

But in today's racialized, Islamified immigration debate, for many Americans, these principles are not applicable—particularly those living in conservative regions of the country. To put it more bluntly, conservative white Americans aren't worried about justice and equality for immigrants they see as an economic or security threat. When it comes to immigration (or even threats of terrorism), law enforcement in politically conservative regions of the country are expected to follow in the tough law-and-order footsteps of Sheriffs Joe Arpaio or David Clarke Jr. Arpaio, notorious for his unrelenting targeting of immigrants in Arizona's Maricopa County, shapes the conservative narrative on immigration by claiming (with no corroborating evidence) that immigrants enter the country with disease, or, for example, unceremoniously forcing 220 undocumented immigrants to march, shackled, from a county jail to his infamous "Tent City."[25]

Meanwhile, Sheriff Clarke of Milwaukee County has made a career of doubling down on the theory that immigration leads to increased threats of terrorism. Speaking to the conservative, fearmongering website World-NetDaily, Clarke said, "we do have to look at immigration as a national-security threat."[26] He went on to ponder on how US citizens could play a role in the fight against immigration and terrorism, "You're going to see more attacks, where they target two different sites and expand across the nation in different states. I think we have to find a role for US citizens in this as well but until we get a strategy, that's not going to happen." Fear-mongering website, meet fearmongering sheriff.

All of this makes the job of Republican law-enforcement officials in conservative districts who want to approach the issue differently much more difficult. Understanding what leads conservative leaders to avoid falling into the trap of profiling and stereotyping Muslims and Latinos leads us back to the thesis that for many Americans, the immigration debate is more about culture and values than about politics and policy. The political environment in which many conservative members of law enforcement operate urges that they approach immigrants and immigration through an enforcement-only lens. What I found is that for many conservative law-enforcement leaders, personally and publicly, they rely on their values framework to chart a different course. Whether it is their faith or their belief that smart law enforcement requires a different approach, for many conservative law-enforcement leaders, their core humanity requires them to treat others with a basic level of fairness.

DIGNITY AND RESPECT

Richard Longworth's book *Caught in the Middle: America's Heartland in the Age of Globalism* thoughtfully outlines the Midwest's challenges with globalization and how they are linked to the region's past and future.[27] My assumption was that in these Midwestern cities and towns there were points of tension and backlash, as well as leaders who sought opportunities to make sure their communities thrived. I figured that local leadership's response to immigrants and immigration determined how these cities and towns moved into the future. So one of my first interviews for this project was with Dick Longworth, now a senior fellow with the Chicago Council on Global Affairs.

Longworth grew up in Boone, Iowa, a "self-contained farming and mining town."[28] Other than the "one black family and one Jewish family," Longworth told me, "the rest of the town was big Swedes, a lot of Andersons and Johnsons and people like that. Very homogenous, everybody looked like everybody else."

Through his life experience and extensive travels, Dick learned that local leadership made all the difference. In order to help immigrants within the small-town culture where word of mouth defined someone's reputation, it was the police chief, the mayor, the schoolteacher, and the pastor who understood that "taking a social structure like that and making it look more like America is tricky, and people have a hard time with it."[29]

In this intersection of concerns over immigration and safety, law-enforcement leaders stuck out as truly instrumental. For Longworth, one of the most important stakeholders in the debate was the police chiefs who "are simply saying that immigrants are not in themselves a threat to a community."[30] He concluded, "They [immigrants] are not a big element in crime. [Police chiefs] see the statistics." At a time when security threats looms large on the public's mind, the role of law enforcement only grows more important.

Greg Zoeller, Indiana's Republican attorney general (2009–2017), fit this mold. Born and raised in New Albany, Indiana, Zoeller is a Hoosier through and through. Just across the Ohio River from Louisville, Kentucky, New Albany has maintained a population of approximately 37,000 over the last four decades. Nearly all of Zoeller's father's family lived there; it was home to "hundreds of Zoellers." Greg himself is a humble, soft-spoken person. His graying hair falls gently over his forehead, and eyeglasses peer over a graying mustache. He doesn't talk slowly as much as he talks carefully, and his eyes are as gentle and quiet as his demeanor. Looking back on life in a family of six in a "very staunch Catholic, German Catholic family," Zoeller felt like he grew up in something of a bubble.[31]

His mother's job as a librarian provided an escape. In our conversation, I asked Zoeller if there was a book that stuck with him through the years. I expected an answer as substantive, cerebral, and serious as his demeanor. Instead, without a pause, Greg mentioned none other than Mark Twain's *Huckleberry Finn*. Zoeller told me that this book led to hours on the shores of the Ohio River, looking across at bustling Louisville, with "daydreams of getting on a boat and paddling."[32] The dreams of boys on riverbanks.

In order to make money during college summers, Zoeller made his dream a reality as he found work on the river barges plying their way up and down the Mississippi. "Most of the people on the riverboats are on parole. . . . I may have been the only one not charged with a felony."[33] But he also told me, "I don't think there was a single person [with whom] I couldn't find a way to break down that wall." As he put it, "Most of them had a nice heart somewhere."[34] That statement was a window into Zoeller's heart and perspective on people.

Bucking the Catholic tradition that at least one child would go off to seminary (his brother got close but ended up a musician), Zoeller received a scholarship to attend Purdue University and intended to study computer science. Instead, he was called to study law because "A lawyer is supposed to serve their clients' interest above their own, and that had kind of a vocational sense to it."[35] This sense of vocation was deeply linked to Greg's Catholic faith. "I do think that you treat people with dignity and respect. If you believe everyone is a child of God, it's pretty hard not to."[36] Greg didn't grow up in a diverse community so, unlike someone who grew up in a more secular, urban environment, he didn't have a set of experiences or relationships to define his sense of justice. So his faith provided that compass. Which, as a law-enforcement official in a conservative state, who is charged with protecting the rights, freedoms, and safety of citizens of the Hoosier state, came with high-risk, high-profile, decisions.[37]

Greg first appeared on our radar in 2011, as the toxic plume of Arizona's SB 1070 was working its way across the country. Despite the success of the Utah Compact, there were many state legislators across America who wanted to pass legislation along the lines of the Arizona law. Zoeller heard about the Utah Compact through the Alliance Partnership, a bipartisan coalition of state attorneys general who, among other things, worked with their counterparts in Mexico to strengthen their criminal-justice system. Utah's attorney general, Mark Shurtleff, and his colleague, Lynne Ross, spoke very highly of Zoeller; he and a group of fellow Hoosiers thought the Utah Compact was something they might replicate.

The Indiana Compact followed a similar trajectory as Utah. Spearheaded by the industrious Angela Smith Jones, of the Greater Indianapolis Chamber of Commerce, and Angela Adams, a private immigration attorney in the region, the group was created in response to state legislative efforts to pass immigration-enforcement legislation. Neither were faith leaders, but they understood what would lead Indiana lawmakers to explore a different approach to immigrants and immigration. Soon, a coalition was built around the leadership of Archbishop Daniel Buechlein, along with a large number of faith, law-enforcement, and business leaders.[38]

Archbishop Buechlein's leadership was crucial for two reasons. First of all, 18 percent of the state was Catholic, so church leadership lent the effort a level of immediate legitimacy.[39] Second, Buechlein and Zoeller were close friends. Zoeller told me, "by the time [Archbishop Buechlein] was in, I was all in."[40]

This meant the archbishop had the opportunity to give Zoeller a little political advice at the February 9, 2011, announcement of the Indiana Compact:

> We're on the stage at this press conference. There was a very well-known rabbi, a number of other clergy. But I looked up and down, we're in the statehouse and there's not a single [other] elected official up there. So the archbishop standing right next to me said, "Greg, you are the only elected official up here, do you think this is a good idea for you politically?" I'm attorney general, I'm supposed to know what I'm doing, so I said, "Well, when the archbishop gives you political advice, you are in it pretty deep."[41]

In Indiana, as in Utah, this combination of conservative faith, law-enforcement, and business leadership created enough political opposition to water down anti-immigrant legislation, leaving it open to a federal injunction and eventual irrelevance once the Supreme Court of the United States ruled on Arizona's SB 1070.[42] It was another signal to Congress that conservatives were grappling with a changing America in constructive ways. Little did Greg Zoeller know that in the years ahead, as the immigration debate took on a national-security bent, he was going to be drawn in even deeper.

Over the course of the summer of 2015, the Syrian-refugee crisis dominated the news. In reaction to deeply unsettling images and news from the Middle East and Europe, as well as pressure from US organizations, in early September 2015, President Obama agreed to increase the number of Syrian refugees admitted to the United States by 10,000.[43] A small increase in the context of the overall crisis, much less the history of US refugee resettlement, as discussed in chapter 2. In November 2015, Republican presidential hopeful, former Florida governor Jeb Bush voiced politically courageous support, "I don't think we should eliminate our support for refugees. It's been a noble tradition in our country for many years."[44]

Of course, Trump pounced on the controversy. He claimed, "You look at the migration, it's young, strong men. We cannot take a chance that the people coming over here are going to be ISIS-affiliated."[45] He was lying; this characterization of the refugees was inaccurate, to say the least. According to the United Nations High Commission on Refugees, between January 2012 and October 2015, there were approximately four million Syrian refugees registered in Egypt, Iraq, Jordan, Lebanon, Turkey, and North Africa. They found that 77 percent of registered refugees were women and children, an overwhelming majority.[46] Since self-reported data was first collected in 2002, a far larger number of Christian refugees have entered the United States than have Muslim refugees.[47]

Refugees who seek resettlement must pass through a thirteen-step security process that often takes two years or longer to complete.[48] The process includes in-person interviews, cross-checks with domestic and international databases, and medical screenings. The fact is that a refugee undergoes a greater level of scrutiny than any other individual admitted to the country. In spite of letters from national-security experts and testimony by Department of Homeland Security officials, opponents to the resettlement of Syrian refugees would not relent.[49] The fear ran so deep that no policy argument could block the emotionally charged political attacks.

But as 2015 progressed, opponents of refugee resettlement attacked the Obama administration for any settlement of Syrian refugees.[50] This debate escalated after media reports that one of the perpetrators of the November 2015 terrorist attack in France entered Europe through the flow of Syrian refugees streaming through Greece. Although it was difficult to confirm whether or not this was true, any linkage of the horrific Paris attack to Syrian refugees was all that opponents in the United States needed.[51]

Three days after the Paris attacks, on November 16, 2015, twenty-five Republican governors (one of whom you met back in South Carolina) vowed to block entry of Syrian refugees to their states.[52] Indiana Governor Mike Pence joined his colleagues and issued a statement, "In the wake of the horrific attacks in Paris, effective immediately, I am directing all state agencies to suspend the resettlement of additional Syrian refugees in the state of Indiana pending assurances from the federal government that proper security measures have been achieved."[53] Of course, the federal government's exhaustive security measures had been explained in great detail. Fear was more powerful than policy.

The next day, a Syrian family who had waited for three years in Jordan to complete the security process was due to land in Indiana. They were to start their new life with the help of Exodus Refugee Immigration, a refugee resettlement organization in Indiana. Pence successfully redirected the family to Connecticut. Carleen Miller, executive director of Exodus Refugee Immigration, told the *New York Times* that finding the family a new home on such short notice was "one of the hardest things I've had to do in the eight years [I've been] here."[54]

Pence sought to suspend refugee resettlement by halting the allocation of specific, discretionary, federal grants to organizations aiding refugees. The *Washington Post* reported, "According to court filings, Indiana would not deny Syrians benefits such as Medicaid based on their country of origin and the state would still use federal refugee resettlement grants to pay for services such as English-language instruction for refugee children in schools."[55] But since the state also managed federal funding for resettlement efforts by passing it on to local organizations, his decision impacted the organizations in Indiana that were the actual recipients of federal dollars. Without those resources, these organizations struggled to resettle any refugees who came to Indiana. Almost five years removed from the controversy around the Indiana Compact, Attorney General Zoeller once again found himself in the middle of the debate.

Zoeller understood the source of the anxiety. "The public fear of terrorism is somewhat based on the fear of the unknown. . . . Add to this the lack of understanding of the Islamic faith of Muslims by many in the United States, and you have a mix that engenders a strong fear of the unknown."[56]

Positions hardened; just over a week after the initial announcement, the governor's office released a statement that claimed, "Governor Pence took decisive action a week ago to put the safety and security of the people of Indiana first by suspending the state's participation in the resettlement of Syrian refugees."[57] Soon, the ACLU of Indiana filed suit on behalf of Exodus Refugee Immigration.[58] The ACLU charged that Pence's actions violated the US Constitution and federal immigration laws because they discriminated based on national origin and sought to take unilateral steps toward federal immigration policy.[59]

Zoeller, in his role to defend the state's action in the court of law, and a member of the Catholic Charities Board of Directors (one of the key refugee resettlement agencies in the state), was in the middle. His office released a statement on the same day: "We are reviewing with our State clients the ACLU lawyers' complaint; and part of that review is whether the lawsuit raises any actual legal question for a court to decide or is instead a dispute over policy that might not belong in the courts."[60] Zoeller met his legal responsibility to represent the state and approach the case on its legal merits; he turned to his faith on how to personally engage in the debate. Of course, there was little separation between personal and professional: Catholic Charities was involved in the resettlement of Syrian refugees in Indiana.

Two weeks later, Archbishop Joseph W. Tobin, now leading the archdiocese of Indianapolis, announced the resettlement of a family of Syrian refugees on December 8, 2015, "Three years ago, this family fled the violence of terrorists in their homeland of Syria. After two years of extensive security checks and personal interviews, the United States government approved them to enter our country."[61] The statement continued, "For 40 years the Archdiocese's Refugee and Immigrant Services has welcomed people fleeing violence in various regions of the world. This is an essential part of our identity as Catholic Christians and we will continue this life-saving tradition."[62]

As he related the story to me, Zoeller told me he weighed in with Governor Pence. He told the governor, "If you don't want to pay, just tell the archbishop that, because we'll be glad to pay [for the resettlement services]."[63] The governor's order was enjoined by a federal court, allowing access to the state-managed federal resettlement funds while Pence appealed the ruling. As of this writing, the case has yet to be resolved.[64] A few days later, Zoeller attended an interfaith ceremony welcoming refugee families to Indianapolis.[65] And, about a week later, Greg published a short op-ed in the *Pharos-Tribune*, making the case that "the Hoosier hospitality that has long welcomed newcomers is part of that character, a heritage handed down from the early generations. So is joining to build a common bond with our neighbors, to face fears together and stand firm against dangers, both known and unknown."[66]

He concluded with, "We can face our fears better together than we can alone."

We talked almost six months after this event, just as Zoeller was in the middle of a heated primary campaign for the state's 9th congressional district. He told me, "I'll just take whatever grief I get out of it. That's just part of the deal."[67] Zoeller never lashed out at the opponents to refugee resettlement. He made his case to the public and treated people with the dignity and respect they deserved.

Zoeller put it best: "It's easier to fear something you don't understand."[68] He felt that "leaders [who] appeal to the 'better angels of our nature' as Lincoln once said, rather than appeal to the dark forces of fear and anger, as is currently being practiced, need to step forward. Immigration reform will be difficult until public fears are addressed by better leaders."

My sense is that we need more law-enforcement leaders like Greg Zoeller.

HEART OF A SERVANT

I think of Fresno as hot and dusty, bustling with agricultural and energy interests. About 225 miles north of Los Angeles, Fresno County runs east–west across California's Central Valley along the southern range of the Sierra Nevada. Founded in 1872 by the Central Pacific Railroad Company, Fresno began as a small farming community settled by Scandinavian immigrants. Soon after, the community became home to Chinese railroad workers, as well as Germans, Russians, Armenians, and Japanese immigrants. It is now the fifth largest city in California and home to half a million people, 47 percent of whom are Hispanic.[69] Fresno County, approximately five thousand square miles itself, is home to 1.88 million acres of farmland.[70]

While California is seen as a politically liberal, deep-blue state, the Central Valley has long been a conservative stronghold. Outside of the Bay Area, as Eric McGhee of the Public Policy Institute of California wrote, "California is more conservative and less consistently defined by geography than conventional wisdom would sometimes suggest."[71] These regions tend to be more business-friendly, skeptical of environmental protections, and resistant to the demographic changes of the state. As a result, county and congressional seats in the region are reliably Republican counterweights to the more liberal urban strongholds on the coast.

Born in San Joaquin, a small town thirty miles west of Fresno, Sheriff Margaret Mims carries herself with the pride and strength of a woman who has traveled a long road. But as Sheriff Mims told me, that journey never took her "more than sixty miles from where I was born."[72] With her short brown hair and forest-green uniform displaying four stars on the shoulder and a golden badge on her chest, Mims commands the respect of her (mostly male) colleagues.

Margaret's parents were Dust Bowl migrants from Arkansas and Oklahoma. Her formative experience in the region's economy came when the family moved from a dairy farm in San Joaquin to another farming community, Caruthers. There, Mims had her very first job: "That's how we paid for our school clothes. I was twelve, my sister was eleven, my brother was six, and we all went to [my uncle's] grape vineyard and picked grapes every summer."[73]

Family farming remains a part of her life as sheriff of Fresno County. She is often reminded of her time on her uncle's vineyard as she passes plots of fruits and vegetables nearly every day. These plots are tended by immigrant families from Southeast Asia, Mexico, or beyond—the modern-day Dust Bowl migrant to the Central Valley of California. "There will be rows of very diverse crops. They will have kids, mom, dad, and grandma and grandpa, they are all out in the fields working, working very hard."[74] Mims saw herself in the immigrant families she saw working in the fields; there was a human connection that went beyond her law-enforcement responsibilities.

As a nineteen-year-old single mother, Mims began her public-service career working in the local school district. In the fall of 1979, Mims practically stumbled upon a career in law enforcement. Her father, then a sergeant with the Fresno County sheriff's office, asked Mims to join him at a retirement dinner because her mother had a headache. With the agreement that mom would babysit the little one, Margaret joined her father at the dinner. There she met the incoming chief of police for the town of Kerman, California (remember that town), who said he was looking for a female police officer. On the way home that night, Margaret told her dad she was going to apply. She got the job, started the training process, and a new career began.

Yes, Mims told me, without her mother's headache, there may never have been a Sheriff Margaret Mims. She paused for a second to smile, then her face grew serious. "I'm a woman of faith. I know nothing happens by accident. Things happen for a reason."[75]

Combined with the life experience she shared with the immigrant families in the fields, her faith was an important guide for Mims. Her sense of humanity complemented her faith, providing a way to approach her job that was different from other Republican sheriffs such as Arpaio and Clarke. She told me, "I don't care if it's professional or personal, and you do things with the heart of a servant and even when you are in a leadership position, you have to have the heart of service and being a servant because that is the basis for everything, every decision you make from there on."

She was the first female deputy sheriff to supervise field patrol units;

she was also the first female deputy sheriff to attain the ranks of lieutenant, captain, and assistant sheriff; and, in November 2006, she became the first to be elected to the office of sheriff in the history of the Fresno County Sheriff's Office, since its inception in 1856.[76]

Mims developed a tough, no-nonsense approach to law enforcement and how she led her department. She made space for smart, strategic-minded approaches that are particularly important in a far-flung place like Fresno County, with a sprawling, incredibly diverse population. Margaret went back to her early career in education when she said, "if it's growing up working in a school, [I'm] keeping kids safe. Now in law enforcement, we're keeping people safe."[77]

To protect almost one million people across six thousand miles requires the development of a high degree of trust with the community, with civic institutions, and with fellow elected leaders. Sheriff Mims understood that the dynamic of fear we saw in South Carolina would not serve her mission to serve and protect the entirety of the community. She realized that her faith and sense of humanity aligned with smart law-enforcement practices: "[if immigrants are] afraid of law enforcement, . . . they can't thrive, having to look over their shoulder all the time [and] wondering if they are going to be deported."[78]

Mims valued the skills and contributions of the immigrant community to Fresno County, but she has her lines in the sand. While simple mistakes are not what she's worried about, "What we don't want are people that prey on [the immigrant] community, that prey on others, that may be here illegally. . . . If you're a wife beater [guilty of] domestic violence, is that a simple mistake? Not in my book. You will get booked for that."[79] This "booking" can lead to deportation.

The history of immigration to the Central Valley of California is not what one would expect. The diversity goes beyond the large Mexican community in the region to now include stable Southeast Asian and South Asian communities.[80] Margaret described growing up in the "very, very diverse" region: "after the Vietnam War, the administration at that time promised the Laotian people that they could come to the United States and we could give them sanctuary basically, and that's what's happened over the years."[81]

Kerman, the town where Mims began her law-enforcement career, grew by over 60 percent in the 2000s, driven in large part by a wave of Punjabi immigrants.[82] Originally, as Mims told me, Kerman was a Russian settlement. "Russian, Italian, Hispanic. It was very mixed. It was agriculture and oil." These days, Punjabis make up a small, tight-knit ethnic community in Kerman, a town of just thirteen thousand—they also hold two out of five city council seats.[83] A South Asian population growing up in the politically and socially conservative Central Valley faces many challenges. Language, culture, and identity are just a few. These are exacerbated by the belief that the turbans Sikhs wear indicate that they are Muslims, one of the great cultural misunderstandings in America. Turbans are a traditional headdress for Sikh men. But they make for easy marks for people looking to exact physical or verbal abuse on those they believe committed the crimes of September 11, 2001, or more recent acts of terrorism.

Mims and I spoke a few months after a horrific attack on an elder Sikh man waiting to go to work as a farmhand.[84] Mims told me that they have a problem with "people attacking Sikh members because in their mind they see Osama bin Laden with a turban. Completely different country, completely different religion." The real problem is "just ignorance. As my grandma would say, 'Pure old ignorance.' It's sad."[85]

Of course, there is no "right" or "wrong" target of violence. But hate crimes directed toward the Sikh community are surprisingly undercounted. While the *New York Times* reported that hate crimes against Muslim Americans and mosques had tripled in the months after the November 13, 2015, attacks in Paris, the FBI only started tracking hate crimes specifically against Sikhs in March 2015.[86] In their own count of hate crimes against their community, the Sikh Coalition found five cases in December 2013, seven in December 2014, and eighteen in just the first three weeks of December 2015.[87] One of the nation's leading South Asian civil rights organizations, South Asian Americans Leading Together, found that between 2011 and 2014, there were seventy-six documented incidents of hate violence directed toward the Sikh community; 80 percent of them were motivated by anti-Muslim sentiment.[88]

Local law enforcement lives in this tension between homeland secu-

rity and the fair treatment of people. For Mims, her public-safety responsibility comes first. "Who is coming into this country and why are they
here? What are their contacts? Are they good, law-abiding, hardworking
people or people that want to come here for an education, or do they have
an agenda?"[89]

Fresno County is a mix of urban, suburban, and rural. Sheriff Mims's
deputies are isolated by the sheer size of the territory they must cover. Out
there in the hot and dusty land, where oil flows and food grows, things can
get interesting, which makes communication and trust with the community
so important.

But her strategy goes beyond the deployment of valuable law-
enforcement resources and engagement of state and federal partners.
Mims also realized her community was changing and that racial diversity was different from cultural diversity. The sheriff's department needed
to change with the community. "As I looked at the diversity of [a recent
Fresno County Sheriff's Department swearing-in ceremony], I had almost
two hundred people on the stage, and [I realized] that we had some diversity, but we really need to do a better job."

Mims says they need to do a better job even to meet "our needs, just
our needs. Deputies are out in the middle of nowhere, and they need to
speak to somebody who speaks Punjab or Laotian or Spanish, for that
matter. Wouldn't it be much better if we had somebody that could speak
directly to them?"[90]

These needs were starting to be met in the county. Officer Manpreet
Tiwana, a Punjabi resident, was one of the Kerman Police Department's
recent hires. Officer Tiwana shared with *California Report* the importance
of her role on the force: "They found somebody who can communicate
with them, and they can tell their issues to. They want to lay it out and tell
me all the problems."[91] Officer Tiwana's service humanized law enforcement for her community, and humanized South Asians for the broader
community. She was a bridge between both worlds.

In this multipronged approach to keep Fresno County safe, Sheriff
Mims has learned one thing: "If all politics is local, all law enforcement
is local."[92]

WHEN FAITH CONFLICTS
WITH POLITICS, FAITH WINS

Sheriff Mark Curran is deceptively tall, at six-foot-five-inches. His close-cut gray hair and serious eyes loom high over you. The even-keeled, Midwestern cadence to his voice offers only a glimpse of his deep and passionate convictions.

I first met Curran through the good people of the Illinois Coalition for Immigrant and Refugee Rights. In typical Chicago fashion, they had developed a politically bipolar relationship with the sheriff. They pressured him to support immigration reform and loved him when he did; but they weren't sure if they should love him, because he was a Republican.

Born in Pittsburgh, Pennsylvania, Curran has spent most of his life in Lake County, a racially and economically diverse region north of Chicago. A county of just over 700,000, its surprisingly large Hispanic population makes up over 20 percent of the overall population.[93]

After getting a law degree at Chicago-Kent College of Law, Curran went on to serve as a prosecutor at the county, state, and federal levels. Hardwired for politics, as he put it, Mark began to size up a run for the state general assembly in 2006. As a pro-life Democrat running against a pro-choice Republican, Curran thought his chances of victory were good. But the Democratic Party intervened and decided to run a pro-choice Democrat against Curran in the primary. On the recommendation of friends, he took his skills as a prosecutor and ran as the Democratic candidate for sheriff. He won, and he was sworn into office in 2007—a year after seismic shifts in the nation's understanding of immigrants and immigration.

For the nation's immigration debate, 2006 was a turning point. Looking at the political map, Lake County was between a rock and a hard place. Just across the state line, slightly to the northwest, Congressman James Sensenbrenner (R-WI) was chair of the House Judiciary Committee and had advanced legislation that came to be known as HR 4437. It passed the House on December 16, 2005, and aimed to dramatically strengthen interior immigration-enforcement laws and enact additional border-security measures.[94] The legislation took unprecedented steps, such as criminalizing faith leaders who did something as simple as providing transportation to an undocumented immigrant. In spite of efforts by President George W. Bush, Senator John McCain (R-AZ), and other Republicans, HR 4437 came to be seen as the GOP immigration calling card. Republican leaders at the local and national level fell into line with the enforcement-centric approach.

HR 4437 sent two political shock waves. For the segment of the population advocating an enforcement-only, deportation-heavy approach, the legislation was precisely what they were looking for. The immigrant community across America, meanwhile, took HR 4437 as a clear and present danger to their families. Lake County was in between a community to the north that supported HR 4437, and a major metropolitan region to the south that was insulted and incensed by the legislation.

On March 7, 2006, in one of the largest mass marches of recent history, over 100,000 immigrants and their allies streamed into downtown Chicago to protest HR 4437. One of twenty key organizers of the effort, Gabe Gonzalez, told me, "Before the marches, we were a set of disparate organizations, with the same general purpose but little cohesion. After the marches, we were a movement."[95] HR 4437 put the movement on the offensive. Gonzalez concluded, "Our struggle, which began as a defensive one, grew. Now it was about rights, and dignity. [The year] 2006 gave us that. Dignity."

The combination of HR 4437 and the energy from the immigrant community created the political tension necessary for legislative movement. Senators Ted Kennedy (D-MA) and John McCain (R-AZ) formed a bipartisan coalition in the Senate to pass comprehensive immigration reform in the Senate. Their bill served as a blockade to HR 4437, which had passed through the House of Representatives; the House and Senate never reached a compromise on the conflicting pieces of legislation, and the immigration-reform stalemate continued.

The year 2007 was Curran's first in office, and immigration was at the forefront of peoples' minds. As he told me, "I was hearing from a lot of people, 'What are we going to do about all these people? They are not supposed to be here,' and on and on and on. I looked into it, and nobody seemed to be enforcing the law."[96] In response, the newly elected Democratic sheriff applied to the 287(g) program, a federal program in which local law enforcement could take on additional immigration-enforcement responsibilities. The enforcement-only contingent was happy; but the immigrant rights community, not so much. Rock, meet hard place.

As the Democratic Party moved further to the left on social issues of life and marriage, Curran switched party affiliations to become a Republican in 2008. The Republican Assembly of Lake County (RALC) could barely contain its glee. They were thrilled to conflate issues of abortion, marriage, and immigration enforcement to define Curran as the ideal Republican sheriff: "The RALC has been in consultation with Mark advising him to do this. He is Pro Life, Pro traditional marriage, Pro second amendment, Pro enforcement of illegal aliens. He is a perfect fit for the Republican State and National Platforms."[97]

Over the next two years, Curran moved forward with a very conservative plan executing a range of local immigration-enforcement measures. In order to maintain the support of the local Republican Party infrastructure during a high-profile national debate on immigration, this was the path to follow: crack down on illegal immigration. He was no longer a Democrat representing a liberal constituency. He was a conservative representing Republicans. And at that point in time for Mark, it was the right thing to do.

Along the way, Curran had conversations with two people—one political, one spiritual—that led him to realize his fierce pro-life and pro-family positions ran counter to the RALC position of "Pro enforcement of illegal aliens."[98]

First, the political. Jeff Bell had been on the conservative scene for decades. He served as a speechwriter for President Ronald Reagan and ran for US Senate in New Jersey. Curran told me that in 2009, Bell spoke with him about the angry anti-immigrant voter, and he learned: "It's the loud people that you are hearing from, and there are just not that many of them. The people that prioritize deportations are much louder, much noisier, much less respectful. But their percentages are not that high."[99] Over time, Bell's analysis proved correct. While eventually this could have changed his mind, it was Mark's heart that set the core of his beliefs. And his heart followed his faith—which led him to question the anti-immigrant leanings of the local Republican establishment.

Cardinal Francis George served as Archbishop of Chicago from 1997 to 2014. As Cardinal George told Kenneth Woodward of the *Chicago Tribune*, he believed the church in Chicago was still a church of immigrants, "Only the countries they migrated from are different."[100] Around the same time as his discussion with Bell, Sheriff Curran had a conversation with Cardinal George. As Curran put it, "He tried to talk to me about why we needed immigration reform, encouraged me to read some documents."[101] So, like a good Catholic, he read and reviewed materials and research by the US Catholic Conference of Bishops; Cardinal George's recommendation had a profound effect on the sheriff.

"It's hard to describe conscience because it's unique for everybody, but I knew I was wrong. At that point in time, I had total clarity that I should be lobbying, if you will. I should be arguing for immigration reform."[102] This wasn't just a political calculation for Mark. It was a tension that ran deep through him and what he did every day. Over time, Curran struggled to arrive at a new position on immigration.

Back in his day job as an elected sheriff, Curran put this spiritual journey into words and actions. He asked the folks who had so eagerly welcomed him to the Republican Party, the Republican Assembly of Lake County, for a speaking slot at their upcoming meeting, which the *Daily Herald* captured: "Lake County Sheriff Mark Curran endorsed national immigration reform Thursday night before an audience of his fellow Republicans who seemed largely opposed to the idea."[103] In his remarks, Curran endorsed a proposal to provide a path to citizenship for undocumented immigrants, which was a position endorsed by his Democratic opponent in the recent fall 2009 election.

Mark attributed this complete reversal to his Catholic faith. He told the gathering, "When faith conflicts with politics, faith wins every time with me. . . . These are human beings we are talking about here, and God loves all human beings."[104]

More than six years after this speech, Curran told me that that moment "felt like kind of an atonement, that I was right with God because that's where truth was. And that the consequences were not as important as the fact that I could feel good about myself."[105] All of this propelled Curran to a local, regional, and national leadership role on the issue. As a conservative, he was willing to challenge other conservatives, and he brought law and order and faith credibility to the argument.

In this day and age, just like it is incredibly rare to find a progressive elected official who opposes immigration reform, it is odd to find a Republican elected official, particularly one whose responsibility it is to enforce the law, who supports the legalization of undocumented immigrants. Neither secularism nor godliness should be a prerequisite to treating people as human beings. But it is important to respect each person's path.

AUNTY AND UNCLE

Sorry, to break it to you, white America, but you are not the only ones who are afraid. The rest of us are afraid as well. We are worried the police will act rashly. We are worried our families will be victims of terrorism. We are afraid a friend or family member will get deported. No community has a monopoly on fear; we are all afraid. The question is, what do we do with that fear? What do our leaders do with that fear?

At the age of eight months, Greisa Martinez came to the United States from Hidalgo, Mexico. She grew up in Texas, and, in 2015, she joined United We Dream, the nation's leading organization of undocumented youth, as their Washington, DC, advocacy director. Like everyone at United We Dream, Martinez is smart, strategic, and incredibly poised. Undocumented for most of her life, she secured temporary legal status through President Obama's 2012 executive actions, but her mother remained undocumented.

Martinez told me, "If you're an immigrant, poor, black, or brown in this country, the message is clear: you are to be feared, not to fear."[106] For the most part, the assumption by conservative media and policymakers remains that immigrant communities are perpetrators of violence but never victims themselves. Certainly not leaders who seek to mitigate violence. Certainly not communities whose members are serving overseas in the armed forces. And, above all, not people who are afraid.

Like nearly every other American, her fear began on September 11,

2001. Martinez remembered sitting in class at thirteen years old, "as bodies and towers burned and fell." Her parents took the family to the church. She told me, "[I] looked for reassurance in my dad's eyes but found none. He was scared, I could feel it.

"Slowly the church began to fill up with other immigrant families. After singing and praying together, the adults naturally gathered in corners, whispering, strategizing on how to keep their families safe. I walked around the corner, hoping to find out more about what caused the attack. But what I overheard was not fear of terrorist attacks, it was fear of police retaliation, fear of ICE '*la Migra*' [Immigration and Customs Enforcement] raiding immigrant homes looking for someone to blame."

Their fears were separate from white America's fears. They didn't fear another attack. They feared America itself.

"That night my family and I slept at church," Martinez told me.[107] "I didn't realize it then, but my family was seeking sanctuary in our own church." She concluded, "That night at the church marked the first time I remember feeling the weight of responsibility to keep my family safe and the beginning of the questions, Where can we be safe? What does safe feel like? How do I break free from the corner of fear?"

These days, Greisa and her community of undocumented, or temporarily documented, immigrants are afraid of President Trump. His campaign rhetoric calling for a "deportation task force," to ensure that on "Day One, my first hour, those people are gone," and ending the "illegal executive actions" that protect Greisa from deportation left a deep imprint.[108] The fear echoed across my Twitter feed, filled my inbox, and was the subject of every conversation in the weeks after the election. Greisa and her community are prepared to fight for their community, but conservative allies such as Greg Zoeller, Margaret Mims, and Mark Curran are more important than ever. They have spent their careers in law enforcement balancing fear, safety, and human dignity. How they help conservative America, whether they are law-and-order voters or religious voters, they understand immigrants are people to be valued is crucial to our future as a nation.

This brings us to the 2016 Democratic National Committee convention in Philadelphia. On something of a lark, I made my way to the city of brotherly love to take in the political theater and festivities. More than that, I wanted to hear how Democrats were addressing the fear that Trump was clearly agitating within the American electorate.

It was the final night of the convention. The arena was packed to the gills by 5:30 p.m., and I couldn't get a seat. So I headed back downtown to watch the speeches from the bar at the Sofitel Hotel.

The handful of us in the bar were all looking forward to Secretary Clinton's acceptance speech. Up to this point that week, there had been a number of speakers who spoke positively about the contributions of Muslims in America. All challenged Trump's call to halt the immigration of Muslims to the United States. These were all applause lines within longer speeches. Important applause lines, but applause lines nonetheless.

Then came Khizr Khan and his wife, Ghazala. We sat on a high bench while we finished our dinner and sipped our beverages. Chatting, checking our phones. I glanced up at the CNN broadcast on the television and was surprised by the two people walking to the podium. Khizr wore a black suit, white shirt, and navy blue tie. He was balding, with a light crown of black hair. His wife, Ghazala, came up to his shoulder, and she had a navy-blue *dupaatta* draped over the back of her head. Her black hair peered out underneath, her wire-rim glasses sat on a profoundly sad face. If I ever met them, I would call them Uncle and Aunty. Behind them, on the massive stage screen, was a picture of their son, Captain Humayun Khan.

Khizr spoke with the deep, slightly accented voice of so many Pakistani immigrants. He started, "Tonight, we are honored," and paused. Ghazala looked down. "To stand here as parents of Captain Humayun Khan," he continued. Ghazala glanced up at Khizr and undoubtedly saw the reflection of her son's image on the wall behind them.[109]

Khizr paused a beat and continued. "And, as patriotic," he raised his right hand and pointed his right finger, "American Muslims." The emphasis carried through those two words as he opened his hand and gestured to the audience.

At that point, twenty-two seconds in, the Khans received their first standing ovation, accompanied by a chant of "U-S-A, U-S-A." It went on for at least ten seconds until Khizr motioned the crowd to quiet. Ghazala looked out over the applause, her solemn look never leaving her face. Looking closely, you could see her lips moving, "U-S-A, U-S-A . . ."

For me, those twenty-two seconds, the image, the voice, and the words, were mesmerizing. What left the deepest imprint for me, though, was the religion. In most political speeches, Democrat or Republican, Christianity or Judaism are the go-to religions. In this case, it was Islam. And a liberal audience was chanting "U-S-A" in response. In a year of upside-down politics, it was an upside-down moment.

I was transfixed by this scene of my parents' generation taking hold of the political world and owning their identity. Their action powerfully laid the foundation for an entirely new conversation on Muslims, national security, and the concept of fear.

The hotel bar grew quiet as all eyes watched the Khans.

Khizr's voice lowered slightly as he said, "If it was up to Donald Trump, [my son] never would have been in America. Donald Trump consistently smears the character of Muslims."[110]

Scattered yells of "yea" from the crowd.

Khizr went on, his voice getting deeper, "He disrespects other minorities; women; judges; even his own party leadership. He vows to build walls, and ban us from this country."[111]

The crowd booed.

"Donald Trump, you're asking Americans to trust you with their future," Khizr continued as his voice boomed. "Let me ask you, have you even read the United States Constitution?"[112] Khizr asked, right hand in the air, the rest of him stock-still.

Cheers rose from the crowd as Khizr paused and reached into his jacket pocket with his right hand.

"I will . . . I will gladly lend you my copy," as he pulled out a worn pocket version of the Constitution and held it up to the wildly cheering crowd.[113]

Ghazala looked out at the cheering crowd, then down, the sadness still on her cheeks.

This was not political theater. This was an American Muslim, grieving parents of an American hero, powerfully repudiating Trump's fearmongering.

I was not the only one with tears in my eyes.

No one in my family has served in the US military. There are few of us who even identify as practicing Muslims. But at that moment, the Khans spoke for me. They spoke for my family.

In a speech of less than seven minutes, this humble husband and wife were who I wanted to be. This couple had made the ultimate sacrifice, and on that stage they embodied American values: patriotism, family, respect, and courage.

They were Americans. They were Muslims. And they were not afraid.

CHAPTER SIX

IDENTITY, INTEGRATION, INFLUENCE

To a large degree, the first half of this book has delved into the individual and institutional relationships that are the foundation through which Americans negotiate the cultural changes that come with immigration. Without them, well, there goes the neighborhood.

Today, segmented news feeds, a globalized economy, and political candidates who exploit cultural divisions make it harder for culturally isolated communities, immigrant or native-born, to manage the prejudice that comes with American immigration. In these cases, the capacity of neighborhood-based organizations that facilitate the integration of immigrants is minimal and leadership has no way to engage fast-diversifying communities.

So this chapter is a little different. Let's take a step back to better understand how immigrants navigate American society, the legislative efforts that brought us to this point, and what the future looks like as the public and private sectors play larger roles in facilitating these changes.

NAVIGATING AMERICA

In early 2010, my colleague Katherine Vargas and I were in Los Angeles for a handful of meetings to lay the groundwork for a legislative push later that year. We had an afternoon appointment with the editorial board of *La Opinión*. The leading Spanish-language daily newspaper in the country, *La Opinión* reaches two million readers monthly in print and online.[1] It is the mothership of Spanish-language media, and it has defined and represented the political identity of Spanish-speaking Americans for generations.

There are 55 million Hispanics in the United States, accounting for 17 percent of the nation, which is a large-enough market to warrant specific media.[2] These days, from thriving Spanish-language radio stations to major television networks such as *Univision* and *Telemundo*, the Latino community is informed and connected to the news of the day.

All of this underscores the groundbreaking role of *La Opinión*, a ninety-year-old news organization dedicated to serving the Latino community. For decades, the *La Opinión* newsroom has looked like every other newsroom in America—except that everyone speaks Spanish. Through these years, *La Opinión* has turned data into information for the fastest-growing population in the country. This entrepreneurial organization understood early on that information is power, so it made sure its audience was the best informed, and, as a result, the most powerful.

Initially, Spanish-language media served as the primary source of news from Mexico for a very new immigrant community. As their readers settled into America and became Americans, these outlets served as the principal tools through which immigrants identified as a community, integrated into America, and, ultimately, influenced institutions.

Vargas, who had left the National Immigration Forum to serve as President Obama's Hispanic Media Director, told me, "Spanish-language media is the navigator map for immigrants who are trying to understand their new country. They help immigrants settle and understand their new country by explaining how the political process works and how to navigate the healthcare and education systems, which may vary significantly from their home country."[3]

As surprising as it may seem, this means the United States is doing something right when it comes to the integration and assimilation of immigrants into society. As a nation, we are always building and rebuilding the institutions through which the American story is expanded. This doesn't happen by magic. It takes a commitment from every ethnic media outlet that serves as the communications go-between for immigrants and America. Immigration naysayers claim that Spanish-language media, like bilingual education, is indicative that immigrants do not want to assimilate into society. This could not be further from the truth. I have traveled to countries like Belgium and France and met with members of their immigrant communities who have limited access to local, language, or culturally specific media. Their language-specific information sources are Internet-based and tend to report on news from home countries. Consequently, immigrants have can't access to local information and, just as important, receiving communities have limited opportunities to learn about their newest neighbors.

That 2010 afternoon at *La Opinión*, Katherine and I sat at the center of a long conference table and began to discuss the issues of the day. There were a handful of editorial board writers across the table lobbing questions in our direction on the politics of immigration and the likelihood of immigration reform. A few minutes into the conversation, out of the corner of my eye, I noticed someone new in the room. She had brown hair and was using a notepad, and she listened intently to the conversation. She didn't lean forward with a question or lean back with nonchalance. She sat straight up, took in the conversation, and quietly dissected our answers from the far end of the conference table.

One of the reporters noticed and invited the newcomer to introduce herself. In a very measured way, she said, "Hi, I'm Monica Lozano. Publisher of *La Opinión*."

HOW WE GOT HERE

Doris Meissner, former commissioner of the US Immigration and Naturalization Service for President Clinton and now with the Migration Policy Institute, explains, "We say with great pride that we're a nation of immigrants. And we are. But we tend to like immigration in retrospect, rather than when it's actually happening."[4]

This sentiment manifests itself in the battle cry, "Take our country back."

Who is taking the country back from whom?

America's Baby Boomer generation was born just after World War II, between 1946 and 1964. These days, Boomers range from fifty-two to seventy years old, and they live in a nation unlike the one of their youth. Boomers grew up in an America that was majority-white. The African

American population was immorally confined to the margins of society and integrated into the mainstream only through the struggles of the civil rights movement. For the most part, parents (and grandparents) of Baby Boomers arrived in America as a result of immigration at the turn of the century, primarily from Northern and Western Europe. The experience of Boomers and their parents was one of a white Christian America that controlled and managed almost all levers of society.

This is the generation whose anxiety has been triggered by today's changing America. A March 2016 analysis of the 2015 American Values Atlas found that 43 percent of Baby Boomers (aged 50 to 64) and 44 percent of seniors (aged 65 and older) felt that immigrants threaten American customs and values. Meanwhile, only one in five (19 percent) of young adults (aged 18 to 29) felt the same way.[5] Herein lies the challenge.

The demographics of this new America are a result of fifty years of steady, incremental change that began with the legislative changes of 1965.

The 1960s, a decade of both cowardly and courageous actions, changed the course of life for millions of Americans. At the decade's midpoint, the summer of 1965, the changes were far-reaching. First of all, the US political process was fundamentally changed by voting rights for African Americans. Later that year came legislation that changed what America looked like: the 1965 Immigration and Nationality Act, which Senator Edward M. Kennedy (D-MA) believed was "knocking down walls of discrimination."[6]

Since 1924, America's immigration system was controlled by quotas set at 2 percent of each nationality's foreign-born population as of the 1890 census. This meant the system heavily favored Western and Northern European countries. The 1965 Immigration and Nationality Act, originally known as the Hart-Celler Act (the original authors), negotiated over the course of that summer, replaced the national-origins quotas with immigrant visa categories based on skills and family relationships. It effectively laid the foundation for a very different America—the America we see today.

Thirty-three-year-old Senator Ted Kennedy was asked by the leadership to serve as the legislation's floor manager. As he was still grieving the loss of his brother, President John F. Kennedy, these must have been emotionally and politically trying times for the young senator; on top of that, immigration was deeply personal to his family.

During my time in Massachusetts, I heard Senator Kennedy tell the story of looking out his Boston office window to see the stairs where his family walked off the boat from Ireland. As one of the great political storytellers, Kennedy always described this scene with passion and conviction. It was also an issue deeply ingrained into the senator's philosophy. As Kennedy said in a Miller Center oral history project, conversations with his grandfather, John "Honey Fitz" Fitzgerald raised the issue of immigration policy for him. "Grandpa talked about the unfairness of the immigration rules—I remember that, long before everybody got into the immigration—how the immigration [system] worked, discriminated against people about where they were born."[7] Kennedy concluded, "He was very strongly against that." The Immigration and Nationality Act of 1965, and Kennedy's intense commitment to immigrants and immigration over the course of his career, would have made his grandfather proud.

While this bill changed history, it was not explained to the public as groundbreaking. With the Statue of Liberty looming in the background, President Lyndon B. Johnson signed the legislation into law on October 3, 1965, asserting, "This bill that we will sign today is not a revolutionary bill. It does not affect the lives of millions. It will not reshape the structure of our daily lives, or really add importantly to either our wealth or our power."[8] (Pretty good soft sell on the part of the president.)

He saw the act as a practical solution to a system that was broken. "For over four decades the immigration policy of the United States has been twisted and has been distorted by the harsh injustice of the national origins quota system. It has been un-American in the highest sense, because it has been untrue to the faith that brought thousands to these shores even before we were a country."[9]

While the Immigration and Nationality Act rode the era's wave of civil rights legislation, immigration itself was not seen as a civil rights issue. In fact, David S. FitzGerald and David Cook-Martín of the Migration Policy Institute make a strong case that geopolitical concerns played a larger role than many realize. They point out that white ethnic organizations and representatives attacked the quota system for discrimination against the Italians, Greeks, Portuguese, Poles, and other Europeans waiting in line for oversubscribed quotas. FitzGerald and Cook-Martin tell us, "White ethnic voices had become much more influential by 1965 than in previous legislative debates. John F. Kennedy had become the first elected Catholic president in 1960, and the 89th Congress (1965–66) was the first in US history to be majority Catholic."[10]

Author of the book marking the fiftieth anniversary of the 1965 Immigration and Nationality Act *A Nation of Nations: A Great American Story* Tom Gjelten wrote in the *Atlantic* that as a result of the act, "The share of the US population born outside the country tripled and became far more diverse. Seven out of every eight immigrants in 1960 were from Europe; by 2010, nine out of ten were coming from other parts of the world."[11] The Pew Research Center calculated that among immigrants who have arrived since 1965, half (51 percent) are from Latin America and one-quarter are from Asia.[12]

This was not what the legislative authors intended. As Gjelten wrote, a last-minute amendment to the act added language "giving visa preferences instead to foreigners who were seeking to join their families in the United States."[13] The amendment aimed to skew future immigration in favor of US citizens with European family roots, weighting the legislation to favor the ethnic white community that pushed for the legislation.

The net result was a legal immigration system that emphasized family connections. On one hand, this played into the common belief that we are a "nation of immigrants," as the legislation's authors believed family ties (at least European family ties) were the past, present, and future of the country. On the other hand, the amended legislation baked the concept of family reunification deep into the nation's immigration cake.

As it turned out, naturalized citizens from Africa, Asia, or Latin America were most likely to take advantage of the opportunity to move and to bring their families with them. Gjelten wrote, "Within a few decades, family unification had become the driving force in US immigration, and it favored exactly those nationalities the critics of the 1965 Act had hoped to keep out, because those were the people most determined to move."[14]

The infusion of talent and energy as a result of the new law cemented the position of the United States as an economic powerhouse. As opposed to what President Johnson said, the 1965 Immigration and Nationality Act affected millions of lives. It also infused the nation with immigrants who ranged from engineers to farmworkers, and whose determination generated jobs for all Americans. As we know too well, and as I mentioned above, this has created a level of anxiety among those who grew up in a different America. In these changes, some of us see an exceptional future where America represents and leads a global society. Others, however, see a future where America is losing its culture in the face of growing diversity.

The 1965 Immigration and Nationality Act scrambled America's eggs. Our future will look dramatically different from our past. According to the Pew Research Center, the white population in the United States has shrunk 22 percentage points since 1965, while the Hispanic population has increased 14 points; and the Asian population, 5 points. Among the projected 441 million Americans in 2065, approximately one in three will be immigrants or have immigrant parents, compared to one in four today.[15] With no projected racial or ethnic majority by 2055, the golden age of the hyphen is near.[16]

Given the current backlash against Latinos, Asians, and other new Americans, the forces behind the 1965 Immigration and Nationality Act are important to understand. Leading up to this legislation, white ethnic immigrants *identified* as American, *integrated* into society, and then sought to *influence* the system to meet their needs. Replace Latino and Asian ethnic communities with white ethnic communities, and you have twenty-first-century America. These are the three *I*'s of becoming American: identity, integration, influence.

A NEW LATINO IDENTITY

Within the complicated history of Mexican migration north to the United States (or as some in the Mexican American community will joke, the movement of the US–Mexico border south) is the story of *La Opinión* and the evolution of Mexican identity in America.

Francine Medeiros's study "*La Opinión*, a Mexican Exile Newspaper: A Content Analysis of Its First Years, 1926–1929" provides a helpful glimpse into the paper's founding.[17] Ignacio Lozano, Monica Lozano's grandfather, immigrated to San Antonio, Texas, from Marín, Nuevo León, in 1908. Working as a writer, Ignacio saved enough resources to launch his own weekly, *La Prensa*, in 1913. As the Mexican community began to grow in Los Angeles, he opened *La Opinión* in 1926. In less than five years, the paper's circulation reached communities in Texas, New Mexico, Oregon, Kansas, Arizona, Utah, and Illinois. This tremendous growth continued: today, *La Opinión* is the longest-running Spanish-language daily in the United States.

So there was a reason I sat up straight during that editorial board meeting. The Lozano family had been doing this for a long time.

Monica Lozano joined *La Opinión* as managing editor in 1985. She became the paper's publisher in 2004 and was appointed CEO of its parent company, impreMedia, in 2010.[18] Over the course of her career, she has served on several corporate and civic boards, including the Walt Disney Company, Bank of America, and the University of California Board of Regents. There are few Latinas as powerful, influential, and humble as Monica Lozano.

As a third-generation US citizen, she infused *La Opinión* with a new type of relevance. During summer 2016, years after that first editorial board meeting, as we talked over breakfast in Los Angeles, Lozano said that her approach "was really to ground *La Opinión* in the local community, to make it a metropolitan daily newspaper that understood the background of [its] readers."[19] She continued, "The fact is they are here now and very likely will stay, and so how do we become a vehicle for integration, for understanding the systems around them, and how do they access those systems?"[20] Under Lozano's leadership, *La Opinión*'s goal moved beyond informing its readership. It sought to empower its readership. In which case, it was a straightforward question that Lozano asked over breakfast: "How do we translate [the Mexican community's] presence into influence?"[21]

La Opinión's power and influence grew with its audience. Just between

1980 and 2010, California's Hispanic population grew over 18 percentage points.[22] The majority of Latinos in California were of Mexican origin, and in Los Angeles County the Hispanic population grew from approximately 2 million in 1980 to over 4.2 million in 2000 (44 percent of the county's population).[23] But these changes were not as simple as they looked to the outside observer.

Driven by growing political instability and economic despair, families fled Central America and began to head north in the 1980s. According to the Migration Policy Institute, between 1980 and 2013 the size of the Central American immigrant population grew from 354,000 to 3.2 million. The population more than tripled in the 1980s, almost doubled in the 1990s, and continued to grow more than 56 percent between 2000 and 2013 due to a range of factors that include gang violence and political instability.[24] Many Central American immigrants moved to Southern California, where there was already a large Spanish-speaking population.

Although the Reagan administration actively discouraged Salvadorans and Guatemalans from applying for political asylum—their visa approval rates were less than 3 percent in 1984, compared to 12 percent for Nicaraguans, and far below the rates for Poles (32 percent) and Iranians (60 percent)—their numbers continued to grow.[25] Given the choice between a deadly civil war and a difficult life in cities such as Los Angeles, they chose to remain in the United States. Some were able to attain legal status as refugees, while others blended into the region's undocumented population. Either way, as political refugees, not immigrants, they had a very different vision for their time in America. They didn't have a choice: They saw the United States as their new home, even if they had yet to attain legal status.

One community was ready to integrate into American society; the other held onto its identity. As Monica put it, Central Americans were "much more focused on sort of rooting themselves here, their kids were going to be born here. . . . It just wasn't possible to go back." Meanwhile, the sentiment of the Mexican community was, "I want to buy my little ranch [back in Mexico], and I'll never become a [US] citizen."[26]

To those outside the Latino community, everyone was from Mexico. But a common language was not necessarily a common identity. As the

Latino community diversified, immigrants from Latin American countries faced a broader question of identity. The question "Where are you from?" took on an entirely new meaning.

Lozano explained that many families went through "identity cycles." She gave an example of a hypothetical family's journey. First, they come to America from Mexico and only consider themselves Mexican. Over time, they start to see themselves as Latino, "part of something bigger and broader."[27] From there, the family starts to consider themselves American, then the hyphenated Hispanic-American. Finally comes the comfort with which first- and second-generation Latino-Americans (or Hispanic-Americans) shift between cultures and give birth to a new, "ambicultural," understanding of identity.[28] This is not so different from white ethnic Americans who went through a very similar identity cycle. For example, Italian immigrants became American citizens and then Italian-Americans. But these generational changes came with growing pains. It has never been a simple "speak English" process of integration. From discrimination in the workplace to physical attacks to political decisions that erect legal barriers, immigrants to the United States have always faced challenges as they adapted to their new home.

REAGAN'S NEW CITIZENS

By 1980, the population of undocumented immigrants in the United States was estimated to be two to four million, and pressure for immigration reform that provided legal status began to grow.[29] On November 6, 1986, Reagan signed into law the Immigration Reform and Control Act. The law granted legal status to approximately three million undocumented immigrants and prohibited employers from hiring unauthorized immigrants. Reagan said, "Future generations of Americans will be thankful for our efforts to humanely regain control of our borders and thereby preserve the value of one of the most sacred possessions of our people, American citizenship."[30]

What followed was a massive opportunity for immigrants to assimilate into American society. Community-based organizations certainly played a large role in this work, but media institutions were positioned as the backbone of this integration process. Without these institutions, who were trusted by the immigrant community, it would have been impossible to successfully implement the law. In 1989, *La Opinión* announced a new partnership with the *Los Angeles Times* to provide information on naturalization programs and services. The March 13, 1989, supplement, "Staying Legal," was a guide to the second phase of Reagan's immigration program, applying for legal permanent residence after the first-phase temporary status, for immigrants that was jointly produced by the papers.[31] Lozano shared with me that half a million were distributed with the *Los Angeles Times* in English and Spanish, with another one and a half million in Spanish only.

It was a clear pivot by the paper to serve and advance the interests of its readership. This audience, Lozano believed, would best be able to flex its political muscle as US citizens. In 1990, just over a year later, the *Los Angeles Times*'s parent company, the Times Mirror, purchased a 50 percent stake in *La Opinión*. While the companies maintained wholly separate operations and staff, they clearly understood their spheres of influence had the potential to expand.[32]

The community *La Opinión* reported on, represented, and informed had changed dramatically. No longer was it a community of Mexican immigrants who hoped to return to their home country: it was a community knit together by language and made up of families with a range of future hopes. They had taken another step in the cycle Monica described; they were becoming Mexican American and saw the United States as a permanent home.

Over the course of the 1980s, as the Latino community reckoned with its identity, President Reagan opened the doors to citizenship, and public and private-sector institutions facilitated an entirely new phase of social integration. But before these new Americans could even begin to influence broader systems, the powers that be lashed out.

THE TURNING POINT

The California of today, deeply diverse and politically progressive, is not the California I grew up in. In the 1990s, California was the leading edge of a cultural backlash to diversity. Whether or not we realized it, the controversy that beset the Golden State was a turning point for the United States, and Cecilia Muñoz was a big part of it.

Born in Detroit, Michigan, to parents from Bolivia, Muñoz spent twenty years with the National Council of La Raza, rising to senior vice president of research and advocacy. In 2008, she was recruited by President Obama to join his administration, and eventually she served as assistant to the president and director of the Domestic Policy Council—the principal forum used by the president of the United States to consider domestic-policy issues.[33]

In many ways, Muñoz speaks to the past, present, and future of America when it comes to immigrants and immigration. She worked in California (1984–1986) just as Reagan's immigration-reform legislation made its way through Congress, confronted local and federal efforts to pass anti-immigrant laws, and elevated the influence of Latinas in government. Her footprint is much bigger than her feet.

Muñoz also has a level of political savvy, influence, and grace that eludes most people. For many years she has been a friend and a mentor, so it was an incredibly special opportunity to interview Muñoz in her West Wing office. Looking out her window at the White House residence just feet away, I realized that it was a powerfully ironic place to talk about California Governor Pete Wilson's failed efforts to scapegoat Latino immigrants.

The Proposition 187 campaign arrived nearly eight years after the passage of Reagan's Immigration Reform and Control Act, and five years after *La Opinión* and other institutions prioritized the civic engagement of the state's Latino population. According to the Congressional Research Service, Proposition 187 was "a 1994 ballot initiative to deny illegal aliens state benefits and to require reporting of illegal alien applicants for benefits to federal immigration officials."[34] To put it more bluntly, less than a decade after millions of immigrants were on the path to integration as full-fledged members of society, Pete Wilson and a burgeoning nativist movement struck back.

In his gubernatorial reelection campaign, Governor Wilson's claim that undocumented immigrants were bankrupting the state allowed him to zero in on immigration as a polarizing issue to mobilize voters to the polls.[35] Muñoz saw how Wilson contorted himself to ride the wave of anti-immigrant backlash to further his own political ambitions. She told me, "[Wilson] overturns himself and rides this wave of ugliness back into the governor's mansion. He won, he got the short-term benefit."[36] Much of the heated campaign was waged on college and high-school campuses. I remember the loud rallies on my college campus and the heated rhetoric in the news; it was a tense time to be a Californian. On November 8, 1994, Proposition 187 passed by an overwhelming 59 to 41 percent margin.

At that time, California's population was 57 percent white, 25 percent Latino, 9 percent Asian American, and 7 percent African American. But voters on that day were 75 to 80 percent white, and only 8 to 10 percent Latino.[37] To underperform so dramatically was what Lozano called "a total political awakening" for California Latinos.[38] It was only with the passage of Proposition 187 that Latino voters in California realized that as long as Latinos were residents of the United States, the political system could work for or against their interests. Returning to Mexico to buy a nice home was no longer the goal; immigrants in California wanted to integrate as US citizens and become voters with a say in their future. It was not a lesson the community would forget.

While implementation of Proposition 187 was blocked by a federal judge, long-term political damage was done to California's Republican Party.[39] "The clear long-term implication was Latinos got really energized in California," Muñoz told me.[40] In the ensuing years, the community "naturalized in record numbers, registered to vote in record numbers. Suddenly you have all these Latinos in the state legislature. You have the first Latino Speaker of the assembly, and California turns blue."[41] In fact, the percentage of eligible Latinos registered to vote in California jumped 15 percent in just six years—between 1990 and 1996, it rose from 52 percent to 67 percent.[42] By 2015, some twenty years after the Proposition 187 battle, California's state legislature was 19 percent Latino, compared to only 6 percent in 1990.[43]

These days, Latinos dictate the terms of the debate for California Republicans, and California Republican officeholders are much more likely to support a path to citizenship for the undocumented than not. This is no longer Governor Wilson's Republican Party.

Lozano summarized the period: "Ten years [after Reagan's immigration reform], you have this moment in time where people are now eligible to become citizens and basically understood that the power of the ballot to take your rights away could only be protected by the power of your vote."[44]

Just like ethnic whites from the twentieth century who pushed for the 1965 Immigration and Nationality Act, Latinos identified themselves as a community, integrated as Americans, and exerted their influence as voters. One of them even became the director of domestic policy for the United States of America. That is the American dream and the American reality.

MORE-ENCOMPASSING IDENTITIES

Progressive activists and pundits often claim that demographic change makes policy change inevitable. The assumption is that the size of minority communities will create congressional districts more representative of the nation's ethnic and racial diversity. As a result (so the thinking goes), members of Congress will represent electorates that support immigrants and immigration reform.

This "wait them out" strategy is as appealing as it is short-sighted. It assumes that over the next few decades, immigration-enforcement programs will be curtailed and states will move forward with their own constructive approaches. But in the meantime, immigrants are left in the lurch; they are detained and deported by a federal enforcement system too well-funded and entrenched to shut down, and there are relatively few states with legislative bodies politically prepared to pass pro-immigrant measures. As a result, the millions of immigrants living in politically moderate or conservative states would be forced further and further to the margins. On the other hand, all the immigrants in the country can just move to California. Or maybe not.

Waiting for demographic majorities also ignores culturally isolated white Americans legitimately struggling with these changes. They would be left to their own devices to understand this new landscape. In the best case, they would gravitate toward the thoughtful conservative leaders they trust and seek a path forward based on a common set of values. (Like we saw in Utah or South Carolina.) In the worst case, they are drawn to extremists, racists, and "Alt-Right–ists," who fill this vacuum with their stream of nationalist, anti-immigrant venom. If the 2016 electoral race and the reality of President Donald Trump proves anything, it is that these dark forces are alive and well.

Best known for his seminal work, *Bowling Alone*, a deep dive into the decline of American engagement in civic life, Robert Putnam has bridged the world of academic researcher and policy wonk.[45] Putnam released a new study in 2007, *E Pluribus Unum: Diversity and Community in the Twenty-First Century*, that caused waves among press, policymakers, and advocates. Based on an exhaustive survey of roughly thirty thousand individuals in 2000, Putnam's research surfaced the challenges communities face when their populations diversify.[46] He found that in the short to medium run, immigration and ethnic diversity challenged social solidarity and inhibited social capital. Or, as communities became more diverse, relationships between new neighbors were difficult to establish because they did not share the same experiences or history. But as time passed and integration took place, "successful immigrant societies create new forms of social solidarity and dampen the negative effects of diversity by constructing new, more encompassing identities."[47] A shorter version: diversity is hard. It requires people from different backgrounds to get to know each other and, over time, develop a collective identity that includes a little from everyone involved.

Putnam's findings cut against the progressive belief that diversity is automatically a net benefit to society. As I told the *Boston Globe* in 2007, "We can't ignore the findings. The big question we have to ask ourselves is, what do we do about it; what are the next steps?"[48]

The challenge of developing "more-encompassing identities" is vexing, but the path forward Putnam proposed in 2007 remains relevant. He makes the case that for society to manage and deal with diversity, a decidedly local approach is required. Institutions such as community centers, churches, and schools are crucial gathering points. These are the places where relationships are established, skills (i.e., English-language learning) are developed, and immigrants are able to acculturate. Through these steps, and certainly others, we may be able to address what Putnam framed as "the central challenge for modern, diversifying societies . . . to create a new, broader sense of 'we.'"[49]

These institutions have catalyzed important changes in the Northeast and West, where the immigrant population is more established. But in the Southeast or Midwest, institutions have adapted and emerged slowly while economic and cultural tensions grow. In this vacuum, the public sector needs to play a larger role.

Unfortunately, the vacuum has grown and the tensions have increased because policymakers on both sides of the aisle ignore poor and middle-class white America. Democrats and progressives, in their efforts to build a powerful multiethnic political coalition based in urban centers and coastal states, never dug deep to understand the economic and social challenges faced by white working-class families. Republicans and conservatives, in their efforts to slash entitlements and winnow tax rates, ignored the reality that a larger number of white Americans' economic sustainability depends on access to government programs and services.

As a result, a not insignificant number of white voters feel that Democrats ignore them because they are white, and Republicans ignore them because they are poor or middle-class. Into this breach stepped Donald Trump. He gave this slice of the electorate permission to vent their cultural and economic anger. As Derek Thompson wrote in the *Atlantic*, "Economic anxiety and racial resentment are not entirely separate things, but rather like buttresses in an arch, supporting each other in the creation of something larger—Donald Trump."[50]

In August 2016, Jonathan Rothwell, a senior economist with Gallup, shed important light on this issue through a working paper, "Explaining Nationalist Political Views: The Case of Donald Trump."[51] Rothwell's paper was based on a massive sample of over 93,000 American adults, and it made for one of the most comprehensive pictures of this population.[52]

Keep in mind that up to that point, Trump's central campaign strategy was to loudly oppose trade and immigration. He bashed trade deals, called for mass deportation of the undocumented, and pledged to severely limit legal immigration. For the Trump campaign, the way to "Make America Great Again" was to scapegoat the "other." But Rothwell's analysis uncovered some unexpected characteristics of Trump's voters.

Rothwell wrote, "Surprisingly, there appears to be no link whatsoever between exposure to trade competition and support for nationalist policies in America, as embodied by the Trump campaign."[53] Trade or competition for local jobs was not the issue that agitated his followers. In fact, Trump supporters were more likely to be self-employed and had higher household incomes than non-Trump supporters.[54] Instead, Trump's support was highest in areas far from the Mexican border that are ethnically and racially isolated from black, Asian, and Hispanic populations, and with few college graduates.[55] The fear of the other wasn't necessarily the immigrant next door. It was the immigrant they'd never seen.

Ryan Lizza hit the nail on the head: "The Trump voter, according to [Rothwell's] research, is driven not by simple economic self-interest but by something deeper and more psychological."[56] This something deeper is a fear of the other—for the sake of their children. All of this feels very reminiscent of California in the early 1990s. The toxic combination of fear based on race and class touched a powerful nerve. Regardless of the year, politicians such as Pete Wilson and Donald Trump were happy to take advantage of these fears.

To a certain extent, America will follow California's trajectory. With every election cycle, the power of the Latino and Asian vote becomes greater. But Latinos make up nearly 40 percent of California's population, so they have a natural heft that brought major changes in just a generation. There aren't many other parts of the country that are going to see that kind of percentage, and therefore that rapid a change. The rest of the country may grow more diverse, but it isn't going to look like California for a very long time.

All of this means that the "wait them out" strategy will take a long time. We can't just wait. A strategy to engage white America in this cultural conversation about identity, integration, and influence is paramount to real change.

THE POLITICS AND POLICY OF CHANGE

There are few people who make politics as fun as Ron Brownstein. A walking, talking encyclopedia of statistics, he can rattle off poll results, demographic changes, and batting averages like a shopping list. Brownstein was one of the first in Washington, DC, to dissect the meaning of changing demographics on the country's political structures. As early as 2006, Brownstein saw the surge in Latino support for Democrats.[57]

Brownstein is one of the few political pundits who understand how cultural change impacts voters. On Britain's decision to leave the European Union, known as Brexit, Brownstein wrote a widely cited June 30, 2016, article, "Culture Is Replacing Class as the Key Political Divide." Even though the demographics of the countries differed significantly, Brownstein concluded, "The Brexit vote pointed to a reshaped U.K. political order that revolves more around cultural affinities—particularly attitudes toward immigration and diversity—than economic class. The Clinton-Trump race is poised to fast-forward that same shift across the Atlantic."[58] The world will not be defined by party politics alone. Increasingly, the cultural changes beneath political change will have deep, long-term repercussions.

Brownstein refers to this as class inversion: "The GOP primary has become more populist—as the growing base of blue-collar whites challenges the hegemony of the party's traditional white-collar base. Simultaneously the Democratic primary electorate has grown more consistently liberal, as the growing populations of minorities, Millennials, and white-collar whites replace the working-class whites shifting toward the GOP."[59] Blue-collar white GOP voters don't care about tax cuts for the rich, and culturally diverse Democrats question the motives of working-class white Americans. Again, political parties are racing past an important segment of the population—which makes for a tricky mess.

Roughly speaking, opponents of immigrants and immigration break into two camps. One group traffics in openly nativist rants and promises a return to a culturally isolated and homogenous United States. That group is a lost cause. Others, more populist than nativist, believe the American-born worker can only thrive if fewer immigrants come to the United States. The common denominator lies in their plan to limit the number of low-skill immigrants to America. I'm not saying all populists are racists, and I'm certainly not saying any racists are well-informed. But they both believe the ticket to America's salvation is to keep farmworkers and janitors out.

Two of the nation's prominent conservative thinkers, Ross Douthat and Rehan Salam, coauthored "A Cure for Trumpism," a July 2016 essay for the *New York Times* that offered a range of policy proposals to address cultural anxiety and economic fear. Douthat and Salam did not scapegoat low-skill immigrants; rather, they were quick to limit their human potential. "While less-educated immigrants are no less admirable and hard-working than those who have managed to acquire the skills most prized in our polarized labor market, there is clear evidence that they and their children need more of a helping hand from social programs, and that their descendants are more likely to assimilate downward when that help does not suffice.

"Given these problems, an immigration policy in the national interest should explicitly try to attract immigrants who will be in a strong position to provide for their families in a difficult economic environment. It should encourage a market in which employers have to compete more for less-skilled labor, to slow the alarming retreat from paying work among native-born working-class men."[60]

They went on, "Republicans should make any path to permanent legal status [for undocumented immigrants] conditional on steady year-over-year cuts in the pace of low-skilled immigration, both legal and illegal."[61]

Let's take a second to unpack this. Douthat and Salam base their conclusions on a study by the Center for Immigration Studies, an organization advocating for reduced immigration. Laura Reston from the *New Republic* found that the study, "exaggerates the number of immigrants on welfare by using households as the unit of analysis; as long as the head of household is an immigrant, they consider it an immigrant household."[62] And, in the original study, the Center for Immigration Studies counts a household as, "using welfare if any one of its members used welfare during 2012."[63] All of which means that if a United States citizen child of immigrant parents receives a subsidized school lunch, the entire household is on welfare.

The canard that low-income immigrants are a drain on public resources has been proven wrong time and again. In fact, the libertarian Cato Institute found that poor immigrants use public benefits at a lower rate than poor native-born citizens. For example, more than one-quarter of native citizens and naturalized citizens in poverty receive Medicaid, but only about one in five non-citizens do so. Additionally, about two-thirds of low-income citizen children receive health insurance through Medicaid or CHIP (Children's Health Insurance Plan), while about half of non-citizen children do so.[64]

Moreover, in the July 6, 2015, issue of the *National Review* (of which Salam is executive editor) Linda Chavez cited a 2011 National Bureau of Economic Research study, "that found immigrants with income less than 200 percent of poverty were less likely to take advantage of safety-net programs than the native-born."[65]

Of course, immigrants pay into the public programs and services through tax contributions. The Institute on Taxation & Economic Policy found that undocumented immigrants pay approximately $11.64 billion in state and local taxes, a contribution that would increase approximately $2.1 billion should they receive legal status.[66] And the president's Council of Economic Advisers found that, in 2012 dollars, the average immigrant contributes nearly $120,000 more in taxes than he or she consumes in public benefits.[67]

While I understand some may feel that non-citizens just should not be eligible for any public programs or services, even if they pay into them, it is unclear why Douthat and Salam continue to drive a narrative that immigrants are a net loss when it has been so thoroughly disproven.

Finally, the economy is not a zero-sum game. Nonpartisan economic think tank Regional Economic Models, Inc., conducted a state-by-state analysis of the impact of immigration reform across high- and low-skill visa programs. It found that an expansion of lesser-skilled visas, with regulations to ensure American workers are not undermined, would lead to increased economic productivity and output.[68] This is the basic outline of every reasonable immigration proposal that has advanced through the United States Congress. Create a balanced approach to immigration that promotes the interests of American workers while shoring up labor needs across the spectrum.

In their essay, Douthat and Salam speak to the need to preserve entitlement programs such as Medicare, Social Security, and the Affordable Care Act (with reforms, of course). They call for an end to tax cuts for those making more than $250,000 per year.[69] But they do not believe in attempts to lift all boats. The authors assume low-income white Americans gravitate toward Trump's identity politics because, like low-skill immigrants, they have reached the extent of their own human potential and want nothing more than access to entitlement programs. Nothing about training American workers. Nothing about making sure our schools are providing a quality education.

Just reduce the number of low-skill immigrants, cut taxes for those making less than a quarter of a million dollars, sound more inclusive, and *voilà*, a new American prosperity.

Their entire argument is based on a belief that success in America is also a zero-sum game: What you have is what I don't have. This is a feedback loop that imagines a world where goods, information, money, and people do not move and economies do not grow. It is a strategy that deepens the cultural isolation of both immigrants and the native-born. Intellectual populism like this is the glide path to a shrinking America.

Even worse, underlying this sentiment is the lack of value we attribute to the work people do. Whether someone has been building houses for generations in Texas or cleaning homes in South Carolina for the three years since she arrived in the United States, their work is of equal value to their families and to the nation. It is a self-fulfilling prophecy to limit the potential of our people and our economy.

COMPANIES ARE PEOPLE TOO

February 2, 2014. Super Bowl XLVIII, Denver Broncos versus the Seattle Seahawks. Super Bowl Sunday is one of the few times in America where we all watch the same thing. Sit on the couch, drink a beer, complain about the halftime show, and watch very large men run into each other at very fast speeds. The 2014 Super Bowl, to borrow from Bob Putnam, expanded the identity of America.[70]

Instead of a botched call on the field, Coca-Cola was the one who caused a Super Bowl–sized meltdown. Their one-minute commercial, a multilingual, multicultural rendition of "America the Beautiful," sung in eight different languages by men and women representing the diversity of the country, triggered a massive response.[71] Social media lit up with excitement and anger. The commercial presented America with a cultural challenge.

There was no other institution that could have confronted us in the same way. We love our Diet Coke and we see it in a very particular way. For Coca-Cola to acknowledge and amplify the power of a changing America rattled our senses. Coca-Cola knew a segment of the US population would not take kindly to the commercial, but it also knew that others would gravitate to its message. It was a quintessential example of immigrants who identify as American, integrate through an incredibly recognizable American song (and delicious beverage), and influence a great American institution.

If culturally isolated communities lack the neighborhood institutions to facilitate culture change, and government cannot play that role, the private sector is positioned to fill that vacuum. Culture change reaches scale when governments and corporations internalize the changes to the country and follow suit. Coca-Cola responded to community changes articulated by ethnic media and others to reach hundreds of millions of people in one sixty-second spot. That is the cultural power of the private sector.

Monica Lozano explained the shift in business relationships with consumers as *La Opinión*'s readership grew: "The private sector really understood the consumer opportunity, the business opportunity attached to this consumer base."[72] As Lozano expanded the paper's relationships, the cor-

porate approach to new communities went "from being transaction-ori-
ented to relationship-oriented. And [corporations] are not just selling them
a product, you are actually developing something that will go through the
life cycle of—they're consumer life cycles."[73] Spanish-language media
provided a way for corporations to understand this new population. They
weren't selling to a Latino mother or a father, they were selling to a Latino
family that included consumers across the age spectrum. By understanding
this new population of consumers, corporations could shape product allegiances over the course of a lifetime.

Soon, she noted a change in approach from corporations. "Then they
start targeting in more authentic ways, so they get deeply involved in education, they get involved in healthcare."[74] Corporations were sponsoring
community events across this range of issues in order to get their brands
in front of this new consumer population. "There's this awakening of the
private sector," Monica told me.[75]

This new consumer base influenced the identity of private-sector institutions. In 2001, Wells Fargo & Company was one of the nation's first Fortune
500 companies to take decisive action. Led by Lynn Pike, regional president for Wells Fargo in Los Angeles, the bank partnered with the Consulate
General of Mexico to announce that Wells Fargo, "will accept the Certificate
of Consular Registration (the *Matricula Consular* card), as an acceptable
form of primary identification for opening new accounts and over-the-
counter transactions at its more than 3,000 banking locations in 23 states."[76]
The *Matricula Consular* was made available to all Mexican nationals
residing in the United States, regardless of their immigration status. Lozano
understood the heart of this change. By accepting one of the few identification options available to undocumented immigrants, "they weren't just
opening up checking accounts, they were empowering [the community]."[77]
Yes, Wells Fargo had a vested interest by accepting the *Matricula Consular*
as a legitimate form of identification for the undocumented immigrant community. But it was a high-risk, high-reward decision.

Announced just a few months after the September 11 terrorist attacks
in New York City and Washington, DC, Wells Fargo was, as she put it,
"out on a limb," and the target of heated criticism. But Wells Fargo saw

the growth potential of the market, so it forged ahead. Two years later, in February 2003, it announced that its audio-capable ATMs also included Spanish-language settings.[78] A simple but substantive change, it continued to open channels of banking to the immigrant community. Unsurprisingly, the moves were a great business decision. In October 2004, the company announced that the number of accounts opened with the Mexican *Matricula Consular* topped 500,000.

Wells Fargo, hundreds of billions of dollars in size, was now a different institution because it realized the community it served was different. *La Opinión* and the readership it served defined that change and its importance. It was a marketing strategy that led to institutional and community change.

What also made this possible was savvy corporate leadership connected to these communities; this starts with the board of directors and senior management. Lozano told me, "Companies that are successful don't just embrace the strategy, they let somebody within the organization that really knows have decision-making over that strategy. Then things will change."[79] Corporate leadership who have lived the immigrant experience, directly or through their families, have a different perspective on these issues and may be more likely to push for such changes.

Leadership is the next frontier for immigrants to influence American companies. In 2011, 74.4 percent of corporate directors were white men, followed by white woman at 13.3 percent. Only 2.4 percent of corporate leaders were Latino men and 0.7 percent were Latina.[80] A new America needs a new, more diverse corporate profile. The experience and qualifications to be successful in corporate America are different now. As Lozano told me, "You have to expand your definition of qualified now. . . . I think some companies get it better than others. But it's a challenge. . . . More than ever, immigrants and the generations that follow them identify and integrate into society as Americans. Influence within the private sector, at leadership levels, will lead to long-term change. Monica told me, "The board can say we really want you to think about your Hispanic strategy, but in terms of designing it and implementing it, that happens at the management level. We need CEOs. We need executives in companies."[81]

A MORE INCLUSIVE AMERICA

As powerful as the private sector is, there is really no bigger change agent than the federal government. The strategic and policy decisions to deploy public resources are key, and so are the people who make those decisions. Different perspectives with different experiences bring about different decisions. In this manner, the Obama administration's efforts to bring new people into the public sector will have a long tail of influence. As Muñoz reflected on her time within the Obama administration, she said:

> One of the things they accomplished is they brought up a whole genera-
> tion of organizers. Many of them came to work in the administration and
> who are well positioned for leadership now going forward. As organizers
> in the Obama world they then learned how to operate, many of them,
> within government so that they're organizers, they are political campaign
> people, and now they are experienced government operatives with policy
> jobs, with outreach jobs, with broader connections to a range of other
> constituencies.[82]

Now that young people have developed an expertise on how to work within government, they will impact the trajectory of the United States for generations to come. In 2016 the *Washington Post* reported that for the first time in history, the majority of top policy appointments within the executive branch are held by women and minorities.[83] Young, immigrant, minority staff I know who cut their government teeth working in the Obama administration have gone on to work for state and local government or run for public office. For Muñoz, "It gives me huge hope for the future."[84]

Ultimately, this goes beyond the idea of diversity. It is to participate and make decisions of consequence in the public or private sector. As Lozano put it, "The inclusion agenda . . . isn't just to be at the table, it's to be a decision maker."

Monica's comment can be interpreted as exclusionary for white, or even black, America. But our understanding of being American is changing. As the country diversifies, "inclusivity" has become a recurring theme of poli-cymaking and economic processes. The basic idea is that communities of color must be included in processes and decisions that impact their lives—which, more and more often, is just about any decision of import. This is a balancing act institutions across the country have pulled off before. It is one we must pull off again.

The immigrant cycle of identity helps this balancing act. Immigrants go from Mexican to Latino, Vietnamese to Asian, Pakistani to South Asian. Then, as a new language and culture takes root, the integration into American society becomes deeper and immigrants play a greater role in institutions, big or small. Finally, they seek to influence these institutions, public or private. Directly as legal immigrants with influence, or indirectly through the relationships or experiences undocumented immigrants share with decision makers. With the right people making and informing decisions, these institutions better serve this population of new Americans.[85]

By no means is this a guarantee that immigrants, or those who understand the immigrant experience, will align their decisions accordingly. But as we enter an era of political polarization that may pit liberal, diverse cities against conservative suburban and rural white regions, representation at decision tables will become more important. Our experiences shape our personal identities; and it is those identities we bring to the decisions we make.

Who would have thought in 1913, when Ignacio Lozano launched *La Prensa*, that the Latino population would grow to such size and diversity? As Monica Lozano put it, *La Opinión* "went from being a Mexican-owned business to an American institution."[86]

Who knows what immigrant family will create the next great American institution?

CHAPTER SEVEN

THE NEW TEXAS

I remember the first time my mom took me with her to vote. We drove in the family station wagon to the polling place at Notre Dame High School. My parents immigrated to the States from Pakistan in 1971. When they arrived, they stayed in Livermore, California, for a few months at my uncle's home. Soon they moved to Santa Cruz (my birthplace), where my dad found a job that helped him acquire the hours necessary for his physical-therapy license. In 1975, we moved to Salinas, California, and my parents opened a private practice.

This was my first trip to Notre Dame, the all-girls high school in town, so I was pretty excited. Sadly, it was also my last time in the building. (Different book.)

We waited briefly to check in with the volunteers and were assigned a booth in the school cafeteria. The blue velvet curtains were heavy and thick with that rarely used smell as we entered the booth. I stood next to my mom as she inserted her ballot, clicked the mechanical switches, and pulled the lever with a satisfying sound. While we use pens or computer screens these days, every time I vote, those lines, smells, and noises come to mind.

We were a bit of an anomaly in Salinas. The relatively small city did not have a big South Asian population. It was mostly my sisters, my parents, and me. Most of my friends were Mexican or white. I was none of the above, but I got along with all of the above. In retrospect, this dynamic played a pivotal role in my ability to work and relate across ethnic and political lines.

We grew up in a comfortable, middle-class neighborhood with the usual dramas of life, nothing too serious. My parents were politically active in that we knew there was a world bigger than Salinas. Maybe this was easier as an immigrant family, since our conversations, relationships, and travels would take us out of the country. While my parents were certainly politically aware, we were not instilled with a spirit of activism. The public-policy debates of the time rarely, if ever, made it to our dinner table.

Voting, I suppose, was my parents' activism. They came to America to become Americans. Participating in the American political system as voters was one way to ensure that my sisters and I had a better life. I admit that I have sometimes taken for granted the right to vote. I didn't always appreciate the impact of the political process on my life, nor did I always work to impact that process through my vote. In doing so, I let my parents down as much as anyone else. Now I realize that, as a US citizen, as a child of immigrants, if I don't vote, I don't matter. Which, I think, is why my mom took me with her to vote. She believed that she mattered. It is the same reason new American citizens are voting in increasingly large numbers.

HARD TO PIGEONHOLE HOUSTON

The story of metropolitan Houston is a story about the United States. As we will see, underneath the social and economic differences within the Houston metropolitan region lie political similarities. As the identity and composition of each city changed, immigrant communities integrated themselves into the political structures, leading to new alliances that influenced the region. In some instances, the alliances were strong enough to bridge cultural differences. In other cases, there was more work to do. As we talked about these changes to the political structure, and the new immigrant and minority leadership that defined them, Mustafa Tameez, a local political strategist, told me, "What they have in common, though, is the sense that it is our time, and that they are more reflective of the cities that they [seek to lead]."[1] Houston's civic leadership was changing to represent the diversity of the region itself.

Born in Karachi, Pakistan, Mustafa moved to Queens, New York, when he was eight years old. He left for Houston in 1994 and built a successful career in communications and marketing. Graying at the temples,

Tameez is soft-spoken, walks with a slight limp, and has a sense of humor I can appreciate.

As we sat in a hipster Houston gastropub, he eyed my kombucha, the latest fad in fermented, effervescent drinks, and asked the waitress, "What is this stuff he has, kombucha?"

"It is a flavored drink with active enzymes. It's really good," I remember her saying as I nodded my agreement.

"I'll try one." After the waitress walked away, Mustafa leaned over, with a bit of a smirk, "You know, in Karachi, we just call that water. And the enzymes clean you right out."[2]

In 2001, a friend from the Houston Muslim community asked Tameez to contribute to Mayor Lee Brown's reelection bid. Mustafa was in the marketing business and had never been politically involved. After a gentle "do it for the community" twist of the arm from his friend, Tameez made his donation and found himself sitting next to Mayor Brown at a fundraiser. He innocently asked the mayor how he planned to use the funds to engage Asian voters—the donation was "for the community," after all. The mayor didn't have an answer, but his campaign manager soon followed up. To make a long story short, his question led to a campaign job in which he designed and executed Brown's Asian-voter outreach program.

That 2001 election deep in the heart of Texas (read: anywhere in Texas), was a bellwether moment. The race pitted Brown (the city's first African American mayor, who was in his third and final term and was strongly supported by the national Democratic Party) against Orlando Sanchez (a Cuban-American Republican supported by then president George W. Bush and his vast network). Since neither candidate earned a simple majority of voters in the general election, they were slated to meet each other in a December runoff.

To the uninitiated, Houston was the last place one would expect a high-stakes race for mayor between two people of color. In a runoff election, with no national or statewide race to attract attention, the campaigns knew victory required an all-out effort. In the final four weeks of the runoff campaign, spending was estimated to be as high as $4 million, as both parties furiously deployed money and spokespeople to Houston.[3] Richard Bond, the former chairman of the Republican National Committee, told the *New York Times*, "We'd love to have this guy."[4]

As a result of the massive investment, voter turnout in the 2001 runoff was up about 12 percent over the 288,000 votes cast in the November 6 election. Richard Murray, University of Houston political science professor, estimated that Brown "won with support from the black community and about one of every four Anglo voters."[5] As a result of Tameez's strategy, 80 percent of Asians voted for Brown; 72 percent of Hispanics did as well.[6] All told, the coalition of black and brown voters earned Brown a 52 to 48 victory.[7]

Consider the alternative: A Sanchez victory based on a coalition of conservative white and Hispanic voters. That alignment that would have provided a Hispanic Republican mayor of the state's largest city a powerful platform to shape the trajectory of Republican politics across the state and, perhaps, the country. Sanchez could have led Republicans toward a new type of politics from one of the most conservative states in the union.

Instead, Houston remained in the hands of Democrats, who, over the years, methodically built a multiethnic coalition that coalesced around a new American identity. And just four years after the Sanchez loss, congressional Republicans passed legislation, HR 4437, criminalizing the undocumented—and anyone who helped them.[8] This led to a decade of coalition work by Democrats and a steady stream of Republican-led legislative attacks on immigrants and immigration at the local, state, and federal levels. At the risk of oversimplification, their stances could be described as follows: Democrats sought to welcome and integrate immigrants, while Republicans looked to marginalize and ostracize them.

As we sipped our hipster kombucha and nibbled on our hipster quinoa, Tameez reflected on Houston as "a city with lots of contradictions. We create more millionaires than any other city. We also have the most amount of low-wage jobs that have been created here than anywhere else in the United States."[9] The changes to the city have been significant. Between 1990 and 2010, the percentage of Latinos in Houston grew fifteen points to 35 percent, while the Anglo (the term of choice for white Texans) population dropped eighteen points to just under 40 percent.[10] The African

American population remained fairly stable at around 17 percent. Over that same period of time, Houston mayors toggled between white and African American leaders, including two women and one of the nation's first openly gay mayors.

The city's leadership understands that its collective economic and political success requires cultural crossover, especially since, as Tameez told me, the future purchasing power of the region is controlled by the 51 percent of people under the age of twenty, who are Hispanic. "Therefore, the power structure will have to yield and change."[11]

A NEW SHERIFF IN TOWN

Born and raised in Houston to Mexican immigrant parents, Adrian Garcia's life and career mirrored the city's demographic, economic, and political changes. Over a steaming plate of enchiladas, Adrian told me that his parents came to the country because "one of my brothers was gravely ill."[12] And because the elder Garcia had been a guest worker, "he was able to petition for another work visa."[13] Now, the younger Garcia lives less than a mile away from where his father worked.

Adrian followed in his brother's footsteps to join the Houston police force in 1980, and he served for twenty-three years. In 2003, he left the department to run for Houston City Council to represent District H, which was over 70 percent Hispanic. Foreshadowing a plucky political career, Garcia defeated Diana Dávila Martínez by a mere 841 votes in a December runoff.[14]

His own political influence grew with the influence of the predominantly Hispanic district he represented. He capitalized on his law-enforcement expertise to chair the council's Public Safety and Homeland Security Committee, and in 2007, Mayor Bill White appointed him mayor pro tempore.

As his stock rose, so did the possibility of significant voter interest. In 2008, Adrian decided to run for sheriff of Harris County. Houston city proper covers 579 square miles with a 2015 population of just over 2 million people; Harris County is the most populous county in the state and third largest in the nation.[15] Its population of 4.337 million people located in 1,777 square miles make Harris County larger than half the states in the union.

This meant that Garcia's population of eligible voters grew dramatically from 131,825 (66 percent of whom were Hispanic) in District H to 1.9 million across Harris County (16 percent of whom were Hispanic).[16] Winning an expanded election required an expanded strategy. The path to victory was moderate voters who needed a reason to put rule-of-law priorities over concerns they might have with a liberal Hispanic sheriff. As Garcia put it, "I'll go work [with] moderate Republicans and try to pull them over."[17]

Garcia went on to win the sheriff's seat by thirteen points.[18] Aided to a certain degree by misstep-prone opponents, his campaign showed "rule of law" values could recruit moderate Anglo voters he did not immediately identify with—particularly since the 2008 "Obama effect" only brought a 2 percent increase from the previous presidential cycle.[19] Garcia parlayed his law-and-order, smart-management message to build a diverse coalition of support. Little did the new sheriff know that his combination personal story, law-enforcement expertise, and elected office experience would put him in the middle of America's identity crisis.

Under President George W. Bush's administration, the Department of Homeland Security created an immigration-enforcement program that permitted state and local law enforcement to enforce civil immigration law under the supervision of US Immigration and Customs Enforcement agents. Local law enforcement decided whether or not to join and implement the program. Further adding to local discretion, the program's authority could be implemented across the entirety of law-enforcement functions, or it could be limited to specific areas, such as correctional facilities.

Immigration advocates believed local law enforcement took advantage of this "287(g) program" to profile people of color and arrest immigrants on minor charges to detain and deport those who proved to be undocumented. Supporters felt local law enforcement should be allowed to assist in the detention and deportation of undocumented immigrants. Wherever the program was implemented, it was a controversial flash point. Immigrant communities could not help but feel that they were under suspicion by anyone who had a badge. As a result, trust between immigrants and law enforcement diminished. But in 2008, Adrian Garcia, who cut his teeth representing one of the largest Hispanic districts in the city, was the one with the badge.

The Harris County Sheriff's Department agreed to participate in a version of the program—limited to correctional facilities only—in August 2008, months before Garcia took office. By the end of his first year in office, Garcia signed onto the Obama version of the 287(g) program, Secure Communities. The program was designed to prioritize the removal of criminal aliens, legal and undocumented, who had committed high-priority deportable offenses. As summarized by the Migration Policy Institute, Secure Communities prioritized removals across three levels.[20] Immigration and Customs Enforcement considered Level 1 offenders the highest priority, those convicted of major drug offenses or violent crimes. Level 2 offenders included those convicted of minor drug offenses and crimes such as burglary, larceny, or money laundering. And Level 3 offenders had been convicted of other crimes.

Due in large part to programs like 287(g) and Secure Communities, the *Washington Times* reported that, "According to a Syracuse University study based on federal records, the Houston-based [US District Court for the Southern District of Texas] handled nearly 23,000 immigration prosecutions in the first nine months of fiscal 2009—by far the most of any district court in the country and a projected increase of 22 percent over last year."[21] The story of a newly elected Hispanic sheriff from a majority Hispanic district detaining and deporting immigrants at a record pace cut both ways. Moderate, white, law-and-order voters respected it. Hispanic voters, Garcia's base, felt disrespected.

All of this complicated life for the new sheriff. He was electorally dependent on an ethnically and politically diverse coalition, but his personal values were rooted in the Hispanic community. As a modern-day crossover candidate, Sheriff Garcia embodied the new Houston Mustafa had referred to. Squaring his role as the chief law-enforcement officer of Harris County with his past efforts as a city councilor and community advocate would be a challenge.

So Garcia used his influence as a Latino Democrat elected to serve as the sheriff of the fourth largest department in the nation to press the Obama administration. He realized he had "made the mistake of believing the administration, that the focus of the programs would be [Level] 1 violators."[22] Therefore, Garcia renegotiated his memorandum of understanding with federal immigration enforcement to force "transparency" and "reporting."

Explaining this to his Hispanic constituents was easier than expected. "When I would go to the Hispanic community, I would ask them for their vote and I would tell them, 'Look, we're going to continue to keep programs in place that are intended to keep everybody [safe]. Remember that some of the people that harmed you tend to look like me.'"[23] When the issue came up with white audiences, Adrian would say, "Look, I'm in the information business. In order for me to do my job well, I need people to come forward and share information. Right now, if I do any more than what I'm doing, I'm likely to shut down a pipeline of information."[24] At a time when he could have leaned in one direction or another, swayed by identity, Garcia relied on his primary purpose to serve and protect with the whole of his broad political coalition and community.

This decision to work across the spectrum and create a political center paid off when he ran for reelection in 2014. Adrian was from, and represented, Houston's Hispanic community, but he was able to reach across the ethnic and political aisle to create a consensus. "When I was up for reelection, the fact that I had worked down the middle made the success of that reelection easier as a crossover. I saved money, [and] people liked the policy I was doing, the work I was doing," Garcia continued. "So it was easier to maintain that crossover status."[25]

The strength of his diversity as a Latino law-enforcement official working across community lines shined through. Sheriff Adrian Garcia's leadership allowed the Harris County Sheriff's Department to be an institution that brought the community together. Similar to a business that marketed to different consumers, a school that served a diverse student body, and a church that brought different ethnic ministries together, this was a law-enforcement agency that was helping Houston move forward as a united city. In this instance, the department captured the promise of Houston.

Less than a year after his reelection as sheriff, Garcia set his eyes on the mayor's office. Fourteen years after Orlando Sanchez's defeat, in May 2015, the *Houston Chronicle* highlighted the importance of Garcia's campaign, "While Garcia will now have to turn in his gun and badge and resign as sheriff, he could end the year elected as the first Hispanic mayor of the most diverse city in America."[26]

But broader culture and politics intervened. In May 2014, with Mayor Annise Parker's support, the Houston city council passed the Houston Equal Rights Ordinance (HERO) in an 11 to 6 vote. Social conservatives organized a ballot initiative to put the ordinance in front of the voters. According to *Ballotpedia*:

> The ordinance, which was on the ballot as Proposition 1, would have banned discrimination based on sexual orientation and gender identity— criteria not covered by federal anti-discrimination laws—especially "in city employment, city services, city contracting practices, housing, public accommodations, and private employment."[27]

The proposition sparked an intense, often ugly, campaign that pit social conservatives against gay-rights advocates and progressives. The local issue quickly became a national hot button, with conservative faith leaders among the most outspoken opponents.

In spite of the ruckus, Garcia's campaign seemed to be going well. Helped by name recognition and the fundraising networks of his recent sheriff's campaign, an October 7, 2015, poll showed Garcia in a tie for first with fellow Democrat Sylvester Turner.[28] The poll also included "questions about the Houston Equal Rights Ordinance (HERO) and showed a majority of Houstonians in favor of it."[29]

As the *Houston Chronicle* wrote less than a month later: "the man many thought could have been Houston's first Hispanic mayor is out of the running and out of a job."[30] Voters had overturned the ordinance 61 percent to 39 percent and sent Republican Bill King to the December mayoral runoff with Democratic State Representative Sylvester Turner—Garcia was a distant eight points back. Conservative anger regarding the ordinance spiked turnout, overwhelmed a crowded field, and split a Democratic vote between several contenders. In other words, culture drove the day.

In the final runoff, Turner, an African American with deep roots in Houston, eked out a 4,100 vote victory over King. According to *Governing Magazine*, "King took 71 percent of the vote in the city's majority-white voting precincts, where residents also turned out in the highest numbers. Turner won a whopping 93 percent of the vote in majority-black precincts, however, erasing King's turnout advantage."[31] Republicans narrowly lost once again.

Let's return to the 2001 Brown versus Sanchez runoff. If Sanchez had won, the ranks of Hispanic conservatives surely would have grown. The older generation, at least, could have opposed Proposition 1. Instead, without a moderate Republican leader in 2015, the Texas Republican Party was dominated by anti-immigrant legislators. In fact, there was a drop-off of about 48,000 votes in the runoff election.[32] It is not difficult to argue that culturally conservative Latino voters, who may very well have opposed HERO, were turned off by anti-immigrant Republicans; they either voted Democratic or stayed home (contributing to the drop-off in turnout). Once again, were Hispanic voters the margin that kept the nation's fourth largest city in Democratic hands?

The ink had barely dried on the 2015 mayoral election before Garcia announced his third campaign in three years with a run for Congress. This time he challenged two-decade incumbent Gene Green to represent the 29th congressional district—the fifth most Hispanic district in the country. Garcia sought to serve a district he described as "the third worst ranking on educational attainment. It ranks lower than state average and national average on homeownership rates. It ranks worse than the state average and national average on children living in poverty."[33]

Early on in the campaign, as the dynamics of the race were taking shape, Emily Deruy of the *Atlantic* asked the question, "Is it more important for a majority-Latino district to be represented by a Latino, or is a long-serving Caucasian ally just as fit for the post?"[34]

As I watched the race from the cushy confines of Washington, DC, it felt like Garcia was thrashing from campaign to campaign, looking for a job. But it was different. He was testing the ability of Hispanic voters to exert their political identity and influence. Although Garcia ultimately fell short in his campaign against Green, his was yet another challenge to the region's power structure.

As we reflected on his political career over that lunch in Houston, Adrian described the string of events that led him to join the police force. These included the "Chicano Brown Power" movement, the high-profile beating and eventual death of a Hispanic Vietnam veteran in Houston, and subsequent outreach by the police department to diversify its ranks.[35] Early in his law-enforcement career, as he felt Hispanics were telling him, "I guess you are not one of us if you joined them," he committed himself to a path where he could increase his influence in order to benefit his community.

While he was out of politics for the moment, this path to influence was still clear to him. It was the path of understanding, he told me, "the quest of identity, the quest of integration, the quest of influence, is still alive and well. It's still occurring in different ways."[36]

THE IMPORTANCE OF THE CROSSOVER

Just east of Houston lies Sugar Land, Texas. With its manicured lawns, gleaming business parks, and clogged traffic, Sugar Land has all the signs of suburban American economic growth. The Town Square, an open-air business district built in the late 1990s, is a multiblock shopping complex with restaurants, high-end boutiques, and a Marriott hotel.

From 1910 until 1959, Sugar Land was a company town that revolved around the Imperial Sugar Company and the housing, healthcare, and businesses it provided for the workers and their families.[37] Beginning in the 1980s, a number of large corporations opened offices in Sugar Land. Its corporate footprint grew to include the headquarters of Minute Maid, Schlumberger, Tramontina USA, Fluor Corporation, Bechtel Equipment Operations, Noble Drilling, Money Management International, and Aetna.[38]

It was midafternoon on a Thursday in downtown Sugar Land, but the Baker Street Pub and Grill buzzed like a Saturday. Through the open windows I saw a group wearing matching blue T-shirts as they laughed and drank, clearly in some kind of celebration. Further down the street, I spotted more people in the blue Clements High School shirts, this time a gaggle of black, white, and Asian parents drinking beer and munching on appetizers. Downtown Sugar Land, it seemed, was the United Nations of beaming parents.

In the twenty-plus years since 1990, the Sugar Land population had nearly doubled to top 87,000 in 2016, and the suburb became the third largest in the metropolitan area (behind Houston and Pasadena). At the same time, Sugar Land became the largest city in Fort Bend County, which Rice University sociology professor Stephen Klineberg called "the most ethnically diverse county in America."[39] Just as Sugar Land resembles an America we will see in the next fifty years, its political dynamics foreshadow those we will see elsewhere.

I met KP George for breakfast at the Avalon Diner on the eastern edge of Houston. As we sat in a booth, sinking into overstuffed vinyl-upholstered benches, George told me his story: he grew up poor in a South Indian village, immigrated to the United States in 1993, and became a citizen in 1999. Since then, he has mounted campaigns for Fort Bend County treasurer, the 22nd congressional district, and a winning effort to serve on the Fort Bend County Independent School District School Board. As an independent certified financial planner, father, and elected official, George was a full-fledged owner of the American dream.

In his rapid-fire South Indian accent, George excitedly described the school district's population, "Ninety-five languages are spoken in Fort Bend. The population is African American about 27 percent, Hispanics around 25.5, and Asians are almost touching 24; . . . you don't see in many places that kind of demographics. And the Caucasian population is about 19 percent, so they are the minority."[40] Fort Bend County is not on a path to the old Texas. It is a county on the cutting edge of economic and social change. And its school system, from the leadership to the students, was one of the places where communities were learning to coexist.

As the largest city in Fort Bend County, Sugar Land had undergone dramatic changes itself. In the first ten years of the new century, the white population shrunk 5 percent, the Asian population grew 78 percent, and the Latino community grew enough to make up 10 percent of the total population.[41] According to the US Census Bureau, the Asian community grew from just under 8 percent of the population in 2000 to over 35 percent in 2010.[42] Political diversity has not accompanied ethnic diversity; the city remains a Republican stronghold. For elected leadership to represent the diversity of the city, the trick was to find a candidate representative of the immigrant community who was able to cross over and earn the support of conservative white Republicans.

Harish Jajoo was that person. He immigrated to Sugar Land in the 1980s from India, was fiscally conservative, and worked as an engineer for the city of Houston. He and his wife (a doctor) had raised their two sons in Sugar Land when it was a small, scrappy Houston suburb.

Jajoo and I sat in the lobby of the Marriott hotel just across the street from City Hall. He told me he and his wife came to Sugar Land for the "good schools, good neighborhoods . . . [and] for the medical center."[43] Well before KP George's time, what drew Jajoo to public service was the local school system. So in 1994, Jajoo ran for school board in Fort Bend ISD. He said, "I was the first Asian American, Indo American, whatever American to run for any public office. We didn't have a clue what we were doing."[44]

While Jajoo was defeated by his eighteen-year incumbent opponent, he felt good about the campaign. "At the end of the day, I still gained 1,800 votes. He had only 3,500, so it wasn't totally lost. So I made 1,800 friends, and I was really excited about that."[45]

What Jajoo remembers from that first campaign is the road he paved. I couldn't help but agree with him when Jajoo echoed my earlier conversation with George: "That was a watershed moment, I think, in the South Asian community; . . . nobody ever did it. I was the first one. Unfortunately, it was not successful, but it paved the path for a lot of other people to follow, too."[46]

Sixteen years and a Sugar Land Zoning Board appointment later, Jajoo retired from his job as an engineer with Houston to try another run for office. This time, he was better prepared. In 2011, Jajoo competed against another South Asian, Farha Ahmed, to secure the District 4 City Council seat.[47]

As Jajoo approached his term limit in 2016, he geared up to run for mayor of Sugar Land. As Jajoo put it, "As the mayor, I can set the path to what you want to see the city as. It's my city. It's your city. It's everybody's city. Nobody owns the city. The city is the people."[48] The challenge was to translate this vision of representing a diverse city to a campaign strategy that reached across race and ethnicity.

Jajoo received enough votes in the general election to run against Joe Zimmerman, a white man with the endorsement of the outgoing mayor, James Thompson. He had also served as Sugar Land's Position Two at-large city councilor since 2012. In June 2016, Jajoo lost the campaign, but he was still paving new paths to try to bring diverse representation to his city.

I saw the same energy and entrepreneurship in Vy Nguyen. Personally recruited in 2012 by the Fort Bend County Democratic Party chair, Nguyen ran for Texas State Representative in District 26 at the age of thirty-four. As a small-business owner, Vietnamese American, and single mother, her story was powerful. "My family came here at the fall of Saigon when the Communist government took over the country," Nguyen told the *Sugar Land Sun*.[49] "My grandmother was killed trying to come to this country. I was named after her. When I think of immigration I'm grateful because I wouldn't be alive if this country wasn't generous enough to let us in."

District 26 covers the overwhelming majority of Sugar Land and stretches north a little into Mission Bend and west into Pecan Grove and Richmond. It is an extraordinarily diverse district. Forty percent of its residents speak a language other than English at home. As with Jajoo, if Nguyen could cross over to reach other ethnic communities, she could win.[50]

Over the course of her campaign, Nguyen saw things she didn't expect from candidates who did not share her immigrant heritage, particularly when it came to reaching out to the diversity of the county. "I saw that the white politicians who are officeholders in Fort Bend County were also at the mosques. When I was there, they were there, too, because they realized how important it was to be more embracing and to open their eyes to the reality and the beautiful diversity that we have out in Fort Bend County, instead of trying to ignore it and suppress it or degrade it."[51]

Issues of voter education and engagement surfaced: "You drove through Sugar Land, [and] there was an early-voting poll at every church. It was ubiquitous. It was everywhere."[52] But ten miles to the north in Mission Bend, a more middle-class town, "they only had one early-voting poll. . . . It was in a small, little, tiny park that was buried in the back of the back streets of Mission Bend."[53]

For Nguyen, she broke ground and inspired others: "I think seeing an Asian candidate was refreshing for [Vietnamese women]. I think it was almost like a lot of the Vietnamese women . . . had never seen that before."[54] Most important, Nguyen was invited into the political infrastructure, "To this day, people ask me to help with political events, [with] this and that, and I always feel very humbled by that. I think to myself, 'Well, I didn't win, but I'm glad to know that people thought that we ran a good campaign.'"[55]

George, Garcia, Jajoo, and Nguyen: these are the stories of four immigrants to America who work to make their communities better places through civic participation. All three were economically successful to one degree or another, but they integrated into society and saw themselves as part of a bigger conversation about the future of America. They identified as American, they integrated into society, and they sought to influence the system as elected officials. They won some races and lost others. But this was the American dream in action.

THROWING AWAY THE UMBRELLA

Just thirty miles to the east, I was a world away. As I left Sugar Land, with its $104,939 median household income, I saw that that income brought with it the spoils and status of the region's energy economy.[56] Meanwhile, as I arrived in Pasadena, with its $48,004 median household income, I was greeted with the dust and grit of the same economy.[57]

Pasadena is bordered by the Houston Ship Channel to the north and

Galveston Bay to the southeast. North of downtown, refineries border the highway, with looming oil tanks and belching smokestacks. The evening air filtered the setting light and illuminated a landscape that was flat and gray—little of the green I saw in Sugar Land. Instead of sit-down restaurants and boutique shopping, the roads were peppered with fast-food restaurants and auto-repair shops. Pasadena City Hall was a low-slung building set off from the street and surrounded by municipal buildings. Pasadena isn't a burnt-out, empty city. It is a blue-collar, working city.

It was early evening when I arrived at Pasadena City Hall, and the dusk light had cooled the air. Before my last interview of the day, I took a second after the long drive to gather my thoughts and check my phone. I locked the car door and turned around to find Ornaldo Ybarra walking up. With a buzz cut and a trim figure, Ybarra's business casual clothes belied a serious demeanor. He had the Texas twang of, well, a Texan, and the look of a Hispanic immigrant. Born and raised in Pasadena City, Ybarra was the US citizen child of immigrants and another face of the new Texas.

Ybarra's city council office was immaculate. He sat behind a large desk, with nary a random piece of paper to be seen. Pinned to the wall behind me were various campaign signs from a range of candidates. Thirty-seven years old, looking young enough to "still get ID'd when I buy beer," Ybarra was in his third, and last, two-year term on the city council. He was a neighborhood kid who had done well.[58]

The Ybarra family arrived in Pasadena from Mexico in the early 1970s. Ybarra recalled, "It's a good place to grow a family. To me there were no issues. The schools were there. They were good. I feel that I got a good education there. It was a good place to grow up."[59]

In 1996, after graduating from high school, Ybarra enlisted in the United States Marine Corps. Upon his return, Ybarra earned a degree from San Jacinto College and went on to join the Pearland Police Department, where he now serves as a sergeant. "You know what, I'm about to get my master's degree this semester, and I still find that my military service was the best thing," Ybarra told me.[60]

Where Sugar Land is an ethnic amalgam, Pasadena is racially binary, with Latino and Anglo populations on opposite growth paths. The city had a population of 153,784, over 60 percent of whom were Hispanic, ranking it well within the top twenty most populous cities in the state of Texas and the second largest city in Harris County.[61] This is a far cry from the Pasadena of the 1970s, when the city was home to a Ku Klux Klan bookstore and reveled in its Wild West, roughneck identity. These days, Mexican restaurants and Latino grocery stores define Pasadena's culture.[62]

"I remember when I was a kid in elementary [and] intermediate [school], the stores were predominantly Anglo convenient stores," Ybarra told me. "Everything that you see now, as far as Mexican restaurants, snack places, the meat market, all that is just—over the last, I'd say, at least fifteen years. [It] has just dramatically changed from when I was a child."[63]

The Pasadena Independent School District illustrates this point further: in 1986, the student population was 60 percent Anglo and 31 percent Hispanic. By 2007, the student population had flipped to 73 percent Hispanic and 14 percent Anglo. As superintendent Dr. Kirk Lewis told the press, "If we're going to have a community that's viable, then all of the children must be educated."[64]

Of course, these demographic changes took place in the context of economic cycles. While Pasadena's unemployment rate had plummeted to 4.3 percent in October 2007, just as the numbers of Hispanic residents climbed, the rate spiked to 10.9 percent in January 2011.[65] But since this high-water mark, Pasadena's unemployment rate has steadily dropped as the state's economy regained its footing. Yet, an economy susceptible to energy prices makes for a constant threat of turmoil. That, on top of demographic change, provides a consistent undercurrent of economic tension. But in the case of Pasadena, that wasn't the issue.

For Ybarra, maybe it was his military service and the responsibility that came with it. Maybe it was growing up in a city as it changed to look more like his family. Either way, Ybarra had a plan on what to do when he got back to Pasadena, he wanted to help the city continue its transformation from a white working-class community to a diverse community with access to good jobs and services. He told me, "I always knew that I wanted to get into politics, just seeing the issues and the problems, I said, 'You know what, I'm going to run.' I knew I was going to do it eventually for something."[66]

So in 2009, at the age of thirty, Ybarra ran for Pasadena city council. "I went out there, and I remember because I had no help," Ybarra shared.[67] "I mean, I didn't know how to get a block walk list or how to campaign. So all I did, I remember, was just basically going to the county-voter registration website and then looking at the precincts in my area." In a city where all the council seats were district-specific, the task was manageable with the right focus (more on this later).

The strategy worked. Ybarra defeated second-term incumbent Ralph Riggs by eighteen points.[68] "I was the first [Hispanic] in almost two decades that got elected," Ybarra said with quiet pride. He didn't ask his constituents about their immigration status. As he put it, he was their representative, regardless of immigration status:

> I think a lot of people don't understand at the policy level either, even though you have got 65, 70 percent Hispanic, when you break it down, whether they are here illegally, undocumented, whatever you want to call it, they still require representation. You still have to represent them. I mean, 22,000 people that live in my district, I still have to represent them . . . whether they vote or not.[69]

After six and a half years in office, and as a newly recruited mayoral candidate, Ybarra talked about what he was most proud of: "To have people actually call now to report things, to say, 'Hey, look, I have an issue with something.' For them to come to City Hall and they feel comfortable doing it, there's nothing better than that to me."[70] He paused behind his big desk, looked away for a second, and remembered that the experience brought "a big smile" to his face.

It is hard to overstate what it takes for an immigrant family, documented or not, to engage their local government for a particular service, particularly in a place like Pasadena. It is the quintessential proof point that an immigrant—as a taxpayer—sees his or her contribution as an investment in the public good that warrants something in return. Of course, there are likely a small number of undocumented who look to game the system. But, more often than not, people coming to city hall to ask for help is not looking to take advantage of something; they see themselves as part of the community and contributors to the greater good. They are on the path to integrating as full members of civic society and seeking to influence its decision makers. Again we see identity, integration, and influence.

In this case, Councilor Ybarra was the linchpin. He was from the community, looked like the community, and lived in the community. Going to Ybarra for help was going to a familiar face. Ybarra was changing the face of the council and changing the faces of people who came to city hall for assistance. His victory brought new voters to the polls and new residents to city hall.

In the face of these demographic and political changes, Pasadena's entrenched interests took notice. *Entrenched* is an understatement. Ybarra and his allies faced Jonny Isbell, a fixture who first joined the Pasadena city council in 1969, served twelve years as a councilman, and then served another twenty-five as mayor. In addition to this generations-long death grip on the mayor's office, Pasadena power brokers, all white men, also maintained a majority of seats on the city council.

These power brokers knew that Ybarra's 2009 city council victory empowered a new set of voters whose elected representation would more closely examine the allocation of resources. Where money was spent and for whom would be closely watched. As the political fight intensified, Isbell and others developed strategies to disenfranchise the Latino electorate. Through their decision on the Voting Rights Act of 1965, the Supreme Court of the United States was complicit in this effort.

When President Lyndon Johnson signed into law the Voting Rights Act of 1965, he said:

> This act flows from a clear and simple wrong. . . . Millions of Americans are denied the right to vote because of their color. This law will ensure them the right to vote. The wrong is one which no American, in his heart, can justify. The right is one which no American, true to our principles, can deny.[71]

Just like the 1965 Immigration and Nationality Act that followed later that year, the Voting Rights Act is rightfully lauded as one of America's landmark legislative efforts; it shaped the nation's future and secured the right to vote for millions of blacks, Latinos, and Asians. According to the Leadership Conference on Civil and Human Rights, the act was designed to prohibit "discrimination based on race, and requires certain jurisdictions to provide bilingual assistance to language-minority voters."[72]

Deriving its power from a formula outlined in section 4 of the act, section 5 had proven itself a powerful tool, holding certain states and local governments to a higher level of scrutiny for changes to their voting laws. Again from the Leadership Conference, "Section 5 of the VRA requires federal 'preclearance' before covered jurisdictions (i.e., specified jurisdictions with a history of practices that restrict minority voting rights) may make changes in existing voting practices or procedures."[73] Based on past discriminatory practices, section 5 applied to a number of states, including Texas.

In the summer of 2012, Shelby County, Alabama, filed suit against the United States, challenging the constitutionality of congressional renewal of the Voting Rights Act in 2006. Amy Howe of *SCOTUSBlog* summarized Shelby County's argument: "Even if the states covered by Section 5 may have discriminated in the past, it argues, that does not automatically mean that they are still discriminating now, and Congress shouldn't have passed new legislation renewing Section 5 until 2031 unless it put together evidence showing that the extension of the law was actually necessary— which it did not."[74]

On June 25, 2015, the Supreme Court agreed with this argument and gutted the Voting Rights Act. It banned preclearance requirements and gave jurisdictions free reign to change voting regulations and districts, regardless of past practices. Justice Ruth Bader Ginsburg spoke for many Americans when she wrote in her dissent, "Throwing out preclearance when it has worked and is continuing to work to stop discriminatory changes is like throwing away your umbrella in a rainstorm because you are not getting wet."[75]

A majority of justices believed America had resolved its identity crisis and moved beyond the discrimination of past generations. The justices could not have been more wrong, especially when you take into account what happened in Pasadena at practically the same time.

For years, Isbell and others had attempted to redistrict Pasadena city council seats and establish a mix of single-member districts representing specific neighborhoods and at-large seats. Their efforts to "better represent the voters,"[76] as they put it, were always proposals that diluted the influence of Latino-heavy districts. As recently as 2012, the Department of Justice had blocked a similar effort under the Voting Rights Act's section 5. But once the Supreme Court skewered that section, Isbell and company moved quickly to advance their plan.

In November 2013, less than six months since the court's decision, the charter amendment based on the council redistricting proposal was presented to Pasadena's voters. Congressman Gene Green opposed the measure, as did four members of the city council.[77] The *Houston Chronicle* remarked, "Just as important as the possible racial aspects to the measure is a deep geographic divide, a kind of civil war between the northern, more Hispanic part of [Pasadena] and the more affluent southern end of the city."[78] It was a fight between the new Pasadena and the old.

The proposition passed by a margin of just 79 votes out of the 6,429 cast, with "Hispanic majority precincts voting on average 68 percent against the proposition, and Anglo majority precincts voting on average 67 percent for the proposition. . . . The average turnout in majority Hispanic precincts was 9 percent compared to an average turnout of 12 percent in majority Anglo precincts."[79]

While the outcome was not what they sought, opponents of the proposition were pleased with the new level of engagement. Resha Thomas, an organizer with the Texas Organizing Project at the time, told me, "I think it's important to show even in an election that we didn't win, there was still engagement and movement of people who never voted."[80]

Soon thereafter, Mayor Isbell unveiled a proposal to reduce the number of single-member city council districts from eight to six, which (unsurprisingly) reconfigured two of the majority Hispanic districts into one. Eliminating single-member districts in this way served to reduce the influence of Hispanic voters in the city, diluting their power across the entirety of the city. As Ybarra put it, "I don't think what people realize is that [a] single-member district is not just solely about race and minority opportunity. Single-member districts work very well because regular, middle-class people can run for that seat because you don't need that much money to run."[81] Isbell successfully disenfranchised voters and made running for office a more difficult proposition. Latino voters didn't matter to him and others deeply entrenched in the Pasadena power structure.

Oscar Del Toro was unfazed. I met Del Toro at Tostada Regia, an expansive Mexican restaurant on the edge of Pasadena. Oscar immigrated to Pasadena from Mexico in 2001 with his wife and children in order to join his parents. In an interview with the *New York Times* magazine, Del Toro described his movement from a "golf playing member of the NRA Republican to a Democratic volunteer for Wendy Davis."[82] Why the change of heart? Del Toro told the *Times* it was a combination of Isbell's demagoguery on immigration as well as Republican Party's positions on abortion and marriage: "I always admired the United States in that respect, you are fine the way you are. You don't have to be something else."[83] Clearly, he was an example of a Hispanic Republican the Texas GOP had lost. (See Houston mayoral elections, above.)

Bitten by the political bug after volunteering on a couple campaigns, Del Toro decided to run for one of the city's new at-large districts. He knew it was a long shot, but as he told the *Times*, "sometimes you have to fight a lost cause to win something."[84] While he managed to earn over 1,600 votes, it was just less than 40 percent of the total.[85] Clearly, Oscar did not have the Anglo support necessary to secure victory. They might have seen him as a fringe candidate. But he wasn't running to win a race, he was running to win an argument. He wanted to make the case that eventually Pasadena's elected government would represent the diversity of the city's population. It wouldn't happen in one electoral cycle. It might take many cycles. As Del Toro told me, "I was trying to send [Isbell] a point that I'm not afraid of them. I don't care if this is your friend or whatever, I don't care."[86] He continued, "my message was clear: From now on, things are going to change."[87]

THE IMPORTANCE OF A STORY

The stories of Adrian Garcia, KP George, Vy Nguyen, Harish Jajoo, Ornaldo Ybarra, and Oscar Del Toro are the future of American politics. They represent a new Texas and a new America.

The immigrant constituents they sought to represent identified with them; the Anglo constituents often saw them as candidates from other communities. Adrian Garcia managed to cross over and secure enough votes from both communities to serve as sheriff, and KP George did the same. But once the others moved beyond their base, they encountered challenges. There was more work to do to build relationships, to strengthen institutions, that facilitated the necessary interpersonal connections. Regardless, each of them reached across the ethnic aisle in their efforts and, along the way, staked out new political territory and fought for greater diversity in representation.

How does Texas navigate this response? Who facilitates that response? Who crosses over from the native-born community? For Garcia, law enforcement as an institution of personal and organizational relationships provided the platform. For George, it was his participation within the culture of the school district that validated his leadership. Both institutions represented the values of the local community, and, over time, the institution took on a role as a cultural change agent.

In a place like Texas, just as socially and politically conservative as South Carolina, the church is another institution with the credibility to establish relationships between native-born and immigrant communities. According to the Pew Research Center's Religious Landscape Study, Texas is the eleventh most religious state in the nation: 64 percent of adult Texans consider themselves "highly religious" and 63 percent say they pray daily.[88] Such a landscape puts people like David Fleming, senior pastor of Champion Forest Baptist Church, in a unique position to lead Texas forward.

Champion Forest Baptist Church's main campus sits on forty-nine acres in northwest Houston. The city was still recovering from the floods of April 2016, and I passed submerged crosswalks as I drove into the still-damp parking lot. I felt like I was entering a community college or high school campus after a thunderstorm.

A member of the Southern Baptist Convention, Champion Forest's congregation of 13,000 is spread over three campuses, and the church's weekly attendance of 5,400 easily puts it in the category of megachurch.[89] Built like a running back, with a graying goatee, Fleming became senior pastor of Champion Forest in December of 2006. He grew up in Central Florida and was licensed to preach at the age of seventeen at First Baptist Church, Winter Garden, Florida. Ten years later, in 1992, he was ordained by New Zion Baptist Church in Covington, Louisiana. Fleming has been doing this a long time.

As Fleming and I took the five-minute walk from the cavernous foyer to his office, we passed clusters of chairs and couches of men and women reading and discussing the Bible. Fleming smiled and casually greeted folks as we passed. It cannot be easy to be a pastor. The conflicts between the spiritual and the secular, the conservative and the liberal, the believer and the nonbelievers must be a never-ending dilemma. As I sat in his office, Fleming summarized the tension as a question, "How do you do what's right both in the area of justice and in the area of mercy and compassion?"[90] He continued:

> For me, I come from a Christian tradition and a biblical worldview. There are lots of those opposing perspectives. The sovereignty of God and the free will of man; which is it? If you let go of one or the other, you end up in an error. If you hold both in tension, it keeps you in balance. So I have had those—is God love? Yes. Is God just? Yes. Which? Both. Justice does not trump His love. His love does not overshadow His justice. He's perfectly one in both, perfectly mingled together.[91]

In a place like Houston, with its thirty-seven megachurches, the church has the potential—some might argue the responsibility—to knit together different communities and ease the tension that comes with demographic change.[92] This requires pastors to push out from their comfort zones with goals and strategies that may or may not grow their congregation. As Fleming put it, "It is my job to serve those within the shadow of the church's steeple."[93]

With this guiding principle, he engaged his community on issues related to immigrants and immigration. It was a difficult road to take, because conservative white evangelicals were more likely to listen to the media than their pastor when it came to immigration.[94] As he told ABC News on April 3, 2013, "White evangelicals have been listening to the voice of the [immigration] extreme. Give education to our people, they are changing their minds on this issue."[95]

Like many who are not immigrants, or don't come from an immigrant family, a personal experience changed Fleming's perspective. Back in central Florida, Fleming experienced the tension of the Mariel boatlift, when thousands of Cubans were brought to the United States, but he felt "neutral" and at "a distance" from the lives of newcomers.[96] That distance was shattered when he met Francisco.

As Fleming related the story to me, Francisco "sat on one of those benches we walked past, and he was broken."[97] Francisco had overstayed his immigration visa, was now undocumented, and had just learned that there were no options for him to legalize his status. Fleming remembered, "So I said, well, man, this is Champion Forest Baptist Church. We've got resources. We've got people. We can fix this."[98]

Fleming was surprised when it couldn't be fixed through his extensive resources and relationships. "My job is to care for this person regardless of what he's done, not in any way that would break the law further for my case or my involvement. How do I help him? How do I love him?" Fleming realized that he "couldn't be neutral after I knew the names and faces."[99]

Around the time he got to know Francisco, Fleming reached out to Champion Forest's Spanish congregation. The ministry had been around for a while, maintaining a membership of about forty. Fleming recalled asking the congregation's pastor, Ramon Medina, "But what would it look like if maybe we just didn't have a [Hispanic] mission, but we just sort of were one church. We drop the mission and receive you as members, and you become a member on our staff."[100]

The growth was transformational. "So in eight years we've gone from forty to 2,800 Spanish-speaking [members] from twenty-three different countries."[101] That would be enough people to make up their own mega-church, but they are instead part of one whole. Fleming found that allowing

Hispanic congregants to identify as Hispanics was crucial. "I think that we didn't know the message we were sending, but the message was [that] this is a place you can come and be a part and yet not ask to not be who you are. That's been huge. You can still be Hispanic. You can still speak your heart language. You can worship in your heart language. There is a respect for who you are, and yet you are a part of the church."[102]

Respect. It's such a crucial sentiment. And it's so easy to overlook. Fleming did not want to be the white savior of a small Hispanic congregation. The story of Francisco, and his eventual deportation, was proof that he alone could not solve this problem. He wanted to bring people together and welcome, respect, and partner with congregants of all backgrounds. The culture was different, but the values were not. As he described the feelings of Hispanic congregants, Fleming said, "I can speak English, but here is a church that embraces my culture. Because it's not just a language difference, it's a cultural difference. So we embrace the culture and yet you are still as much a part of the church as somebody from Alabama."[103]

Champion Forest did not simply put two congregations under one roof and hope for the best. Fleming wanted to empower his new congregants and make sure the church was influenced by their different cultures. "[Hispanic] people want to know two things when they come to a place like this: Is there anybody here like me? If there is, then I can come and maybe I can stay. But to become involved, I need to see people involved. I need to see people at the table making decisions, on the platform. So we're real aggressive in hiring Spanish-speaking staff—bilingual and some only Spanish."[104] Fleming went on:

> So we never had an issue. I mean, I can't tell you that nobody got upset about it. I can't tell you nobody left. [But] I can tell you this: I don't know their names. I don't know who they are. If there are any, I don't know. Because there was never any movement.[105]

Is David Fleming the crossover Anglo voter Adrian Garcia could have reached? Can their differences around other social issues be set aside? While both men were clear champions of the immigrant community, some questions of culture may still be too far apart to bridge.

Mustafa Tameez tapped into this same thread as we discussed the tension that comes with immigration in our country: "I think we have to have a far gentler conversation, [and realize] that when we use a word like *diversity*, not everyone sees that as a net positive. I think that when you say 'more opportunity for my children,' it is going to be interpreted by some as less opportunity for their children. So there is an obligation by those that care about inclusivity not to exclude that Anglo population."[106] This is the Anglo cultural and economic anxiety that Donald Trump rode to the White House. Overcoming it means both sides need to lean toward each other across the cultural and economic gaps to create points of consensus.

The Houston metropolitan region shows that integration is a two-way street, that communities can lean in each other's direction. Immigrants change themselves and change their communities. Some communities are comfortable with that change in identity, some struggle with it, and some are completely opposed. The tension can be resolved through the prism of one's faith, as we saw with David Fleming and Champion Forest Baptist Church. Or through Adrian Garcia's ability to mold the Harris County Sheriff's Department to create agreement across voters based on a belief in law and order. And, Sugar Land provides an example of how economic success facilitates political diversity, while Pasadena's challenging economic and social history is more difficult to work through.

For Tameez, the progressive Muslim from Karachi who chuckled at my hipster food, it was the hyphen: "We have this hyphen. It is one thing that says we can have dual identities. We can be American and Hispanic. We can be American and Jewish. We can be American and Muslim. We can be anything hyphen American." Of course, a hyphen alone will not ensure all jobs go to native-born Americans. Nor will a hyphen reduce the anger in someone's blood when he believes an immigrant, or someone he believes is an immigrant, is accessing a public benefit without paying taxes.

But a hyphen is our simple way to value our collective identity as Americans and honor our unique histories as immigrants. As Mustafa put it, "The American hyphen is our—it is our salvation in many ways."[107]

CHAPTER EIGHT

MY WORKFORCE IS MY FAMILY

I remember my first trip to Pasco, Washington. The Columbia River, with Interstate 84 alongside, winds its way between Oregon and Washington. With barges on the river and eighteen-wheelers on the road, it is a journey along an economic lifeline of the Pacific Northwest.

Driving east from Portland on the Oregon side of the river, the trip begins with the rolling greenery of the Mount Hood National Forest. Feeder creeks trickle down the mountainside, while fishing spots, hiking trails, and vista points dot the roadside. Logging trucks, stacked high with felled trees, lumber along. As I left the forest, the landscape became arid—more high, dry desert than lush river-scape.

Soon, the river widened and the roadway narrowed as it hugged sloping, dry, brown hills. I reached the junction of the Columbia and Snake Rivers and crossed the Umatilla Bridge into the state of Washington and the town of Pasco, population 69,541.[1]

Highway 124 took me to the eastern edge of Pasco, and soon I was back in the hills. I continued along a two-lane road bordered by a mix of vineyards, tree farms, and orchards. Farmworkers' cars bordered the fields they tended. Instead of logs, the eighteen-wheeler in front of me carried a load of massive wooden crates, each stamped with a name: Broetje. I follow that truck.

The rumbling diesel turned left on to a small road. Through the clear, hot summer air, I saw Broetje Orchards in the distance. As far as the eye could see were neatly arranged lines of apple trees poking out of rolling hills. About a half a mile down the road, a small housing development peeked up on the right. I saw manicured, modest homes behind the small grocery store, gas station, and church. What must have been a city block down the road (I'm a city boy, that is how I measure these things), a modest two-story office building squatted in front of two imposing, metal-sided warehouses. There were dozens of pickup trucks and SUVs in the parking lot, and the eighteen-wheelers I saw on the highway idled at the loading docks. I got a sense of the scale of the enterprise and thought, "This is no mom-and-pop operation."

Oh, but it was most definitely a mom-and-pop operation. Cheryl and Ralph Broetje were in charge. With white hair and a white beard, Ralph fits the part of apple grower. Whether he is in the offices at the orchard, or in meetings in Washington, DC, I always get the sense he would rather be in his truck, with his trees, talking to his workers. Meanwhile, Cheryl's sense of humor and infectious laugh are matched by her sharp business eye. Together, they want to grow apples and grow people. Their conjoined entrepreneurial spirit is embodied in their company's mission statement: "Bearing fruit that lasts."[2]

I've been fortunate to get to know the Broetje family over the past few years (their family foundation supports the National Immigration Forum), and I always look forward to my annual trip to the orchard. Our conversations range from serious discussions about the apple industry and issues their immigrant workforce faces, to hilarious ones in which Cheryl comments on my lack of fashion sense (to her great joy). More than anything, every time I see the family, I learn something new. And this time was no different.

It was a spring afternoon, and everyone was worried about the weather. Well, okay, they are farmers. They worry about weather like city folk worry about traffic: All. The. Time.

In any case, that afternoon I sat in the small, second-floor conference room with Ralph, Cheryl, and their daughter Suzanne. Out the window behind me, the trucks waited to head out with a new load. After discussing the state of the apple blossoms (not a lot for me to contribute there), the conversation turned to both apples and people.

For Ralph, growing apples with a larger mission in mind started with a junior high school daydream, "That someday I would have an apple orchard to be able to help a few kids in India."[3] So he planted his first trees in the northwest of Washington. After fits and starts, the recession of the

1980s hit and financing dried up. Or, as Ralph put it, "God had to hit me with a two-by-four and pretty much take everything away."

The young family moved south to Pasco and started to rebuild, living in a motel for a month until they were able to establish themselves. At this point, the workforce began to change as Latino farmworkers made their way north to work the orchards. According to the University of Washington, Hispanic farmworkers grew from 24 percent of the labor force in 1980 to 43 percent in 1990, and 59 percent in 2000.[4] In eastern Washington, much less the farming communities themselves, for the farmworker community to go from 71 percent white in 1980 to 51 percent white in twenty years, these were significant changes.[5]

Cheryl noticed the change in the workforce in the 1980s and saw it through the lens of her mission work. "We were raised in the church," she told me. "We knew that you were supposed to help people who were poor. We could see these people were coming with nothing. And lots of them. Why? It just seemed like we needed to find out."[6]

So they organized a mission trip to Mexico to better understand where their new workforce was coming from. It was a trip that transformed the family.

That experience led Cheryl to realize, "We're not going to be able to help kids in India or anywhere else if we don't help our employees first."[7] She continued, "They had nothing. They didn't have affordable places to live. . . . They didn't have places to leave the kids, so the kids were being left in terrible situations, in many cases."

For the Broetjes, there was also a sense that they were all immigrants to this desolate place, far from urban or suburban centers. There was a feeling of solidarity in the fact that everyone was from somewhere else. Cheryl told me that early on, they instilled a sense of "Welcome, whether you are the last person in or the first person in, welcome, has become part of the spirituality that is what guides the work we do in this place."[8]

As the orchard began to take root, the Broetjes noticed the workforce was less migratory. No longer were farmworkers circling through the United States, following the harvest from the Southeast, through California, and then up to the Northwest. Higher gas prices and bigger families had led the community of workers to seek more stable working and living arrangements. Over time, this would lead to permanent changes in the region and a raft of challenges that were yet to be fully understood.

Ralph and Cheryl started to think of their workers as they thought of their own family, bringing their sense of mission to the orchard. Their workers needed safe housing, quality childcare, and accessible schools. Ralph and Cheryl hoped that with better services, mothers on the packing line could be near their children, and fathers picking apples could be home for dinner. They started with good housing on the orchard, and the community grew from there. Over the years, Broetje Orchards became a neighborhood unto itself—something those familiar with the agricultural industry very rarely see.

You can find Broetje apples picked by farmworkers across the globe. To get an apple picked by immigrant hands in Pasco, Washington, some 2,700 miles east to a grocery store in New York City, many other hands play a role. In fact, according to economists, approximately 3.1 million "upstream" and "downstream" nonagricultural jobs are dependent on domestic agricultural production.[9] While not related to the agricultural sector, one job in New York City seemed quite dependent on the labor of undocumented immigrants: conservative political commentator. And there are few people who have made a bigger career out of railing against immigration than Lou Dobbs.

CLASH OF CULTURE AND THE ECONOMY

Lou Dobbs's award-winning career began at CNN as host of *Moneyline*, covering financial news for the fast-growing network. In 2001, he launched a new show, *Lou Dobbs Tonight*, covering a broad range of topics. Every evening, beamed into airports, living rooms, and bars across the nation, he would rant against and report on the news of the day. In the mid-2000s, as immigration reform made another run through Congress, Dobbs trained his ire on immigrants. Pro-immigrant forces were no match for the cable-news megaphone CNN provided Dobbs as his audience made thousands of calls into congressional offices.

When I interviewed him in 2016, Dobbs's argument was that trade and immigration were existential threats to the economic well-being of America's middle class. He laid the blame at the feet of power brokers who had little regard for the American worker. Dobbs believed they were willing to export jobs or import people, in the pursuit of profits and at the expense of American workers. Dobbs did not blame the immigrant worker who was willing to work for lower wages. "I'm not saying it's cheap labor's fault. I'm saying it is the elites, it is the corporate establishment, it is the political establishment that are making these judgments and doing so with absolutely as little regard as possible for the consequences [to] a working man and woman in this country and their families and the middle class."[10] He claimed that policymakers were not being honest with the American public as to the impact of trade and immigration.

The impact of immigration on American wages is not complicated. And it would be good for both sides to be a little more honest. From the Congressional Budget Office to a slew of researchers, the consensus is that there is a small short-term negative impact on low-skilled worker wages but a long-term, overall benefit.[11] In 2016, the National Academies of Sciences, Engineering and Medicine issued a comprehensive report finding the impact of immigration on economic growth was positive while effects on government budgets were mixed.[12]

Dobbs has a tendency to skip over this evidence in his efforts to make the case that immigration is a net cost to American workers. But underneath this economic message was something else—something rooted in culture. Our conversation shifted to a debate about the 1965 Immigration and Nationality Act, which was designed to end the national-origins quota and establish an immigration system based on economic needs and family relations. Lou felt that the act was "the incipient point of everything we are talking about."[13]

His argument was no longer about the economy. Dobbs was clearly referring to the cultural impact of immigrants and immigration when he said, "The dynamic is different [now] because, in the '20s and '30s, people knew exactly who the country was. There was a common bond. We are so deeply divided now." Sorry Lou, this magical "common bond" never existed; back then, Irish, German, Italian, and other western European immigrants came to the United States in record numbers and upset the Puritanical majority. That history lesson doesn't change how people feel today—even if their ancestors were told "Irish need not apply."

To be fair, I agree with Dobbs when he says, "There was a time that we all thought of ourselves as middle-class, whether we were a newly arrived immigrant who had just found opportunity or whether we were a highly successful businessman or woman, we were all in it as middle-class Americans because that is where the American dream resided."[14] Yet the nation's eroding middle class isn't the fault of the immigrant, and the solution is not closing America off from the world. Money moves, goods move, information moves. To act like people won't move to find a better life for themselves and their families, and like corporations will not operate across borders, is naive.

We need a new way to understand the global economy: a balance of intelligently regulated immigration systems, balanced trade agreements, and protections for all workers in America so everyone can compete for the same job at the same wage. These days, we have a wholly unregulated immigration system and trade agreements with weak worker and environmental protections. This status quo allows unscrupulous employers to exploit undocumented workers at the expense of law-abiding competitors, native-born workers, and immigrant workers.

I think Dobbs would agree with this prescription, but our starting points are different. I see the 1965 Immigration and Nationality Act as the moment when the United States led the world into the twenty-first century. Dobbs and many others see 1965 as the moment the United States lost its culture.

CROPS AND CARS IN ALABAMA

As John Steinbeck, my local library's namesake, described my hometown, "Salinas had a destiny beyond other towns. The rich black land was one thing, but the high gray fog and coolish to cold weather which gave it a lousy climate created the greatest lettuce in the world, several crops a year and at a time when no other lettuce in the United States matured. The town named itself the Salad Bowl of the World. . . ."[15]

The smell of that high gray fog is seared into my olfactory system; it reminds me of cool mornings, windy afternoons, and miles of lettuce fields. Without those fields, and the farmworkers who bend over them every day, Salinas would have ceased to exist a long time ago. The same can be said of agricultural cities and towns across the country.

In 2014, the US agriculture sector contributed $835 billion to the nation's GDP, a 4.8 percent share.[16] Approximately $177.2 billion of that contribution came from farmwork. The industry employs about 17.3 million people; 66 percent work at "food and beverage places," and 15.3 percent are farmworkers. Until robots are made with very soft hands, this will remain a labor-intensive industry. Access to skilled farmworkers is crucial and presents an ongoing challenge.

The Agricultural Coalition for Immigration Reform's important report, "No Longer Homegrown: How Labor Shortages are Increasing America's Reliance on Imported Fresh Produce and Slowing US Economic Growth," found that labor shortages explained as much as $3.3 billion in lost GDP growth in 2012, as well as $1.3 billion in lost farm income.[17] Without the labor to pick and produce crops, there was no reason to plant them.

Craig Regelbrugge, chair of the Agricultural Coalition for Immigration Reform, cited the National Agricultural Worker Survey's findings that 78 percent of the industry's current workforce is foreign-born. He told me, "That represents a bit of a decline over some past reporting, and likely represents some attrition of the foreign born who 'went home,' as well as a slight uptick in US-born Hispanic workers as part of the overall picture."[18] Either way, the vast majority of the agricultural workforce wasn't born here in America. Most debates on this issue lead to a circular argument of whether or not an American would do that job. Let me be clear, I do not believe there is any job an American *won't* do. To claim that any job is beneath the interests of any person is as unpersuasive as it is insulting. It is not for me to judge what a person will or will not do for work.

However, there are jobs Americans aren't doing. These days, farmwork happens to be one of them. Increased wages doesn't mean more Americans will do these jobs, and mechanization simply does not work for some industries. Growers have tried to offer increased wages, but to no avail. Tasks like picking strawberries takes an expertise no robot can match, and those strawberries are often picked by hardworking immigrants. (Related question: Do we want Americans or robots doing these jobs?)

These are skilled farmworkers putting food on the world's tables, not weekend gardeners pulling weeds. Their contributions should be valued as such.

I'm not saying that every farmer in America is an angel. But farmers lead one of the last great American businesses, and many genuinely care about their workforce. In this way, they are some of the most compelling conservative spokespeople when it comes to immigrants and immigration. Growers live in fast-changing communities and often employ their region's largest numbers of people of color. Their experiences make them trusted, effective messengers. While members of Congress love taking pictures with farmers, they have refused to listen to their labor needs.

Craig has a front-row seat where immigration policy and the agricultural economy intersect. He clearly understood how bad immigration laws were undermining the competitiveness and sustainability of farms across the country. Regelbrugge characterized the problem this way: "Despite these realities, recent years of congressional inaction have prompted several states—like Alabama—to take matters into their own hands. The result? Economic self-mutilation that has hurt farmers and families, and betrayed American core values. As a nation, we can and must do better."[19]

In 2011, just over a year after Arizona passed Senate bill 1070, Alabama moved forward with House bill 56, the Beason-Hammon Alabama Taxpayer and Citizen Protection Act. When the legislation was signed into law on June 9, 2011, Alabama Rep. Micky Hammon said, "This is an Arizona bill with an Alabama twist."[20] If you were an immigrant (or a farmer) in Alabama, this was not an improvement.

The legislation was a toxic sludge of anti-immigrant measures designed to make life as difficult as possible for the immigrant community, documented or not. Under the law, state and local law enforcement were required to attempt to determine the immigration status of a person involved in a lawful stop where reasonable suspicion exists that the person is an alien and is unlawfully present.[21] (Of course, the police officer could not consider race, color, or national origin when implementing the law.) Citizens and legal residents were also allowed to sue states or localities that restrict enforcement of federal law. Public schools (K–12) were required to determine a student's immigration status and submit annual reports to the state education board. It was unlawful for a person to transport an alien; conceal, harbor, or shield an alien; or harbor an alien unlawfully present by entering into a rental agreement if the person knows or recklessly disregards that the alien is unlawfully present.[22]

In a poignant *New York Times* essay, Diane McWhorter asked, "If Alabama, the cradle of the civil rights movement, can retool Jim Crow as Juan Crow, what have we learned?"[23] The law used the veneer of undocumented status to profile immigrants writ large. It was a direct effort to instill a deep sense of fear among immigrant families, hoping they would leave the state.

Alabama's anxiety came from its cultural isolation. In 2010, just under 4 percent of Alabama's population was Hispanic and only 3.5 percent was foreign-born.[24] While the total numbers were small, the speed of the change in Alabama was remarkable. From 2000 to 2010, the number of undocumented immigrants in Alabama jumped from an estimated 25,000 to 120,000 as migrants flocked to jobs in agriculture, meatpacking, and construction.[25] Local tensions were exacerbated and immigrants provided a convenient scapegoat for politicians.

HB 56 was greeted with loud protest from the immigrant rights community. Civil- and immigrant rights organizers streamed into the state from across the country to take a stand against the legislation. Setting the stage for a protracted legal battle similar to what we saw in Arizona after its law, SB 1070, Marielena Hincapie, one of the nation's leading immigrant rights attorneys and executive director of the National Immigration Law Center said, "Today, Alabama effectively turned state workers, peace officers, and school teachers into de facto immigration agents. Immigrants and people of color will be subjected to additional, unconstitutional scrutiny when they take their children to school or interact with local law-enforcement officers."[26]

Once the bill was signed into law, fear settled in across the community and there were widespread reports of immigrant children not attending school; this was music to the ears of supporters. Tea Party Republican congressman Mo Brooks told *Politico*, "Those are the intended consequences of Alabama's legislation with respect to illegal aliens."[27] In other words, if a state law ran counter to the 1982 *Plyler v. Doe* Supreme Court decision that guaranteed access to education for all children regardless of immigration status, well, in this case, the Tea Party was happy to ignore the US Constitution.[28]

While the powerful institutional memory of the Alabama civil rights infrastructure kicked into gear, a different set of allies entered the fray. Beyond ministers, organizers, and civil rights groups, the Alabama business community tipped the scales.

It's important to note that the Alabama economy relies heavily on agriculture; one in five jobs in the state is supported by it.[29] This includes very large poultry and livestock industries, along with traditional fruit and vegetable crops. While industrial manufacturing and transportation manufacturing had decreased in size, like in South Carolina, the sector made a comeback through foreign investment.[30]

In 1996, Mercedes-Benz opened its first US plant in Alabama. Some twenty years after the plant opened, Mercedes claimed to be responsible for 22,000 jobs in the region, with an annual economic impact topping $1.5 billion.[31] According to *Reuters*, the Center for Business and Economic Research based at the University of Alabama found the factory and its local vendors had an economic impact estimated at $6.8 billion and 41,830 jobs.[32]

So you can imagine the state's embarrassment when a Mercedes-Benz executive, Detlev Hager, was arrested in mid-November 2011 under HB 56 because he did not have his passport with him.[33] It was a high-profile face-plant for the new law, and one that brought unwanted international attention; with this incident, the law was proven to be anti-immigrant, not just anti-undocumented-immigrant.

The irony of all this is that one of the reddest of red states in the country passed a law that threatened the jobs they'd successfully in-sourced. But as titillating as this story was, a detained Mercedes-Benz executive was not the person who turned the tide. It was the Alabama-raised farmer.

WBRC Fox News reported on a contentious meeting between local farmers and Senator Scott Beason, who was the original sponsor of the law. "Farmers told Beason the law resulted in their migrant workers leaving the area and leaving them with a depleted workforce. That, they say, could cause economic disaster that could even shut down farmers on Chandler Mountain—farms that have been in the same families for as many as four generations."[34] The German executive making the case against HB 56 was one thing. Alabama-grown farmers about to lose the family plot was quite another.

When Henry Hagood, chief executive for Associated General Contractors of Alabama, called HB 56 "mean-spirited," it was clear business leaders were looking out for more than their bottom line.[35] To use a term like that indicated that Hagood felt the law was unnecessarily targeting people he respected. He was looking out for people he cared about.

Two years later, a combination of smart legal work and powerful organizing by faith, law-enforcement, and business leaders led MSNBC's Benjy Sarlin to write, "HB 56 is in ruins. Its most far-reaching elements have proved unconstitutional, unworkable, or politically unsustainable."[36] Pressure from business, faith, and law-enforcement leaders in the state had a deep impact.[37] From the Supreme Court's decision that components of laws such as HB 56 were unconstitutional to state legislation curbing its impact, HB 56 was dramatically reined in.

AN ENGINEER OR AN IMMIGRANT?

On March 21, 2016, the United States lost one of its great entrepreneurs and citizens when Andy Grove passed away after a long fight with Parkinson's disease. The *Economist* captured the relationship between the United States and Andy as follows: "America was good to the young Andy Grove, providing him with a refuge from totalitarianism and then a first-class education. In return Andy Grove was good for America, by helping it to remain at the very heart of the semiconductor revolution."[38]

But Andy Grove was more than an entrepreneur. In her slight Eastern European accent, Andy's wife, Eva, told me, "Andy was a Jew from Hungary, not just an immigrant. Therefore, his whole perspective came from that experience."[39] His experience as a refugee not only shaped one of the nation's great companies but also modeled civic responsibility for technology leaders today.

Eva was kind enough to spend some time talking to me one afternoon in early fall 2016. Through our conversation, I got a glimpse of what motivated the Grove family to care about immigrants and immigration. My assumption was that the business needs of the technology sector drove Andy's interest in the issue. Instead, as Eva told me, "Andy saw the issue first as being an immigrant himself, then as needing engineers. But that wasn't his first concern."[40]

The Groves were two of the first Silicon Valley business leaders and philanthropists to understand the cultural underpinnings of the immigration debate. (The Grove Family Foundation supports the National Immigration Forum.) I remember meeting Andy for the first time and walking through a slide presentation describing how we arrived at our strategy to engage conservatives and moderates. I expected him to see this as an issue about the technology sector, the business community, and the need for engineers. Instead, he quickly understood that in order for conservative Americans to see the value of immigrants and immigration, we needed to go beyond making the economic case. Andy understood that the issue was a cultural conversation with Americans about a changing America, as much as it was an economic debate among business leaders. Andy asked piercing but supportive questions that pushed us in the right direction.

This was a mind-set that, as Eva described, went back to their arrival as refugees in the United States. When Andy fled communist Hungary, he arrived in the United States in 1956 and enrolled in the City College of New York. Eva, who was on a similar journey, was in New York attending Hunter College. They weren't economic migrants; they weren't undocumented immigrants; they were political refugees whose formative years were in a hustling and bustling New York City that was the leading edge of a changing America. It sounded like a natural integration experience in that life for both of them moved forward seamlessly from those days in the Big Apple. Eva told me, "That experience in New York City allowed us to go on with the rest of our lives and just not think about what happened." The family realized their immigration experience was unique—certainly when compared to the difficulties immigrants and refugees went through today. Eva continued, "[Our integration experience] didn't color our lives. But as life went on we saw that what we see today is different. So, we asked, is that really right?"[41]

While the Grove family was long supportive of refugee resettlement efforts, engagement in the political and cultural debate behind immigrants began to take shape around 2005, when federal immigration-enforcement efforts impacted one of their staff person's children—whose friend's undocumented parents were detained as a result of an enforcement action. "The family became more supportive of immigrants when the Immigration and Customs Enforcement raids started happening," Eva told me. "The whole idea that these things can happen here was wrong, so we figured we needed to do something. That made us realize how bad things were, that as a nation, we aren't really an immigrant-friendly country."[42] So the family expanded its philanthropy and its voice to address social and legal issues facing undocumented immigrants, refugees, and legal immigrants.

Andy and Eva, who were welcomed by immigrant-friendly mid-century New York City and assisted by refugee resettlement policies, contributed more to America than they ever received. But they came to believe, as Eva shared, "We [Americans] have a very ambivalent history when it comes to immigration, both acceptance and rejection."[43] They were going to use their influence to do something about it across the country and within the technology sector.

Unlike manufacturing, service, agriculture, or construction, our connection to technology cuts across socioeconomic lines. More simply, our jobs are spread across a variety of sectors, but just about all of us use the Internet. From Sergey Brin, cofounder of Google, to the stereotyped Asian immigrant engineer on television, we understand the impact immigrants have had on the technology sector.

On the other hand, the dizzying days of the dot-com boom established the industry's reputation as a mix of beanbags, Ping-Pong, and billions of dollars. So in addition to designing applications that, to quote HBO's Silicon Valley, "make the world a better place," the technology sector came to be seen as immigrant-dependent, to a fault.[44]

During the 1990s, the ratio of US-born to foreign-born scientists and engineers nearly tripled; in 1994, there were 6.2 US-born workers for every foreign-born worker in science and engineering occupations.[45] By 2006, there were only 3.1 American-born workers to each foreign-born worker. Despite this influx, one of the greatest public-policy challenges for the technology industry has been access to talent. Just as growers need skilled farmworkers, technology CEOs need skilled engineers.

A focused strategy became necessary as the economy tightened and legislative attacks were launched on visa programs, such as the H-1B program, designed to help the technology sector. The H-1B program provides temporary visas to high-skill immigrants across a range of industries. It is best known for the high number of H-1B visas utilized by the technology sector. According to the Migration Policy Institute, the cap on visas was lifted temporarily to 115,000 visas in 1999 and 2000 as the result of the 1998 American Competitiveness and Workforce Improvement Act and then again to 195,000 visas for 2001, 2002, and 2003 under the 2000 American Competitiveness in the 21st Century Act. The annual H-1B cap reverted to 65,000 in 2004.[46]

Every year, these visas are snapped up in a matter of weeks. In 2006, as immigration-reform legislation was taking shape, Microsoft founder and CEO Bill Gates ventured to Capitol Hill to meet with lawmakers and urge them to expand the number of visas and pass comprehensive immigration reform. Gates told the *Washington Post* columnist Greg Broder that the "high-skills immigration issue is by far the number one thing. . . . This is gigantic for us."[47]

At its current numbers, the H-1B program does not serve the needs of American workers or technology companies seeking global talent. The number of visas available are not adequate, and the program needs reforms that emphasize protections, increased training, and education funding for US-born workers. Quite simply, across the whole sector, we need to do a better job training US workers and competing for the global talent that will keep us competitive.

In their zeal to push Congress to expand the H-1B programs, the technology sector lost control of its message in the buzz saw of cultural fears. The "we need more engineers" argument was seen as self-serving. Congressional opponents and some parts of organized labor framed the sector's demands as wealthy technology oligarchs importing cheap Indian labor to write code Americans could write. As a result, there was a growing cultural disconnect between the everyday Americans who used technology and the Silicon Valley set who designed it.

Something more than economic anxiety was at play. The average middle America voter didn't see an engineer who might design the next big app. They only saw another immigrant coming to America. Even if this person was a legal immigrant, middle America still saw the other. Someone who spoke with a foreign accent; someone who would compete for jobs and compete for resources. Technology leaders were making an economic argument to a country embroiled in a cultural debate.

Just like so many we have met, the entry point to this unfamiliar cultural debate for technology leaders starts with a personal experience. No longer could they see immigrants only as workers here to do a job. They had to understand who immigrants were as people and, more important, tell those stories to the rest of the country.

Laurene Powell Jobs's primary interest has always been education reform. Her business and philanthropic work has long sought to challenge America's education system and improve it for the nation's underserved students. As detailed in a *Wall Street Journal* profile, Powell Jobs started to tutor low-income students in 1995. She realized undocumented students were unable to apply for college because of their immigration status and told the *Journal*, "Year after year we saw potential wasted."[48]

Since she dove into the national immigration debate in 2006, Powell Jobs has remained a staunch advocate for the students she has gotten to know. But she has also come to realize that this is also about convincing native-born Americans that immigrants are their coworkers and neighbors, even if they aren't in the technology or high-skilled sector. She invests her resources in the dreams of undocumented immigrant youth and uses her influence within the technology community to bring others into the fold. Powell Jobs wrote in *Wired* magazine:

> More than ever, we need the contributions of every American—and every American immigrant—to power our next era of growth. But the economic argument for inclusion is not the most fundamental one. Immigrants have not only made our society wealthier and more productive but also more decent. They have enhanced our national character and made us more ethical people. For America, this is our identity crisis: How a society treats immigrants is a great test of its decency, and we are failing. Immigrants, with their hopes and energies, should be seen not as threats but as blessings.[49]

Just like Powell Jobs, Facebook cofounder and CEO Mark Zuckerberg's initial experiences with undocumented immigrants came through volunteer work with youth. Looking beyond the technology industry's economic needs for labor, he sought to better understand the youth in his own community. Working in East Palo Alto, he too realized undocumented youth faced limited opportunities because of their immigration status. As Mark wrote in a *Washington Post* op-ed, he understood the need for border enforcement but he also felt that "we have a strange immigration policy for a nation of immigrants. And it's a policy unfit for today's world."[50]

Soon, Mark expanded his perspective. Zuckerberg gathered his peers in the technology community, including Bill Gates, to launch FWD.us, a public-policy advocacy organization dedicated to mobilizing the tech and business community to support immigration reform. The effort challenged both Democrats and Republicans to look beyond their bottom-line interests to engage in the immigration debate with an eye toward fairness for all.

Another example is Steve Case, who told me in 2016 that his interest in immigration reform started through an "economic prism." As he came to learn more, "It became a little more of a moral fairness issue."[51]

Case, the cofounder of AOL, grew up in Hawaii. As he put it, "Things tend to move slowly there, require sort of a respect for the past, while also kind of figuring out how to lead the future."[52] In retrospect, it was more than surfing and sun for Case. The experience of being a racial and ethnic minority shaped his world perspective and belief in "being more inclusive and bringing more people together and leveling the playing field for more people, [all of which] I think is important."[53] These days, as an investor and a philanthropist, Steve put these values into motion by prioritizing minority leadership in the ventures he supports and shining his spotlight on undiscovered technology communities in between the coasts.

I first met Case in December 2012, when we convened a national meeting of conservative and moderate leaders from across the country to talk about immigration reform. The event was called Bibles, Badges and Business for Immigration Reform. Case was our featured speaker, to be interviewed by the *National Journal*'s Ron Brownstein. I was fairly surprised that Steve, something of a household name, had agreed to participate in the event, and I didn't know quite what to expect. Unfairly, I assumed we would have a high-maintenance technology mogul on our hands who would just want to talk about the need for immigrant engineers.

Midway through the event, Herbie Ziskend, Case's connected and generous staffer, told me Steve was on his way over. Waiting at the registration area, checking my phone (as always), and chatting with guests, I turned around to find Case, the man I recognized from a *Wall Street Journal* dot-matrix portrait, casually dressed, alone, thumbing through whatever was on the table. "Huh, that's Steve Case," I thought to myself.

Case's warm personality came across immediately as we chatted for a few minutes before the panel. I remember he said he was looking forward to the interview. So, I asked him, "What brought you here?"

I remember his smiling, matter-of-fact, reply, "Anything with a Bible, a badge, and a business must be interesting." Which is when I knew we had done two things. One, we had broken through to find new top-tier leadership who wanted to be a part of the conversation. But, two, we had also found a nationally recognized leader who knew what it takes to speak to the full range of Americans.

Instead of immigration reform as a question of the number of engineers allowed into the United States, the issue fit into Steve's broader interests. As he told me, "The last decade, a lot of my interest has gone from democratizing access to information through technology to democratizing access to opportunity."[54] When it came to immigration, the undocumented in particular, I sensed there was something underneath his motivation to engage outside of a purely economic self-interest. Of course, it came down to a personal experience.

Steve shared the story of helping an undocumented woman his family had come to know. Through his networks and resources, Case was able to help the woman attain legal status. The woman's daughter, he told me, went on to graduate at the top of her class at the University of Virginia. Case came to realize this woman and her daughter were lucky. His connections opened doors that led to legal status and educational opportunities. "There are millions of people [for whom] that's not the case, and that doesn't seem to be fair," Case told me. "What about all the other people out there who don't have those networks or connections or what have you?"[55]

Whether or not this young woman ever stepped foot inside a technology company wasn't the point. It was whether or not she had access to the opportunities that allowed her to reach her fullest potential. Steve understood that the more people in America who had the ability to reach their potential, the better it was for the nation overall.

Case saw the moral necessity to treat people fairly. But he also saw that the challenge was to "reframe [immigration] as more of it is in people's interest, their self-interest, to be more supportive of a broader pool of talent at various different kinds of skill levels." [56]

Together, Powell Jobs, Zuckerberg, Case, and others followed the lead of Andy Grove to ensure America gets closer to what Eva called "parity." The issue is not just about visas for engineers. It is about people across a broader swath of society.[57]

Brad Smith, general counsel for Microsoft, and Tom Nassif, CEO of Western Growers Association, put it well in their March 16, 2014, *Sacramento Bee* op-ed, "The fact is our economy needs both the skilled farmworker and the skilled engineer."[58]

MADE IN THE USA

Unless you are reading this book naked, it is very likely you are wearing a piece of clothing manufactured by someone, somewhere. These days, that someone is more than likely located outside the United States.

In 1965, 95 percent of Americans' clothing was made in the United States In 1990, over 12,000 independent clothing manufacturers were based in the country, and approximately 938,000 people were employed in the textile-manufacturing industry.[59] Then came the North American Free Trade Agreement. By the year 2006, that number had plummeted to just under 240,000; by 2010, that number dropped to 160,000.[60]

Marty Bailey has lived through the ups and downs of the textile industry. Bailey, born in Montana and raised in Kentucky, was the first in his family to go to college. His reserved personality has been on the inside of the rise, fall, and realignment of America's garment industry. One summer morning, as we drove east of downtown Los Angeles to play a round of golf, we talked about making clothes in a changing America and a globalized economy.

In his quiet voice, Bailey's story started with a walk-on scholarship with the Campbellsville College basketball team—a scholarship that allowed him to stay in school. "We weren't a wealthy family, by any means," he said.[61] He married and had a child in college, which stretched finances further. "Even as a basketball player, through four years of college, I still kept two and three jobs all the time to pay for my family, whether it was working in the fields picking strawberries or putting up tobacco or hay," not to mention a side-gig playing the guitar and singing songs at a local restaurant.[62]

With a population of just over eight thousand at the time, Campbellsville was also home to the nation's largest Fruit of the Loom manufacturing plant. The same day Bailey took his last final at Campbellsville College, the dean introduced him to Jack Moore, president of Fruit of the Loom. Mr. Moore "hired me that day," Bailey told me.[63]

It wasn't the job offer that stuck with Bailey. It wasn't the circumstance of the meeting. Rather, the "one thing that always stuck into my mind was that [Moore] said, 'I want you to be able to walk through and know everybody's name. I want you to be able to walk through and know something about them, know their kids.'"[64] This piece of advice served Marty well as his career unfolded in the context of a fast-changing global economy.

To say Campbellsville was a company town is to say Fruit of the Loom made underwear. As described in *Fast Company*, Fruit of the Loom called Campbellsville home for a half century and employed 4,200 people at its height. Every other Thursday, payday, $2.5 million poured into town in a single afternoon.[65]

Bailey spent two years cutting his manufacturing teeth at the plant in Campbellsville. He developed an understanding and appreciation of work flow and efficiency. Most important in the piece-rate structure of apparel manufacturing, he learned that a productive workforce was one that made more money for themselves and their company. He saw his job on the sewing floor as similar to that of a basketball coach: get the best out of each player so the team was successful.

The international trade agreements of the 1990s changed economic models, and Fruit of the Loom started closing domestic plants. On August 7, 1997, about thirteen years after Marty walked through its doors, the Campbellsville Fruit of the Loom plant started to downsize.[66] It was the beginning of the end for America's apparel and textile-manufacturing sector.

In the *Fast Company* profile, Karen Brockman's family illustrated the centrality of the factory. "Me and my husband both worked there. My mother worked there. My mother-in-law worked there. My father-in-law worked there. I had three sisters who all worked there, and a brother-in-law, and a sister-in-law also."[67] For Bailey, who went from being committed to knowing everyone on his sewing floor to now closing plants across the company, this was not easy. Particularly since his role had become as global as the company itself.

As we drove, Bailey told me, "When you close a facility [in the United States], it's seven hundred jobs at this place, then immediately in less than six months, you are in a new country, training people to do those same jobs that you took away from the people you go to church with and your kids go to school with." His quiet voice dropped lower, "You really, really go in with a chip on your shoulder."[68]

But "it didn't take long to understand that people, whether in Mexico, Honduras, or El Salvador, they were trying to survive."[69] Marty realized "they were very, very receptive and very inquisitive on how to do this and how to do their jobs and how to be successful, as successful as they could be."[70] He got to know his new workforce, for a period of time spending more time with the families of his staff than with his own family. "Today I understand where folks come from because I was there every week, whether it was Central America, Mexico, Africa, Morocco, Caribbean, whatever."[71]

For someone who grew up in Kentucky and scraped his way through college, this was a life journey he couldn't have expected. Around the globe, he got to know people and places worlds away from Campbellsville. Years later, Bailey and his wife aimed to settle down in North Carolina near her family, but the industry intervened. Soon he was on a plane to Los Angeles to serve as Chief Manufacturing Officer for American Apparel. Marty's career had come full circle; he was back to manufacturing in the United States.

As he modernized American Apparel's manufacturing process, his past came back to find him. With a bit of a chuckle, Bailey told me, "I would have people come up to me [at American Apparel in Los Angeles] and say, 'Marty, Marty, Fruit of the Loom El Salvador.'"[72] The workers he had trained in Central America had brought their skills to Los Angeles. Their skills complemented an untold number of sales, design, production, transportation, and management jobs in the United States. T-shirts were being sewn by an immigrant in America, and in the process more Americans were being put to work.

Eva Grove's characterization of US ambivalence toward immigrants came to mind as my conversation with Bailey turned to an immigration-enforcement audit targeting thousands of American Apparel employees.[73]

I asked Bailey, "Do you remember getting that list for the first time?"

"Yeah," he replied.

"What did it feel like?"

"My heart sank."[74]

In April 2009, the Obama administration announced a new worksite immigration-enforcement strategy; it focused on the prosecution of

employers with undocumented workers, not the prosecution and deportation of workers themselves. I-9 audits of employers' work-authorization
files became the main tool for this strategy.[75] American Apparel was legally
required to have every staff person complete an I-9 form, providing proof
of authorization to work in the United States. According to United States
Citizenship and Immigration Services, "The employer must examine the
employment eligibility and identity document(s) an employee presents
to determine whether the document(s) reasonably appear to be genuine
and to relate to the employee and record the document information on
the Form I-9."[76] American Apparel, like millions of employers across the
country, was not in a position to serve as immigration-enforcement agents.
They reviewed the documents that were presented to them and determined
whether they were acceptable.

The list that sank Bailey's heart was likely a "Suspect Document"
letter, listing employees whose work-authorization information did not
match official records. In this case, he told me the list was "over 2,500
names long."[77] In September 2009, American Apparel fired about 1,800
immigrant employees who could not resolve the paperwork discrepancies
found in the audit.[78]

On the way back to Los Angeles, after I lost many a golf ball, we discussed the impact of the audit. Throughout the process, Bailey told me he
"stood there and took it, whether it was the anger or the heartbreak or the
handshakes or the hugs or whatever."[79] Looking back, he remembered, "It
was a whole array of emotions for weeks while we went through this." Well
before the audit, American Apparel had advocated for immigration reform
that would have provided legal status to undocumented immigrants—not
realizing a number of its staff might be undocumented themselves.

What angered Marty most was that the audit, and the resulting termi-
nations, solved nothing. There were no visas available for their workers,
even though they were skilled tradespeople. And there was no way to help
them attain legal status. In short, there was no line for them to get into.

Employers like American Apparel were forced to make a profit in a
tight labor market with slim operating margins. As a result of their firing,
the talented tradespeople who made tens of thousands of garments were

pushed further underground and into the hands of unscrupulous employers. Those employers would certainly pay far less than American Apparel, which gave $18 million in stock to its employees.[80]

Bailey had stayed true to the advice Mr. Moore gave him during that first conversation in Campbellsville. He had gotten to know his workforce. Marty knew the workers he laid off were not going back home. "I have been where a lot of these folks come from," he told me. "They are not going back. As bad as it is—as bad as it could be here, it's much more than what they left."[81]

HUMAN POTENTIAL

Cheryl and Ralph Broetje's job is to grow apples. Marty Bailey's job is to make T-shirts. Steve Case's job is to develop new technologies. Their job isn't to explain to America that immigrants and immigration, documented, undocumented, or refugees, are a net benefit to society, and our legal systems are unable to address this challenge. They have businesses to run. But they realize this is about more than the bottom line. They realize their changing workforce is indicative of a larger societal change, and that they have a moral, not merely financial, responsibility to address.

For many Americans, these changes feel national, foreign, and unknown. Business leaders who take a moral stand on immigrants and immigration are unique in that they realize these changes are incredibly local. This is particularly true in the exurban or rural areas of the country where business leaders are in a position to advance a constructive approach.

Pasco, home of the Broetje family, lies within the Tri-Cities region, just miles from the Hanford Nuclear Site. To the outside observer, the region is dominated by the billions of dollars and thousands of jobs funding the cleanup of the Hanford Site, where plutonium was produced for nuclear arms. Lori Mattson, CEO of the Tri-City Chamber of Commerce for nearly eight years, saw the economy and population diversify beyond the massive cleanup project. In 2007, the county was nearly 57 percent Hispanic, up from 47 percent in 2000. Between 2000 and 2006, Pasco schools registered 3,700 new students and the district had built five new schools since 1999.[82] The majority of this growth came from an increase in farm labor, and with it came the inevitable growth in stores, restaurants, and other small businesses to serve this very different population.

All of this impacted the economic ethnicity of the area. Mattson's enthusiasm picked up a notch as she spoke of a 2015 report from the Association of Chamber of Commerce Executives, "Eight Influences Shaping the Next Decade for Chambers of Commerce."[83] The report explained that changes "present both complications and opportunities for institutions like chambers, which have been struggling to increase inclusiveness for decades. . . . Chambers will also play a role in ensuring that population demographic shifts are accepted in the region. Chambers need to model evolving pro-social behavior through the types of programs they offer and their own hiring."[84] Mattson told me, "So we are very aware at this moment that the chamber and the Tri-Cities, but certainly as an organization, that we need to become much more inclusive than we are."[85]

My conversation with Lori reminded me of my breakfast with Monica Lozano when she spoke of the need for a higher level of participation from Latino business leadership in corporate management and board rooms. For both Lori and Monica, the inclusion agenda is different from the diversity agenda. And the Tri-City Chamber of Commerce CEO understood that a diverse staff could foster better relationships with Hispanic businesses and, most important, ensure that her board of directors included Hispanic business owners. With greater Hispanic representation within the Chamber of Commerce, the business community overall could better understand the needs of a fast-growing immigrant population. This wasn't going to happen quickly or easily.

To state the obvious, Pasco, Washington, is not Los Angeles, California. Institutional capacity within the immigrant community is just emerging, and local organizations that help immigrants navigate society are still young. Mattson felt that native-born, white business owners had a leadership opportunity, if not a responsibility: "I think that the business community can certainly have a strong influence on issues like [demographic change]."[86]

Let's go back to my favorite mom-and-pop operation, Ralph and Cheryl Broetje.

In 2013, the Broetjes ran out of housing at the apple orchard and looked for plots of land closer to town.[87] Cheryl told me about a meeting with the local power brokers: "They came out here. . . . We [told them that we] had a lot of families that had been with us ten, fifteen years and would like to own an asset. So here is our vision."[88]

These power brokers did not want affordable housing for Latino farmworkers closer to town. "Thank you, but no thank you," was the response they received.

"So, then, what did we do?" asked Cheryl.[89]

They did it anyway. Ralph and Cheryl figured out a way to buy the land from the city themselves, and they broke ground. Over the years, Tierra Vida, as the development was named, proved itself a good neighbor. "People were watching out for each other, didn't let [bad] things happen," said Ralph.[90] The new homeowners became a constructive part of the broader community—so much so that one of the original opponents to the development later sought assistance from the Broetjes for a family he or she knew.

For a fast-growing Hispanic community, hundreds of miles from an urban center, the American dream was flourishing because the Broetjes believe in human potential. Whether it was apples or people, the family was bearing fruit. Fruit that will last.

CHAPTER NINE

MAKING THE FUTURE

I've often joked with friends that I didn't want to write a "smart" book. Rather than yet another book about the data and policy behind immigration, I wanted to look at the moment we're in as a nation, culturally speaking.

I am incredibly lucky to do this work, because every day I meet courageous men and women who step outside their emotional and social comfort zones to help America understand and negotiate our twenty-first-century identity crisis. Every day I am inspired by those who come to this country to improve the American experiment, whether they are my own parents, DREAMers, techies in Silicon Valley, or farmworkers in Alabama. In these stories I've found deep-seated challenges, but I've also found hope.

As I reflect on these stories, starting the final chapter of this book with my first interview feels right.

In 2011, when this project was just a twinkle in my eye, I read Richard Longworth's *Caught in the Middle: America's Heartland in the Age of Globalism*.[1] His account of Midwestern communities grappling with globalization opened my eyes to the larger challenge. So when I decided to move forward with this book, I knew I wanted to talk to Dick very early in the process. During our February 2016 chat in downtown Chicago, Longworth and I talked about the cultural isolation besetting our politics. In his travels, Dick told me, he saw some towns adapt and grow but others that "would rather commit suicide than have immigrants in."[2]

Which explains the popularity of walls. Whether they are literal, such as along the US–Mexico border, or figurative ones along the city limits of culturally and ethnically isolated communities, they seem like an easy answer to a profound challenge.

But America's next fifty years will break down walls. The way we categorize race and ethnicity will become increasingly irrelevant. Longworth made an astute observation that "as more and more intermarriage happens," cultural isolation will be more difficult. "No matter what Donald Trump wants, you can't build a wall against hormones."[3]

THE RETURN OF TRIBALISM

Too often the immigration debate devolves into accusations of xenophobia and racism. I don't mean to say that those sentiments aren't real—but I think accusations of racism are often a simplistic end to an argument. People aren't just one thing; we have to engage with each other as complex and evolving, struggling with questions that are personal and social.

I refuse to assume that every person who disagrees with me is a racist. We all have fears that we are faced with every morning in the bathroom mirror.

Here's a test for you to take. As you are brushing your teeth, pause a second, and while the foam drips out of your mouth, think about the last immigrant you saw, and ask yourself, "Am I a racist?"

Some of you may very well say, "Yep. I'm a racist." In which case, thank you for buying the book. Tell a friend.

The majority of us look in that mirror and say, "No, I don't think I'm a racist. But I'm a bit scared by what is happening around the world and wonder if that will come to my neighborhood."

Cool. We can work with that. Rinse and spit. Get dressed for your day.

As I have argued throughout this book, the fear and anxiety coursing through our nation are a function of cultural change brought on by rapidly shifting demographics. Whether we live in cities or towns, these changes are upon us—they are at our doors, and we have a tendency to react in polarizing ways. The polarization is not limited to the United States; it doesn't take much effort to scan the day's news and see that Western democracies like Britain, France, Germany, and others, are facing similar dynamics.

While I certainly believe there is a simple solution to our national identity crisis, Longworth's hormonal strategy might be a shade too simple.

(And it will take too long.) At its core, demographic and cultural change are our nation's arc through history. No generation is like the one before. The American story is constantly changing, and each person I interviewed grappled with these changes in similar ways.

Whether it was insurance salesman Harold Smith in his comfortable recliner in suburban South Carolina, or technology billionaire Steve Case in his well-appointed Washington, DC, office, I saw very different people, living very different realities, but with similar concerns. Can communities across the United States navigate the changes that come with immigration and culture change? Can we tell a new American story that brings people together?

It is certainly easy to think we are a divided nation: Democrats versus Republicans; people of color versus people of no color; urban versus rural; tote bags versus holsters. Of course, it is easy to list the reasons why these divisions exist. The media. The establishment. The economy. The border.

These divisions lead us to become more tribal. Our segmented Facebook feeds, our neighborhoods, our jobs, and our friends all define our tribe. Robert Jones, CEO of the Public Religion Research Institute, took this a step further when he told me, "partisanship has become tribal."[4] He continued, "It's overlaid with race. It's overlaid with class. It's overlaid with religion. Those are like these deep-seated tribal identities."[5] This isn't gridlock. This is not a stalemate. This is the establishment of emotional walls between groups who think differently. We are loathe to cross these boundaries. We believe our emotional and physical safety is best served on our side of these walls. All this is to say, the anxiety and fear that comes with immigration to America in the twenty-first century is our culture war waged in the media, on the Internet, and in political campaigns.

But as the left and right engage in their versions of trench warfare, I am convinced the majority of Americans seek a different story when it comes to immigration. Some are immigrants themselves, while many have been in the United States for generations. They believe in the principles of family, safety, and prosperity.

Jonathan Haidt's *The Righteous Mind: Why Good People Are Divided by Politics and Religion* is a fascinating assessment of the moral psychology behind today's political discourse.[6] Haidt crawls into the inner sanctum of the mind's eye as he seeks to explain why good people are so darn disagreeable when it comes to politics and religion. Within his exhaustively researched book, Haidt clarifies the narratives of liberalism and conservatism in the United States.

The liberal narrative is summarized as "Authority, hierarchy, power, and tradition are the chains that must be broken to free the 'noble aspirations' of the victims."[7] Meanwhile, the conservative narrative is a defensive emphasis of freedom from government constraint, loyalty to country, and sanctity of family. At times these narratives are articulated with anxiety-inducing anger, and at other times with optimistic aspiration. Depending on the message and messenger, fear or hope can serve as the leading edge of these stories.

Where cultural and demographic change fits in this narrative is constantly changing. Over the last twenty years, liberals and conservatives have both framed demographic change in positive and negative ways. For better or worse, the narrative is defined by the political expedience of electoral goals. In regions where naturalized citizens make up a considerable portion of the electorate, candidates will see immigrants as benefits to society; when the numbers are low, immigrants are threats to society to be politically exploited or simply ignored.

Given the deeply polarizing tone and tenor of the 2016 political campaigns, if you ascribe to the above divisions, one would expect a fall-off in support for immigrants and immigration.[8] But it turns out that the immigrant narrative does not fall along purely political lines. Instead, for all of President Donald Trump's efforts to marginalize and scapegoat immigrants, a September 2016 NBC News/*Wall Street Journal* survey found that 54 percent of registered voters believe that immigration helps the United States more than it hurts, compared to just 47 percent in July 2015.[9] And, less than two weeks before the election, Pew Research released new polling that found by a 4:1 margin (80–18 percent), Americans support a policy that allows undocumented immigrants to stay legally over a policy that does not allow them to stay legally.[10] Since Pew began asking this question in 2013, this was the highest level of support recorded.

Turns out America hasn't given up on the neighborhood quite yet.

NO LONGER LEFT VERSUS RIGHT

If Americans continue to believe in the idea of immigration beyond all the political sniping, then why all the drama?

Michael Lind, a fellow at New America, a think tank and civic enterprise in Washington, DC, discussed the concepts of globalists and nationalists as political actors in a May 2016 essay.[11] Lind surmised that the intra-party culture wars fought over social issues such as abortion and marriage were over. The parties are who they are: Democrats are pro-choice, pro-gay marriage. Republicans are pro-life, pro-traditional marriage. When it comes to these issues, there is no ideological crossover and very little moderation. With the homogeneity of the parties on these issues, Lind postulated, "The culture war and partisan realignment are over; the policy realignment and 'border war'—a clash between nationalists, mostly on the right, and multicultural globalists, mostly on the left—have just begun."[12]

I would offer a friendly amendment that Lind's "border war" is a new type of culture war. Building a bubble around the country, ending immigration as we know it, will not stop demographic and cultural change in America's neighborhoods. The conflict doesn't begin or end at our border. There are social and economic shifts happening at all levels of society: global, national, and neighborhood. America today includes a more diverse mix of people than it did at any other time in our history.[13] We have to adapt at a local level in order to continue to lead at the global level.

I'll put it another way. If we close our borders to never let in another immigrant, yes, the nationalists will have won. But America will still become more Latino, more Asian, more diverse, because that is who we have become as a nation. So the globalists will win in the long-run. The challenge is to get to a place where both sides "win," without taking the extreme and unrealistic step of closing America off from the world—or opening up to everyone, regardless of our national interest.

Haidt built on Lind's concept in a July 2016 essay arguing that the more demographic changes are brought on by globalists, the more authoritarian nationalists become. The simplistic view is that one group wants to let the world in, while the other is trying to turn inward. According to Haidt, nationalists' intense sense of patriotism and identity with country is "a real moral commitment, not a pose to cover up racist bigotry."[14] Globalists, on the other hand, are urban elites who "embrace diversity and welcome immigration, often turning those topics into litmus tests for moral respectability."[15]

As we have seen, these groups do not always cut along traditional political party lines. There are nationalist Democrats and Republicans both worried about trade and job competition, just as there are conservative and liberal globalists who seek a more open immigration system.

Better control and regulation of immigration is necessary and long overdue. Our antiquated immigration system has not met the needs of America's economy and has created an underclass of millions of people. But we should not believe that approaching this as only a border conflict, much less just a policy question, will reduce culture change and the tension between globalists and nationalists.

If we want to stop culture change, close off America from the world entirely—North Korea is one example of this isolationist strategy. For obvious reasons, that does not sound too appealing to Americans. But if a large number of Americans blame/credit the 1965 Immigration and Nationality Act for today's diversity, we know limiting or ending immigration will not solve the problem. With or without new immigration, America is changing and it will take a cultural strategy to navigate our future.

THE STEPS WE TOOK

I started this book with December 18, 2010, the day the DREAM Act was defeated and "Don't Ask, Don't Tell" was repealed. On that day at the United Methodist Headquarters, I decided that the National Immigration Forum needed to do something different. After the wrenching loss, it was clear our politics and policies were unable to cope with the fact that money, information, goods, and people move. Native-born white Americans feel that their world is upside down. So if we were going to pass any kind of immigration reform, we needed to authentically engage conservatives and moderates and create a new space.

In 2010, there were (and still are) great organizations to our political left doing amazing work. They included those led by undocumented immigrants, policy shops, longtime civil rights institutions, and organized labor. These institutions organized the immigrant rights community, registered Latino, Asian, and other new American voters, and ensured the powerful voice of the immigrant community drove the debate. Through media, marches, and campaigns, they made the case to Democrats and progressives that immigrants and immigration were to be valued from a political and social perspective. But while we would never change the law without the leadership of the immigrant community, and the support of progressives and liberals, victory ultimately required conservatives to be a part of the solution.

To our political right, the space was dominated by anti-immigrant groups, along with a handful of business and faith stakeholders such as the US Chamber of Commerce and US Catholic Conference of Bishops. But these allies never matched the volume of the liberal left or anti-immigrant right. As a result, the public understood the debate as a political fight between the hard left and the hard right.

The conservative faith, law enforcement, and business communities had never come together in a coordinated fashion to craft a narrative based on culture and values. They operated in silos, occasionally crossing paths in the context of policy questions. There was little strategic engagement at the local level to build coalitions of conservative and moderate stakeholders. Our theory was that if we convinced middle America (the ones who saw the left and right lobbing verbal grenades at one another) that immigration was a question of culture and values that could be resolved in their interest, we would see the beginning of a constructive public debate.

To build a strategy, we went to the data.

Using as a proxy the 2010 DREAM Act Senate vote, the one Senator Lieberman walked through the snow for, we found limited political support for immigrants and immigration particularly in the Southeast, Midwest, and Mountain West regions of the country. From Idaho to Arizona, across to Kansas, east to the Carolinas and south to Florida, both senators voted against what we thought was our most compelling legislation: legal status for high-achieving undocumented youth. If we couldn't get their vote on the most appealing slice of the legislative debate and we didn't have a strategy to build support in these states, we would never win broader reform.

Yet there was potential for alignment to be found across the Southeast, Midwest, and Mountain West. In each of the three regions we found the highest number of evangelical Christians,[16] the highest number of state and local law-enforcement personnel per 100,000 residents,[17] and, as a proxy for the young and dynamic workforce business sought, the fastest growth in foreign-born population.[18] Overlaying these four maps painted a clear picture. The Southeast, Midwest, and Mountain West had the least amount of political support for immigrants and immigration, the most evangelicals, the most cops, and the fastest growth in the immigrant community. Based on the success of the Utah Compact earlier that year, we saw the contours of a strategy that knit messages and messengers together on culture and community.

So we went to work in these regions to develop new relationships, learn a new language (so to speak), and lay the groundwork for a new direction. I assumed this would be incredibly difficult and that we would run into opposition at every turn.

Instead, developing and implementing this approach was the easiest thing I've ever done, and probably the most interesting thing I will ever do. Beginning with the 2010 Utah Compact, then to Georgia, Indiana, and beyond, we learned how to work and communicate with a new set of allies. From national organizations to local leaders, too many to name, we were welcomed into the conversation. Through many conversations, some awkward and many entertaining, we developed an understanding and trust that gently eased all of us out of our respective comfort zones.

What we learned between 2010 and 2012, as this book describes, shaped a new story we wanted to tell. A story that came into clear relief when I told the *Boston Globe*'s Adrian Walker in June 2012, "If you hold a Bible, wear a badge, or own a business, you want a solution to the immigration dilemma."[19]

With that, a coalition message of Bibles, Badges and Businesses for Immigration Reform was born. It wasn't a poll-tested, focus-grouped message that cost us millions of dollars to research (though if someone has millions of dollars for research, call me). It was a message based on months of getting to know these new stakeholders on their terms, in their language.

Through those conversations, we began to understand what brought them to the issue. It wasn't politics. It wasn't policy. It was a question of values. A belief in God, the rule of law, and the free market. A conservative version of what I wrote earlier: family, security, prosperity. If we spoke their language and respected their viewpoints, over time we would build an approach that resonated with a broad swath of America.

With trust among coalition partners came trust from the public. In Bibles, Badges and Business, people saw themselves, and they saw the leadership they followed. We presented a new narrative to America, that conservative and moderate faith, law-enforcement, and business leaders saw immigrants and immigration as a social and economic benefit to the nation. And, as those who hold a bible, wear a badge, or own a business, they believed Congress should move forward with practical immigration solutions.

Importantly, it was a conservative narrative that did not marginalize liberals. And it was an argument that put our anti-immigrant opposition on their heels. Political and social conservatives were organizing themselves to debate and marginalize the nativist elements of the Republican Party. Bibles, Badges and Business for Immigration Reform became a story about culture change that resonated across the political spectrum.

Over the course of 2013 and 2014, our incredibly talented staff organized hundreds of faith, law enforcement, and business events across the country. Thousands of news stories followed, and the narrative advanced on multiple levels.

My favorite part of these events was never onstage. It was always in the green room before speakers went before the public.

More often than not, the conservatives we gathered may have supported the same Republican candidates, but they had not collaborated on an issue campaign. So they were rarely in the same room, speaking to the same issue. Nobody was entirely sure how the other would speak to immigration, and there was always an awkward tension in the room. No one wanted to get dragged into a political conversation. Everyone wanted to stay within their comfort zone. Each one of these socially and politically conservative leaders had specific talking points in mind. The business and law-enforcement leaders did not want to be a part of a socially conservative event. Pastors did not want to discuss visa numbers for computer engineers; they wanted to talk about the Bible. Law enforcement about public safety. Business about, well, business. Looking around, it was clear speakers assumed they were in for an uncomfortable conversation of politics and policy.

Just like that dinner in Utah, the dynamics quickly changed once the speakers shared stories of immigrants in their congregations, in their communities, and on their worksites. From their different vantage points, time and again, they would speak about immigrants as people to be valued, not as policy points to be argued. A powerful onstage synergy replaced the painful greenroom awkwardness. They needed to trust each other as much as they trusted us. Slowly, a coalition willing to take on culture change began to form.

The audience, whether in person or in news reports, could choose between a range of messengers. They didn't have to trust every speaker; they just had to trust one of the B's on the stage. Whether it was lessons from scripture, the improved public safety that comes with trust between law enforcement and immigrant communities, or the business need for immigrants and immigration, there was a messenger they believed in. More important, the principles of faith, rule of law, and free market eased the cultural anxiety simmering underneath the debate. The coalition began to open the hearts and minds of middle America.

WITHOUT THE BASE, THERE IS NO MIDDLE

If Jorge Ramos is the Walter Cronkite of Spanish-language television, Congressman Luis Gutierrez of Chicago is the Muhammad Ali of the immigrant rights community. His frame may be slight, but his voice is loud; his political punches keep Democrats and Republicans on their toes with a bilingual, bicultural intensity. For millions of Latinos across the United States, he is their personal congressman.

Gutierrez is also the wise sage of the immigration movement. So much of what the Forum has done was based on lessons we took from the congressman's approach. He infused America's stale, partisan, immigration fight with the stories of immigrants as human beings. He lifted their voices, amplified their stories, and represented their dreams in epic political battles with Democrats and Republicans alike. I am just as proud to say I was arrested in front of the White House with Congressman Gutierrez, protesting President Obama's deportation policy (don't tell my mom), as I am to honor his vision to engage conservative faith leaders as a template for our approach.

One afternoon, I sat and chatted with Gutierrez in his Capitol Hill office. Along with his indefatigable chief of staff, Susan Collins, and brilliant communications director, Douglas Rivlin, we talked about the past, present, and future of the debate. Sitting on the edge of a leather couch that doubles as his bed when he's in Washington, DC, bouncing slightly when he wanted to make a point, Gutierrez talked about his early work with Hispanic faith leaders. Even then, he understood that the Latino faith community was a powerful way to organize and define the political base for immigration reform. He could make a case for immigrants and immigration through a cultural prism acceptable to conservative and moderate Americans: their faith. And he could make this case just as powerfully as he made it to union locals, progressives, and secular organizations that fought for immigrant rights. Gutierrez was a crossover advocate.

The basic idea was to organize events in churches where US citizens told their personal stories of family separation due to deportations. Since the events took place in religious institutions, they were more personal than political, more values-based than policy-oriented. In early 2009, Gutierrez launched a national tour he called *Familias Unidas* (Families United), and he traveled to twenty-four evangelical and Catholic churches across the country.

As the tour picked up energy, the pews began to fill. I remember standing in a packed-to-the-doors Catholic Church in Salinas while Gutierrez spoke. Every eye was on him. Reporting on a separate event, the *Washington Post*'s David Montgomery captured Gutierrez's intensity: "He brings no notes. He starts slow. His words surf on crests of emotion, tacking fluidly between English and Spanish, in the singular oratory of a Chicago-born Puerto Rican Catholic who preaches like a Baptist."[20]

The events triggered deeply emotional commitments from Democrats who, at that time, controlled the House and Senate but were hesitant to take on the Obama administration. During a March 2009 event at St. Anthony's Church in her hometown of San Francisco, then Speaker Nancy Pelosi was so moved by the testimonies that she made an unprecedented statement, "[Immigration raids] must be stopped. . . . What value system is that? I think it's un-American. I think it's un-American."[21] There was no way Speaker Pelosi, a practicing Catholic, would make that kind of emotional statement in the sterile confines of the Capitol. She needed to hear US citizens tell stories of deported family members in a Catholic Church to truly understand this issue.

Through *Familias Unidas*, Gutierrez did much more than energize Democrats. He built a bridge to conservatives based on the values of Hispanic evangelicals. For Republican politicians, Hispanic evangelicals are a valuable audience. They are members of vibrant congregations who tend to be socially conservative. Republicans feel that they can compete for conservative Hispanic voters based on issues outside of immigration. The problem is that the Latino community sees Republicans as anti-immigrant. The late Robert Gittelson, working on behalf of a number of different evangelical organizations, saw this opening and was an instrumental player in setting up some initial meetings to create opportunities for dialogue on this issue.[22]

Gutierrez recalled a meeting Gittelson organized with a number of Republican members of Congress. He told me, "I remember the Republicans sitting there, waiting for their turn to go speak. . . . I walked in, and they go—I could just see them, they were like, 'How is it that Luis Gutierrez, this very liberal person, has such a connection to these people?'"[23]

Gutierrez's relationship with evangelical churches cut right into the Republican base—or at least a base they wanted. "Big caucus room in the Capital," Rivlin chimed in, "A room full of evangelicals that [Congresswoman Michelle] Bachmann and [Senator Rand] Paul thought were their guys. And then Luis Gutierrez talks to them, and they were applauding and excited to see him. So at the same time there was a showing members of Congress the power of Luis Gutierrez and the power of this issue."[24]

The relationship Gutierrez built with Hispanic evangelicals went beyond the political. A conservative Hispanic evangelical congregation would agree with Republicans on issues of life and marriage, but he or she was personally impacted by a broken immigration system that deported upward of two and a half million people over the course of the Obama administration.[25] Republicans refused to help fix this problem, and consequently they found it nearly impossible to win conservative Latino support. To put it differently, questions of life and marriage became less important when Republicans also wanted to deport a voter's mother.

Gutierrez wasn't in the church to talk about life or marriage. He didn't initiate these relationships to ask for votes. He was there to listen and talk to the families in the pews about their lives in America and show Republicans that there was a heartfelt need for change. In that way, the events were an opportunity for the community to put forward a constructive story about their social and economic contributions to the United States. As Gutierrez put it, "The other thing was the testimonies. . . . [The churches were] the perfect venue to tell a story about family and love and government."[26]

Like the Utah Compact, Gutierrez's work opened eyes to the potential of a faith-based narrative that resonated with both the political left and the social conservative right. In this case, instead of a conservative crossing over to the left, this was an ideologically anchored liberal crossing over to the right.

IDEOLOGICAL ANCHORS

It is fair to assume the stark partisanship and polarization we see in our politics today will remain for years to come. Or as the Hewlett Foundation's Daniel Stid put it, "Polarization is neither a trend that can be reversed nor a problem that can be solved; rather, it is a predicament with which we need to learn how to cope."[27] Things have gotten so bad that we can't get anything else done. Every issue gets swallowed up in the partisanship of cultural change. In his article, Stid quotes a paper by Steven Teles, Heather Hurlburt, and Mark Schmitt originally published in the *Stanford Social Innovation Review*:

> Some of the most creative advocacy work currently underway builds cross-party coalitions that are anchored not by centrists, but by figures

with unquestioned ideological credibility. We call this style of advocacy "transpartisan," because it recognizes that the critical political gate-keepers are no longer ideologically neutral actors at the center, but the authorizers of ideological orthodoxy at the poles.[28]

Back at the Methodist Church headquarters after that fateful 2010 DREAM Act vote, I didn't think we were about to execute some sort of newfangled political science theory. I just figured there was more support for immigrants, immigration, and cultural change than we were organizing. I felt our political ideology had blinded us to the potential for new allies.

As we built out Bibles, Badges and Business, we found ourselves seeking ideological anchors from the conservative movement. You don't get much more socially conservative than Dr. Russell Moore, head of the Ethics & Religious Liberty Commission of the Southern Baptist Convention. It's difficult to get more rule of law than pro–death penalty attorney general Mark Shurtleff. No one is more pro-capitalism than Tom Donohue, CEO of the US Chamber of Commerce. And few are reviled by the progressive left more than Grover Norquist, CEO of Americans for Tax Reform. But all of these leaders are fully invested in resolving America's identity crisis through a more constructive approach to immigrants and immigration.

Through local and national work (often in churches, just like Gutierrez), the National Immigration Forum aimed to engage these kinds of ideological anchors in order to establish a political center, one whose influence could allow Congress to compromise. A center through which conservative Americans could see new Americans as human beings with value and potential. We hoped that, as Robert Jones of Public Religion Research Institute told me, "Then compromise doesn't become anathema. . . . You are not compromising with the enemy. You are compromising with another party you disagree with. That's different than the enemy we fought and resisted at all costs."[29]

Agreeing to disagree seems like a modest goal.

But the "transpartisan" model doesn't require agreement on issues beyond the current coalition. It doesn't require one to leave one's ideological beliefs behind. In fact, it is better if ideology remains front and center and credibility is maintained. What it does require, though, is a vehicle through which the dialogue and relationships are nurtured. This is what the National Immigration Forum and Bibles, Badges and Business for Immigration Reform strove to provide.

When we embarked on this approach, we spent the better part of a year explaining to our allies on the political left why it was important. Many just didn't get it. They thought agreeing to disagree was a recipe for bad policy. At one point, an advocate from the left even told me, "You will give them too much power." Well, if that was the case, we would have won by now.

Deepak Bhargava, one of the country's most influential progressive leaders, understood the strategy from day one. A close friend and thoughtful advisor for nearly a dozen years, Deepak is executive director of the Center for Community Change, an organization working to build the power and capacity of low-income people, especially people of color, to change their communities and public policies for the better. Under his leadership, the Center for Community Change has become a political force.

If there was anyone who would get weirded out by the idea of social and fiscal conservatives locking arms with the immigrant community, it would be Deepak. So many of his beliefs conflicted with the conservatives we aimed to work with. Like Gutierrez, Deepak understood the cultural context of the debate:

> It is pretty essential for the US to find a way to embrace the best of our immigrant heritage. For that to happen would take the reestablishment of a consensus in the country on immigration. Which means a lot of different constituencies need to find it in not just their self-interest, but at the core of their values and their sense of identity as Americans.[30]

An organizer by training, Deepak understood the importance of a resonant narrative and the importance of ideological anchors. "Bibles, Badges and Business has been a pathway for people and constituencies to find their own meaning on the value of immigration to the country," he told me.[31] "This is hugely significant not just for the legislative debate of the day but for the construction of the American identity in the twenty-first century. The existence of a conservative block that affirms a role of immigrants and immigration is an essential part of the American identity."[32]

While staying true to their values, I see how political poles can bend toward each other.

A ROAD MAP FORWARD

People often ask me how I ended up working on immigration. Was it a deep-seated belief in the immigrant story? Was it a commitment to my own family's history as immigrants? No. None of those. The job was open and the issue seemed interesting.

Over the course of my career, I've had the opportunity to work on environmental and public-health issues. But there is something different about immigration. There are few public-policy questions that touch so many lives so quickly. Not just because it is important to my family and millions of families across the country. Immigration gets at the core of who we are, and who we want to be, as a country. Todd Schulte, president of FWD.us, put it best: "Immigration, more than any other issue, is a referendum on who we are as a nation."[33] This is why the immigration debate cuts across cultural and political lines like few others.

From 2003 to 2010, I spent the majority of my time approaching this debate from the immigrant rights perspective. As I said earlier, without leadership from communities of color, these issues will never be resolved, much less advanced. Over the course of the last five years, since crossing over to engage conservatives and moderates, I've found myself in conversations and rooms I never expected. Some of them were inspiring; others, quite alarming.

The experiences of the last five-plus years, working with an entirely new set of allies and asking for their trust, led me to my own identity crisis. I learned that as a dyed-in-the-wool liberal who doesn't carry a Bible, wear a badge, or own a business, it is hard to engage conservatives on their terms. It is hard to stay true to my own principles while sitting at the table with people who have had very different life experiences.

As the 2016 presidential campaign unfolded, I told the press, policymakers, and anyone who would listen that in politics, clear choices are good. Candidate A's policy position versus Candidate B's policy position. The clearer the difference, the sharper the decision. For much of 2016, the sharpness was provided by immigration and the cultural changes it drove.

But understanding culture change is not a binary process. People don't fear culture change one day and wake up the next day as globalists. As we got closer to Election Day, I realized the cultural debate would not go away with one election. The emotions underlying these fears shift slowly, erratically, constantly reminding us of a past many hold dear.

Over the course of the 2016 electoral campaign, I increasingly felt that we had chosen the right path. Bibles, Badges and Business for Immigration Reform is not a political strategy. Success will not even come with one electoral or legislative win. It is a strategy that addresses culture change; one that demands patience as conservative communities work through a very emotional process. Yes, somewhere along the way we will secure legislative wins. But patience is a painful virtue when there are 11 million people forced to live in the shadows, and the public debate is dominated by scapegoating and fearmongering.[34]

This takes me to a very simple question Cecilia Muñoz, director of President Obama's Domestic Policy Council, posed that afternoon we spoke in her West Wing office, "Do we see each other as Americans?"

These days, I'm not so sure, which makes me sad.

We do an awful job of seeing the human potential in one another. We are quicker to dwell on differences than capitalize on similarities. We treat relationships as negotiations instead of collaborations. We seem more concerned with individual liberties than with the common good.

The forty-fifth president of the United States will lead a nation divided by an entirely new set of political norms. Racism, xenophobia, and misogyny are no longer topics of discussion for the dark corners of the Internet. They are out in the open, since they have been mainstreamed in this election year's bitter campaigns.

It is too simple to claim this vitriol is white America's final grasps for power; it's more than that. It is the fear and anxiety of globalization at our doorstep. Ron Brownstein, a journalist with the *Atlantic*, captures the question many Americans ask themselves: "Are nations more likely to achieve security and prosperity by building walls or bridges to the outside world?"[35] Regardless of the consequences of isolation, some people want walls instead of bridges, because they are afraid the world is storming their gates.

Cities and towns are asking the same question. Local city councils and state legislatures are just as much a political battleground on issues sparked by demographic change as the United States Congress is. The same question applies: Bridges or walls?

In the years ahead, we will witness a realignment of America's politics in ways that are impossible to predict. All we can do is be ready and put our best foot forward. This brings me to the last question I asked almost everyone I spoke with, and the question I now ask myself: "What gives you hope?"

My hope came from President George W. Bush's speech at the opening of the National Museum of African American History and Culture. He said, "A great nation does not hide its history."[36] Our immigrant history may be complicated, but it is personal to practically each and every one of us. Americans are an exceptional people because we learn from our past.

But our national identity crisis isn't just about our history. It is about our future.

The immigrant families working at Broetje Orchards in Pasco, Washington, make decisions about their lives and their communities while sharing stories of relatives dying at the border. Pastor David Fleming in Houston, Texas, ensures his church serves the community and his decisions are influenced by the community. Angela Smith Jones and Angela Adams organize conservative citizens in Indiana to support immigration reform with an infectious zeal. President Dieter F. Uchtdorf encourages Mormons around the world to welcome refugees. Like so many, many others, they are speaking out, and America is listening. It takes people like these at all levels of society, stepping toward one another with courage and hope, to help neighborhoods address the identity crisis that comes with American immigration.

Together, we aren't making history, we are making the future.

ACKNOWLEDGMENTS

The idea to torture the English language with a book came to mind in 2011. As I put pen to paper, opining on the history of immigration and the details of immigration policy, I soon (very soon) realized I was neither smart enough nor disciplined enough to write such a book.

Literary glory shelved, the English language breathed a sigh of relief.

Then, in November 2015, National Immigration Forum board member and good friend Sayu Bhojwani told me to write a book about the new allies we have come to know over the past few years. As I recall, she said to pick five interesting people, interview them, and write about it.

From that conversation, *There Goes the Neighborhood* was born. Over a few months in early 2016, I interviewed more than sixty incredible people who were terribly generous with their time and to whom I owe a great debt of gratitude. Not just for sitting with me and talking, but for all they do, every day, to make America a better place.

Before I get to the people who were crucial to pulling distinct pieces together, let me thank the people without whom this entire endeavor would have been impossible. First of all, the National Immigration Forum board of directors, currently chaired by the brilliant Laura Reiff. The Forum board was kind enough to hire me in 2008 (thank you, John Gay), confident enough to move forward with a new approach, and supportive enough to allow me the time and resources to write this book.

Let me put it this way: the staff (past and present) of the National Immigration Forum are rock stars. Full stop. To a person, they are committed to the organization's mission, passionate about their work, experts in their field, and amazing people to work with. A special thank you to Dawn Byrne, our finance director, for her help and guidance; Cathleen Farrell, our communications director, who helped me work through several steps of this project; Dan Gordon, our communications anchor; and Caroline Leffert, executive assistant, who keeps the trains running.

(And a special shout-out to past Forum staffers Mario Moreno and Guthrie Graves-Fitzsimmons for some clutch South Texas staff work.)

In addition to the Forum's DC-based policy, communications, and organizing staff, I have to thank our organizers of faith, law enforcement, and business leaders across the nation. The stories I shared here are a snapshot of the incredible work they, and numbers of volunteers, do on a daily basis. They are the heart of this work, and it is their commitment that helps communities meet the challenge of American immigration.

From my first days in Washington, DC, three people have been my most trusted confidants and advisors. First of all, the incredible Patty First, a principal at the Raben Group. If there has been one person who understood what was necessary, what was possible, and what the Forum needed to do, it was Patty. She and the founder of the Raben Group, Robert Raben, have been my sounding board, reality check, and dream catcher as we embarked on this work.

In 2010, on a train ride to New York, Deepak Bhargava of the Center for Community Change and I hatched the early contours of this approach—just two South Asian progressives trying to think about how we can pull conservatives and moderates into the immigration debate. (America is a strange and beautiful place.) More than what we discussed on that train ride, Deepak has been a friend and colleague willing to open doors to resources, validate this work among liberals who thought we were "selling out," and, most important, keep me honest to who I am and what I believe.

There Goes the Neighborhood as a strategy, much less as a book, would have been nearly impossible to pull off without Nora Feely. In 2011, just as this approach was starting to take shape, Nora was the person at the Forum who pulled all the pieces together and converted an idea (for which Rich Stolz deserves credit) into a strategy that helped change the way America sees immigrants and immigration. Even though she left the Forum to go on to graduate school, she came back to help edit the manuscript and remind me of missing details.

From a research perspective, Nicolas Montano worked tirelessly to chase down information at a moment's notice. Without the expert transcription services of Kerry Harper, reviewing over sixty interviews would have been completely impossible.

A note of appreciation to *La Opinión*'s Pilar Morrero for introducing me to my book agent, Diane Stockwell of Globo Libros Literary Management. Diane helped shape the book from early on and was a constant source of encouragement and advice as I went through the peaks and valleys of the project. And, of course, the Forum's copier is eternally grateful to Diane for finding the good people at Prometheus Books who published *There Goes the Neighborhood*.

Led by Editor in Chief Steven L. Mitchell, the Prometheus Books team has been wonderful to work with. Jade Zora Scibilia's edits improved the manuscript dramatically; Jill Maxick and Cheryl Quimba of the marketing team have been great partners; and Hanna Etu has tied down every conceivable detail.

And a quick thank you to Cristina Mejia for a brilliant direction in cover design. (And Kristin Rademacher for some last-minute design advice!)

One of my closest friends from growing up in Salinas, Alan Shipnuck, encouraged me to take on the project from day one. A reporter with *Sports Illustrated* and an author of several books, Alan shared contacts and provided crucial advice. Both of us, if I may put words under his pen, owe one of the best English teachers ever, the late Kitty Drew of Washington Junior High School, a debt of gratitude.

In addition to writing a generous and thoughtful foreword, Juan Williams helped think through the project, pushed me to answer critical questions early on, and connected me to friends and colleagues. Robert Putnam, the Peter and Isabel Malkin Professor of Public Policy at Harvard University, provided helpful advice just when the scale of the project dawned on me. Deepa Iyer, author of *We Too Sing America*, has carved out a leadership role for South Asians in America and was a helpful thought partner early in the process as well.

One of the people I turned to early and often as the project took form was Tim King. His understanding of evangelicals in America and his help shaping various chapters was incredibly important. Plus, I think we both got smarter as the nights of bourbon tasting got longer.

Enough cannot be said of the brilliance of Matt Soerens and Jenny

Yang. They are two unsung, tireless, heroes working to help Americans welcome immigrants and refugees into their communities.

In Houston, Mustafa Tameez taught me so much about the region and introduced me to leadership across the area. Jason Mathis opened doors in Salt Lake City. Derrick and Meghan Smith (and their families) helped me understand South Carolina and connected me with warm, gracious people.

Friends provided places to escape in the midst of the writing process. In Chicago, Gabe Gonzalez and Marissa Graciosa opened their house to me at a critical juncture, providing helpful input and welcome respite. Jason Mollring introduced me to the inspirational qualities of British ale during the doldrums of August. My cousin Faisal Noorani allowed me to post up in San Diego for a few days. John Sandweg offered a landing pad and advice when it was most necessary.

Scott Friedman provided a helpful outside eye just as the manuscript was coming to a close. Billy Moore—Texan, golf partner, Washington Nationals fan, and all-around great person—talked through the concept over several miles of me chasing errant golf shots. Manuel Santamaria, the late Amy Hagedorn, Jeanne Atkinson, Roger Bairstow, Jacinta Ma, Michael Thoennes, Amy Low, Todd Schulte, Jonathan Plutzik, Felicia Wong, José Andrés, Craig Regelbrugge, Ben Johnson, Scott Nielsen, Henry Ramos, Frank Smith, Tom Powers, Humberto Garcia-Sjogrim, Roberto Suro, Monica Lozano, David Ayón, David Drury, Kevin Price, Laura Capps, José Cardenas, Angelica Salas, Darren Sandow, Suzette Brooks Masters, Geri Mannion, Leslie Dorosin, Doris Meissner, Jimmy Kemp, Rob McKay The Man Who Cracked His Head Open on a Golf Cart, and many others, you may not have known it, but you provided help along the way. Thank you.

A sincere and heartfelt note of appreciation to Kerry Souza for encouraging me to jump into the immigration debate and pushing me to think differently.

Now, my family.

One of my first social-justice memories is from when I was probably ten years old. I had spent the morning at my dad's office, doing odds and ends at his physical-therapy practice. We went to lunch at a local deli and sat down with our sandwiches on paper plates. Suddenly, my dad picked up his plate and walked out the door.

I had no idea where he went. So I sat there waiting. After a few minutes, he returned, still holding his plate with the sandwich. I asked him what happened.

He told me he saw a homeless man in the deli who had taken the half-eaten sandwich a customer had left. Folks working at the deli had kicked the homeless man out, so my dad wanted to find him to give him his sandwich.

That lesson, that moment, is seared into my brain.

A partner to my dad in many ways, my mother's quiet perseverance was the stability to our family. And her unrelenting belief that all people should be treated kindly, and justly, shapes who I am.

To my sisters, Zeba and Farah, and their beautiful families: I want to be you when I grow up.

Finally, I must acknowledge the immigrant or refugee who comes to America today. You have a courage that exceeds my wildest imagination, and you are the reason I feel so incredibly fortunate to do the work I do. Thank you.

NOTES

PREFACE TO THE PAPERBACK EDITION

1. Megan Brenan, "Record-High 75% of Americans Say Immigration Is Good Thing," Gallup, June 21, 2018, https://news.gallup.com/poll/235793/record-high -americans-say-immigration-good-thing.aspx.

2. Adam Serwer, "The Cruelty Is the Point," *Atlantic*, October 3, 2018, https://www .theatlantic.com/ideas/archive/2018/10/the-cruelty-is-the-point/572104/.

3. Stephen Hawkins, Daniel Yudkin, Miriam Juan-Torres, and Tim Dixon, "Hidden Tribes: A Study of America's Polarized Landscape," More in Common, https://hidden tribes.us/pdf/hidden_tribes_report.pdf.

4. Lynn Casey, "VIDEO: Two Oklahomans Share Story about Being in New York during Bomb Scare," Fox23 News, https://www.fox23.com/video?videoId=860655716 &videoVersion=1.0.

5. Elizabeth Dias, "Beto O'Rourke May Benefit from an Unlikely Support Group: White Evangelical Women," *New York Times*, https://www.nytimes.com/2018/10/09/us/ politics/texas-beto-orourke-evangelicals-women.html?action=click&module=Top%20 Stories&pgtype=Homepage.

FOREWORD

1. Matthew Frye Jacobson, "The Quest for Equality: European Immigration, Part I," YouTube video, 59:58, lecture at the Gilder Lehrman Institute of American History, posted by "Tinkers Thinkers," December 11, 2014, https://www.youtube.com/ watch?v=9HvaR3bnt2o (accessed October 30, 2016).

2. Jay P. Dolan, *The Irish Americans: A History* (New York: Bloomsbury, 2008), pp. 96–98.

3. Jacobson, "Quest for Equality."

4. John F. Kennedy, *A Nation of Immigrants* (1964; repr., New York: Harper Perennial, 2008), pp. 17 and 83.

5. Anna Brown, "Key Takeaways on US Immigration: Past, Present, and Future," Pew Research Center, September 28, 2015, http://www.pewresearch.org/fact-tank/ 2015/09/28/key-takeaways-on-u-s-immigration-past-present-and-future/ (accessed October 30, 2016).

6. "Modern Immigration Wave Brings 59 Million to US, Driving Population Growth and Change Through 1965," Pew Research Center, September 28, 2015, http://www.pewhispanic.org/2015/09/28/modern-immigration-wave-brings-59-million-to-u-s-driving-population-growth-and-change-through-2065/ (accessed October 30, 2016).

7. Matthew Yglesias, "New Poll: Voter Worries about Immigration Mostly Aren't about the Economy," *Vox*, July 6, 2016, http://www.vox.com/2016/7/6/12098622/immigration-worries-economy-security (accessed October 30, 2016).

8. Robert P. Jones, Daniel Cox, Juhem Navarro-Rivera, William A. Galston, and E. J. Dionne, "Citizenship, Values, and Cultural Concerns: What Americans Want from Immigration Reform," Brookings Institution, March 21, 2013, https://www.brookings.edu/research/citizenship-values-and-cultural-concerns-what-americans-want-from-immigration-reform/ (accessed October 30, 2016).

9. Jens Manuel Krogstad, Jeffrey S. Passel, and D'Vera Cohn, "5 Facts about Illegal Immigration in the US," Pew Research Center, September 20, 2016, http://www.pewresearch.org/fact-tank/2016/09/20/5-facts-about-illegal-immigration-in-the-u-s/ (accessed October 30, 2016).

10. "Undocumented Immigrants' State and Local Tax Contributions," Institute on Taxation and Economic Policy, February 24, 2016, http://www.itep.org/immigration/ (accessed October 30, 2016).

11. National Academies of Science, Engineering, and Medicine, *The Integration of Immigrants into American Society* (Washington, DC: National Academies Press, 2016), p. 378.

12. Ibid., p. 328.

13. Ibid., p. 330.

14. Ibid., p. 204.

15. Gihoon Hong and John McLaren, "Are Immigrants a Shot in the Arm for the Local Economy?" (NBER Working Paper Series 21123, National Bureau of Economic Research, Cambridge MA, 2015, 3, cited in Gillian B. White, "Actually, Immigration Can Create Jobs," *Atlantic*, May 1, 2015, http://www.theatlantic.com/business/archive/2015/05/actually-immigration-can-create-jobs/391997/ [accessed December 1, 2016]).

16. Dana Goldstein, "America: This Is Your Future," *Politico*, November 30, 2016, http://www.politico.com/agenda/story/2016/11/political-future-of-america-generations-diversity-tensions-000235 (accessed December 1, 2016).

17. Marcus Noland, Gary Clyde Hufbauer, and Tyler Moran, "Assessing Trade Agendas in the US Presidential Campaign," Peterson Institute for International Economics, September 2016, https://piie.com/publications/piie-briefings/assessing-trade-agendas-us-presidential-campaign (accessed October 30, 2016).

18. National Academies, *Integration of Immigrants*, p. 371.

19. "Three-in-Ten US Jobs Are Held by the Self-Employed and the Workers They Hire," Pew Research Center, October 22, 2015.

CHAPTER ONE: ELECTIONS MATTER . . . CULTURE MATTERS MORE

1. "Constantino Brumidi: Artist of the Capitol," *US Capitol*, https://www.visit thecapitol.gov/sites/default/files/documents/content/brochure/2505/constantino-brumidi -artist-the-capitol-en.pdf (accessed September 3, 2016).

2. Ali Noorani, "US Immigration System at Its Worst," *Boston Globe*, March 9, 2007, http://archive.boston.com/news/globe/editorial_opinion/oped/articles/2007/03/09/ us_immigration_system_at_its_worst/ (accessed July 27, 2016).

3. Thom File and Sarah Crissey, "Voting and Registration in the Election of November 2008," United States Census, July 2012, https://www.census.gov/prod/2010 pubs/p20-562.pdf (accessed July 28, 2016).

4. Mark Hugo Lopez, "The Hispanic Vote in the 2008 Election," Pew Research Center, November 7, 2008, http://www.pewhispanic.org/2008/11/05/the-hispanic-vote-in -the-2008-election/ (accessed July 28, 2016).

5. Doris Meissner, Donald M. Kerwin, Muzaffar Chisti, and Claire Bergeron, "Immigration Enforcement in the United States: The Rise of a Formidable Machinery," Migration Policy Institute, January 2013, file:///C:/Users/anoorani/Downloads/pillars -reportinbrief.pdf (accessed December 3, 2016); Mark Hugo Lopez, "The Hispanic Vote in the 2008 Election," Pew Research Center, November 7, 2008, http://www.pewhispanic .org/2008/11/05/the-hispanic-vote-in-the-2008-election/ (accessed July 28, 2016).

6. Tip O'Neill, *All Politics Is Local: And Other Rules of the Game* (Holbrook, MA: Adams Media Corporation, 1995).

7. Ann Morse, "Arizona's Immigration Enforcement Laws," National Conference of State Legislatures, July 28, 2011, http://www.ncsl.org/research/immigration/analysis -of-arizonas-immigration-law.aspx (accessed July 28, 2016).

8. Bureau of Labor Statistics, "Databases, Tables & Calculators by Subject," http:// data.bls.gov/timeseries/LNS14000000 (accessed December 1, 2016).

9. "A Long Walk for a Cause," *New York Times*, http://www.nytimes.com/2010/04/ 29/us/politics/29students.html (accessed December 3, 2016).

10. Jorge Ramos, in discussion with the author, May 9, 2016.

11. "About," Trail of Dreams, http://trail2010.org/about/ (accessed September 3, 2016).

12. Carlos Roa, "I Am a 'Dreamer.' I Walked 1,500 Miles for the Right to Stay in America," *Guardian*, April 12, 2016, https://www.theguardian.com/commentisfree/2016/ apr/12/dreamer-walked-1500-miles-right-stay-america (accessed June 5, 2016).

13. Ramos, in discussion with the author.

14. Brian Montopoli, "Lt. Dan Choi Arrested at White House during Gay Rights Rally," CBS News, March 18, 2010, http://www.cbsnews.com/news/lt-dan-choi-arrested -at-white-house-during-gay-rights-rally/ (accessed September 8, 2016).

15. Ibid.

16. N. C. Aizenman, "Broad Coalition Packs Mall to Urge Overhaul of Immigration Laws," sec. Politics, *Washington Post*, March 22, 2010, http://www.washingtonpost.com/wp-dyn/content/article/2010/03/21/AR2010032100956.html (accessed September 3, 2016).

17. Paul Kane, "'Tea Party' Protesters Accused of Spitting on Lawmaker, Using Slurs," *Washington Post*, March 21, 2010, http://www.washingtonpost.com/wp-dyn/content/article/2010/03/20/AR2010032002556.html (accessed October 29, 2016).

18. Lawrence Downes, "Two Rallies," *New York Times*, March 22, 2010, http://mobile.nytimes.com/2010/03/23/opinion/23tue4.html?referer= (accessed September 3, 2016).

19. Ramos, in discussion with the author.

20. Ibid.

21. Robert Farley, "Gov. Jan Brewer Talks of Beheadings in the Arizona Desert," PolitiFact, September 8, 2010, http://www.politifact.com/truth-o-meter/statements/2010/sep/08/jan-brewer/gov-jan-brewer-talks-beheadings-th-arizona-desert/ (accessed September 3, 2016).

22. Ibid.

23. Dan Gilgoff, "New Force for Broad Immigration Reform: Conservative Evangelicals," CNN, May 10, 2010, http://www.cnn.com/2010/POLITICS/05/10/immigration.evangelicals/index.html (accessed September 3, 2016).

24. Richard Land, "A Moral and Just Response to the Immigration Crisis," *Christian Post*, May 17, 2010, http://www.christianpost.com/news/a-moral-and-just-response-to-the-immigration-crisis-45196/ (accessed September 8, 2016).

25. "On the Crisis of Illegal Immigration," Southern Baptist Convention, 2006, http://www.sbc.net/resolutions/1157 (accessed September 3, 2016).

26. "Colorado Senate Profile," *New York Times*, December 10, 2010, http://elections.nytimes.com/2010/senate/colorado (accessed September 6, 2016).

27. "Latinos in the 2010 Elections: Colorado," Pew Research Center, October 15, 2010, http://www.pewhispanic.org/2010/10/15/latinos-in-the-2010-elections-colorado/ (accessed September 3, 2016).

28. Ken Buck, "Ken Buck on Immigration," On the Issues, 2010, http://www.ontheissues.org/International/Ken_Buck_Immigration.htm (accessed September 3, 2016).

29. "Colorado 2010 Results," Latino Decisions, 2010, http://www.latinodecisions.com/blog/recent-polls/colorado-2010-results/ (accessed September 3, 2016).

30. Kyle B. Hansen, "Reid Calling for Comprehensive Immigration Reform This Year: Rally Draws Thousands to Urge Changes in Federal Law," *Las Vegas Sun*, April 10, 2010, http://lasvegassun.com/news/2010/apr/10/reid-calling-immigration-reform-year/ (accessed October 29, 2010).

31. Dan Amira, "Sharron Angle Tells Hispanic Students That They Might Be Asian," *New York Magazine*, October 18, 2010, http://nymag.com/daily/intelligencer/2010/10/sharron_angle_tells_hispanic_s.html? (accessed September 3, 2016).

32. "Latinos in the 2010 Elections: Nevada," Pew Research Center, October 15, 2010, http://www.pewhispanic.org/2010/10/15/latinos-in-the-2010-elections-nevada/ (accessed September 3, 2016).

33. Ramos, in discussion with the author.

34. "Nevada 2010 Results," Latino Decisions, http://www.latinodecisions.com/blog/recent-polls/nevada-2010-results/ (accessed September 3, 2016).

35. Mahwish Khan, "Latino Firewall in the West Saves Senate for Democrats," America's Voice, November 3, 2010, http://americasvoice.org/press_releases/latino_firewall_in_the_west_saves_senate_for_democrats/ (accessed September 3, 2016).

36. Nate Silver, "Did Polls Underestimate Democrats' Latino Vote?" *New York Times*, November 3, 2010, http://fivethirtyeight.blogs.nytimes.com/2010/11/03/did-polls-underestimate-democrats-latino-vote/ (accessed September 3, 2016).

37. Edward Schumacher-Matos, "What Democrats Owe Latinos: Pass the Dream Act," *Washington Post*, November 19, 2010, http://www.washingtonpost.com/wp-dyn/content/article/2010/11/18/AR2010111803068.html (accessed September 3, 2016).

38. Julianne Hing, "DREAM Act Fails in Senate, 55 to 41," New American Media, December 18, 2010, http://newamericamedia.org/2010/12/obama-there-was-no-reason-for-senate-to-reject-dream-act.php (accessed September 8, 2016).

39. Jordan Fabian, "Jon Kyl, Kay Bailey Hutchinson Unveil Alternative to DREAM Act," ABC News, November 27, 2012, http://abcnews.go.com/ABC_Univision/Politics/republican-senators-introduce-alternative-dream-act-bill/story?id=17820394 (accessed September 8, 2016).

40. ProPublica, "Senate Vote 278:—Fails to Advance DREAM Act," December 18, 2010, https://projects.propublica.org/represent/votes/111/senate/2/278/?nyt=true (accessed September 3, 2016).

41. ProPublica, "Senate Vote 281:—Repeals 'Don't Ask, Don't Tell,'" December 18, 2010, https://projects.propublica.org/represent/votes/111/senate/2/281/?nyt=true (accessed September 3, 2016).

CHAPTER TWO: UTAH'S HIT LIST

1. Paul Mero, in discussion with the author, April 5, 2016.

2. "2010 Census Population of Uvalda, GA," Census Viewer, http://censusviewer.com/city/GA/Uvalda/2010 (accessed July 7, 2016).

3. Mero, in discussion with the author.

4. Ann Morse, "Arizona's Immigration Enforcement Laws," National Conference of State Legislatures, July 28, 2011, http://www.ncsl.org/research/immigration/analysis-of-arizonas-immigration-law.aspx (accessed June 29, 2016).

5. Jan Brewer, "Arizona Gov. Jan Brewer Explains Signing Nation's Toughest Illegal Immigration Law," *Los Angeles Times*, April 23, 2010, http://latimesblogs.latimes .com/washington/2010/04/jan-brewer-arizona-illegal-immigration.html (accessed June 26, 2016); Mero, in discussion with the author.

6. Rich Stolz, in discussion with the author, April 18, 2016.

7. "Russell Pearce," *Ballotpedia*, https://ballotpedia.org/Russell_Pearce (accessed July 18, 2016).

8. "Mayor & Council," Mesa AZ, 2016, http://www.mesaaz.gov/city-hall/mayor -council (accessed October 25, 2016).

9. "Timeline: SB 1070 History," *Arizona Republic*, April 22, 2012, http://archive .azcentral.com/news/politics/articles/20120422sb0170-history.html (accessed June 29, 2016).

10. "Pearce Claims Mormon Blessing," *AZ Central*, http://archive.azcentral.com/ video/1215608827001 (accessed July 6, 2016).

11. Lee Davidson, "Utah's Latino Population Skyrockets 78% in 10 Years," *Salt Lake Tribune*, February 26, 2011, http://archive.sltrib.com/story.php?ref=/sltrib/home/ 51307553-76/percent-utah-latino-population.html.csp (accessed July 24, 2016).

12. Ibid.

13. "Salt Lake City," Utah Community Data Project, November 18, 2013, http:// ucdp.utah.edu/reports/Place/Demographic_Trends/Demographics_Trends_Salt_Lake _City_city_67000.pdf (accessed July 23, 2016).

14. Jesse McKinley and Kirk Johnson, "Mormons Tipped Scale in Ban of Gay Marriage," *New York Times*, November 14, 2008, http://www.nytimes.com/2008/11/15/us/ politics/15marriage.html?_r=1 (accessed October 25, 2016).

15. "Growth of the Church," Church of Jesus Christ of Latter-day Saints, http:// www.mormonnewsroom.org/topic/church-growth (accessed July 25, 2016).

16. "Mormons," Pew Research Center, 2016, http://www.pewforum.org/religious -landscape-study/religious-tradition/mormon/ (accessed July 25, 2016).

17. Ibid.

18. Michael Otterson, in discussion with the author, April 4, 2016.

19. Ibid.

20. McKinley and Johnson, "Gay Marriage."

21. Michael Otterson and Michael Purdy, in discussion with the author, April 4, 2016.

22. Natalie Gochnour, in discussion with the author, April 5, 2016.

23. Mero, in discussion with the author, April 5, 2016.

24. Ibid.

25. Jason Mathis, in discussion with the author, April 4, 2016.

26. Ibid.

27. Ibid.

28. Lee Davidson et al., "Herbert Calls for Investigation into List of 1,300 Identified

Illegal Immigrants," *Deseret News*, July 13, 2010, http://www.deseretnews.com/article/700047867/Herbert-calls-for-investigation-into-list-of-1300-identified-as-illegal-immigrants.html?pg=all (accessed June 20, 2016).

29. Ed Pilkington, "Utah Firing Squad Executes Death Row Inmate," *Guardian*, June 18, 2010, https://www.theguardian.com/world/2010/jun/18/firing-squad-executes-death-row-inmate (accessed June 30, 2016).

30. Ibid.

31. CNN Wire Staff, "Utah Launches Investigation of Leak of Immigrants' Information," CNN, July 22, 2010, http://www.cnn.com/2010/US/07/22/utah.attorney.general/ (accessed July 1, 2016).

32. Lane Beattie, in discussion with the author, April 5, 2016.

33. Mero, in discussion with the author, April 5, 2016.

34. "'Utah Compact' Urges Guidelines for Immigration Discussion," *KSL*, November 11, 2010, http://www.ksl.com/?nid=148&sid=13237741 (accessed July 1, 2016).

35. "Read the Utah Compact," Utah Compact, November 11, 2010, http://www.utahcompact.com/read-the-utah-compact (accessed October 25, 2016).

36. "'Utah Compact.'"

37. Chris Burbank, in discussion with the author, April 4, 2016.

38. Ibid.

39. "Church Supports Principles of *Utah Compact* on Immigration," Church of Jesus Christ of Latter-day Saints, November 11, 2010, http://www.mormonnewsroom.org/article/church-supports-principles-of-utah-compact-on-immigration (accessed July 6, 2016).

40. Ibid.

41. Michael Otterson, in discussion with the author, April 4, 2016.

42. Ibid.

43. "The Utah Compact," *New York Times*, December 4, 2010, http://www.nytimes.com/2010/12/05/opinion/05sun1.html?_r=1 (accessed June 26, 2016).

44. Ginger Rough, "Group Launches Recall Effort against Sen. Pearce," *Arizona Republic*, January 27, 2011, http://archive.azcentral.com/news/election/azelections/articles/2011/01/27/20110127arizona-recall-drive-against-russell-pearce.html (accessed July 6, 2016).

45. Stephen Lemons, "Russell Pearce Recall Paperwork Filed by Anti-Pearce Group," *Phoenix New Times*, January 27, 2011, http://www.phoenixnewtimes.com/blogs/russell-pearce-recall-paperwork-filed-by-anti-pearce-group-6502455 (accessed July 6, 2016).

46. "Pearce Claims Mormon Blessing," *AZ Central*, http://archive.azcentral.com/video/1215608827001 (accessed July 6, 2016).

47. "Pearce Claims Mormon Blessing."

48. Stephen Lemons, "Russell Pearce Seems Incapable of Telling the Truth, Even about His Own Religion," *Phoenix New Times*, March 29, 2012, http://www.phoenix

newtimes.com/news/russell-pearce-seems-incapable-of-telling-the-truth-even-about-his
-own-religion-6452820 (accessed October 25, 2016).

49. Ibid.

50. "Russell Pearce Recall, Arizona State Legislature," *Ballotpedia*, https://ballotpedia
.org/Russell_Pearce_recall,_Arizona_State_Legislature_(2011) (accessed July 6, 2016).

51. Gary Nelson, "Jerry Lewis Urging Focus on Moderate Immigration Bill,"
Arizona Republic, November 15, 2011, http://archive.azcentral.com/news/articles/2011/
11/11/20111111jerry-lewis-focus-moderate-migrant-bill.html (accessed July 6, 2016).

52. Ibid.

53. Carly M. Springer, "30 Things You Didn't Know about the Conference Center,"
LDS Living, http://www.ldsliving.com/30-Things-You-Didn-t-Know-about-the
-Conference-Center/s/76671 (accessed July 26, 2016).

54. Kelsey Shwab, "What It's Like to Play the Organ for the Mormon Tabernacle
Choir," *Deseret News*, July 8, 2015, http://www.deseretnews.com/article/865632205/
What-its-like-to-play-the-organ-for-the-Mormon-Tabernacle-Choir.html?pg=all (accessed
June 26, 2016).

55. "Donald Trump Calls for Barring Muslims from Entering US," *New York Times*,
December 7, 2015, http://www.nytimes.com/politics/first-draft/2015/12/07/donald-trump
-calls-for-banning-muslims-from-entering-u-s/?_r=0 (accessed December 3, 2016).

56. "Church Points to Joseph Smith's Statements on Religious Freedom, Pluralism,"
news release, Church of Jesus Christ of Latter-day Saints, December 8, 2015, http://www
.mormonnewsroom.org/article/church-statement-religious-freedom-pluralism (accessed
July 26, 2016).

57. Ibid.

58. Natalie Gochnour, in discussion with the author, April 5, 2016.

59. "Mormons Stepping Up Aid to Refugees," news release, Church of Jesus Christ
of Latter-day Saints, September 28, 2015, http://www.mormonnewsroom.org.uk/article/
mormons-stepping-up-aid-to-refugees (accessed July 2, 2016).

60. "General Authorities and General Officers: Elder Patrick Kearon," Church of
Jesus Christ of Latter-day Saints, https://www.lds.org/church/leader/patrick-kearon
?lang=eng (accessed July 25, 2016).

61. Sarah Jane Weaver, "October 2015 LDS First Presidency Letter on Refugees,"
Deseret News, March 26, 2016, http://www.deseretnews.com/article/865650963/LDS
-First-Presidency-letter-on-refugees.html?pg=all (accessed July 2, 2016); "Church
Members Encouraged to Assist Refugees," news release, Church of Jesus Christ of
Latter-day Saints, October 29, 2015, http://www.mormonnewsroom.org/article/church
-members-encouraged-assist-refugees (accessed July 2, 2016).

62. Ibid.

63. Linda K. Burton, "I Was a Stranger," Church of Jesus Christ of Latter-day

Saints, April 2016, https://www.lds.org/general-conference/2016/04/i-was-a-stranger
?lang=eng (accessed June 26, 2016).

64. Ibid.

65. Patrick Kearon, "Refuge from the Storm," Church of Jesus Christ of Latter-day
Saints, April 2016, https://www.lds.org/general-conference/2016/04/refuge-from-the
-storm?lang=eng (accessed July 3, 2016).

66. Ibid.

67. Ibid.

68. "President Uchtdorf Moments from April 2016 General Conference," YouTube
video, 6:04, posted by "Troy Terry," April 27, 2016, https://www.youtube.com/watch
?v=FSzn1DM4oDA (accessed July 26, 2016).

69. Ibid.

70. Michael Otterson, in discussion with the author, April 4, 2016.

71. Sarah Jane Weaver, "President Uchtdorf Visits Refugees; Presents $3 Million
from LDS Church to Help Refugees," *Deseret News*, July 25, 2016, http://www.deseret
news.com/article/865658706/President-Uchtdorf-visits-refugees-presents-3-million-from
-LDS-Church-to-help-refugees.html?pg=all (accessed July 26, 2016).

72. Gerry Avant, "President Uchtdorf Represents the Church in White House
Meeting," Church of Jesus Christ of Latter-day Saints, March 18, 2013, https://www
.lds.org/church/news/president-uchtdorf-represents-the-church-in-white-house-meeting
?lang=eng (accessed July 3, 2016).

73. Tad Walch, "LDS Church Reaffirms Stance on Immigration," *Deseret News*,
April 15, 2014, http://www.deseretnews.com/article/865601049/LDS-Church-reaffirms
-stance-on-immigration.html?pg=all (accessed July 3, 2016).

74. Joseph Smith, "Chapter 24: Leading in the Lord's Way," Church of Jesus Christ
of Latter-day Saints, https://www.lds.org/manual/teachings-joseph-smith/chapter-24
?lang=eng#3-36481_000_028 (accessed July 26, 2016).

75. Purdy, in discussion with the author.

76. "Young, Tolerant, and Surprising: Some Lessons in Practical Conservatism from
the Desert West," *Economist*, May 2, 2015, http://www.economist.com/news/united
-states/21650153-some-lessons-practical-conservatism-desert-west-young-tolerant-and
-surprising (accessed July 26, 2016).

CHAPTER THREE: SOUL FREEDOM

1. Ed Stetzer, "Some SBC Reflections:—A Short Series," The Exchange, June 20,
2016, http://www.christianitytoday.com/edstetzer/2016/june/reflections-on-sbc-annual
-meeting.html (accessed July 15, 2016).

2. Daniel Woodman, "Messenger Increase Predicted for St. Louis SBC," *Baptist Press*, June 1, 2016, http://www.bpnews.net/46958/messenger-increase-predicted-for-st -louis-sbc (accessed August 5, 2016).

3. Gerald Harris, "Do Muslims Really Qualify for Religious Freedom Benefits?" Christian Index, June 6, 2016, http://christianindex.org/muslims-really-qualify-religious -freedom-benefits/ (accessed July 15, 2016).

4. "Dr. Russell Moore Responds to Question at SBC16," YouTube video, 2:14, posted by "Philip Meade," June 15, 2016, https://www.youtube.com/watch?v=BuGx OE0Vy1g (accessed July 15, 2016).

5. "Armorel ESEA District Report," Armorel School District, September 2, 2016, http://armoreltigers.org/postings_33_2117454067.pdf (accessed October 16, 2016).

6. "Armorel High School," *US News and World Report*, http://www.usnews.com/ education/best-high-schools/arkansas/districts/armorel-school-district/armorel-high -school-1231/student-body (accessed October 16, 2016).

7. "Dr. Russell Moore Responds to Question."

8. Ibid.

9. Ibid.

10. Matthew Soerens, Jenny Hwang Yang, and Leith Anderson, *Welcoming the Stranger: Justice, Compassion, & Truth in the Immigration Debate* (repr.; Downers Grove, Ill: IVP Books, 2009), pp. 82–83.

11. "America's Changing Religious Landscape: Christians Decline Sharply as Share of Population; Unaffiliated and Other Faiths Continue to Grow," Pew Research Center, May 12, 2015, http://www.pewforum.org/2015/05/12/americas-changing-religious -landscape (accessed July 16, 2016).

12. Ibid.

13. Robert P. Jones, *The End of White Christian America* (New York: Simon & Schuster, 2016), pp. 49–51.

14. Ibid.

15. Ibid.

16. "Chapter 3: Demographic Profiles of Religious Groups," Pew Research Center, May 12, 2015, http://www.pewforum.org/2015/05/12/chapter-3-demographic-profiles-of -religious-groups/ (accessed August 3, 2016).

17. Laurie Goodstein, "Donald Trump Reveals Evangelical Rifts That Could Shape Politics for Years," *New York Times*, October 17, 2016, http://www.nytimes.com/2016/ 10/17/us/donald-trump-evangelicals-republican-vote.html?_r=1 (accessed October 17, 2016).

18. Daniel Marans and Lydia O'Connor, "Here Are 13 Examples of Donald Trump Being Racist," *Huffington Post*, October 10, 2016, http://www.huffingtonpost.com/entry/donald-trump -racist-examples_us_56d47177e4b03260bf777e83 (accessed December 7, 2016).

19. Bob Smeitana, "2016 Election Exposes Evangelical Divides," Lifeway Re-

search, October 14, 2016, http://lifewayresearch.com/2016/10/14/2016-election-exposes
-evangelical-divide/ (accessed October 17, 2016).

20. Goodstein, "Donald Trump Reveals."

21. Smeitana, "2016 Election Exposes Evangelical Divides."

22. Barrett Duke, in discussion with the author, July 6, 2016.

23. Ibid.

24. Ibid.

25. Ibid.

26. Ibid.

27. Ibid.

28. Jo Anne Lyon, in discussion with the author, February 23, 2016.

29. Ibid.

30. Jeffrey Walton, "Wesleyan Church Reports Record Attendance," Juicy
Ecumenism, September 8, 2015, https://juicyecumenism.com/2015/09/08/wesleyan
-church-reports-record-attendance/ (accessed July 17, 2016).

31. Ibid.

32. Ibid.

33. Ibid.

34. "QuickFacts: Logansport City, Indiana," US Census, http://www.census.gov/
quickfacts/table/PST045215/1844658 (accessed July 31, 2016); "Indiana Presidential
Primary Results by District," *Associated Press*, May 3, 2016, http://www.wfyi.org/news/
articles/indiana-presidential-primary-results-by-district (accessed July 31, 2016).

35. Lyons, in discussion with the author.

36. "We Serve: The Bridge, Logansport, Indiana," The Wesleyan Church, https://
www.wesleyan.org/3062/we-serve-the-bridge-logansport-indiana (accessed July 17, 2016).

37. Ibid.

38. "Chapter 3: Demographic Profiles of Religious Groups," Pew Research Center,
May 12, 2015, http://www.pewforum.org/2015/05/12/chapter-3-demographic-profiles-of
-religious-groups/ (accessed July 31, 2016).

39. "Archbishop Thomas Wenski," Archdiocese of Miami, http://www.miamiarch
.org/CatholicDiocese.php?op=ArchbishopThomasWenski (accessed July 22, 2016).

40. Archbishop Thomas Wenski, in discussion with the author, February 29, 2016.

41. Ibid.

42. Ibid.

43. George de Lama, "Florida Bracing for New Wave of Cuban Immigrants,"
Chicago Tribune, April 14, 1985, http://articles.chicagotribune.com/1985-04-14/news/
8501210598_1_mariel-refugees-new-immigration (accessed December 7, 2016).

44. Ibid.

45. Ibid.

46. "The Miami Mirror: Cubans on the Other Side of the Water Are Slowly Changing Too," *Economist*, March 24, 2012, http://www.economist.com/node/21550419 (accessed July 31, 2016).

47. Chiamaka Nwosu and Jeanne Batalova, "Haitian Immigrants in the United States," Migration Policy Institute, May 29, 2014, http://www.migrationpolicy.org/article/haitian-immigrants-united-states (accessed July 31, 2016).

48. Rebeca Piccardo, "The Archbishop Biker: Thomas Wenski Leads Poker Run across Miami-Dade," *Miami Herald*, February 1, 2015, http://www.miamiherald.com/news/local/article8901071.html (accessed July 26, 2016).

49. "The Red Mass," All Events.in, March 11, 2016, https://allevents.in/key%20west/the-red-mass/1721032754820020 (accessed July 18, 2016).

50. Thomas Wenski, "We Gather Here Today to Ask God for Wisdom," (homily), Archdiocese of Miami, March 11, 2016, http://www.miamiarch.org/CatholicDiocese.php?op=Article_We+gather+here+today+to+ask+God+for+wisdom#.VugIkqYKdUk.mailto (accessed July 18, 2016).

51. Ibid.

52. Adrian Edwards, "Global Forced Displacement Hits Record High," United Nations High Commission on Refugees, June 20, 2016, http://www.unhcr.org/en-us/news/latest/2016/6/5763b65a4/global-forced-displacement-hits-record-high.html (accessed October 18, 2016).

53. Wenski, in discussion with the author.

54. Stephan Bauman, in discussion with the author, May 10, 2016.

55. Ibid.

56. "History of the US Refugee Resettlement Program," Refugee Council USA, http://www.rcusa.org/history (accessed July 31, 2016).

57. Peter Finn, Carol D. Leonnig, and Will Englund, "Tsarnaev Brothers' Homeland Was War-Torn Chechnya," *Washington Post*, April 19, 2013, https://www.washingtonpost.com/politics/details-emerge-on-suspected-boston-bombers/2013/04/19/ef2c2566-a8e4-11e2-a8e2-5b98cb59187f_story.html (accessed August 3, 2016).

58. Ibid.

59. "Angela Merkel Attacked Over Crying Refugee Girl," BBC, July 17, 2015, http://www.bbc.com/news/world-europe-33555619 (accessed August 5, 2016).

60. Joe Parkinson and David George-Cosh, "Image of Drowned Syrian Boy Echoes around World: Details Emerge about 3-Year-Old from Syria Who Died Off Turkish Coast," *Wall Street Journal*, September 3, 2015, http://www.wsj.com/articles/image-of-syrian-boy-washed-up-on-beach-hits-hard-1441282847 (accessed August 5, 2016).

61. Heather Horn, "The Staggering Scale of Germany's Refugee Project," *Atlantic*, September 12, 2015, http://www.theatlantic.com/international/archive/2015/09/germany-merkel-refugee-asylum/405058/ (accessed August 5, 2016).

62. Daniel Cox and Robert P. Jones, "Nearly Half of Americans Worried That They or Their Family Will Be a Victim of Terrorism," Public Religion Research Institute, December 10, 2015, http://www.prri.org/research/survey-nearly-half-of-americans -worried-that-they-or-their-family-will-be-a-victim-of-terrorism/ (accessed July 17, 2016).

63. Molly Ball, "Donald Trump and the Politics of Fear: Trump's Candidacy Relies on the Power of Fear. It Could Be the Only Way for Him to Win," *Atlantic*, September 2, 2016, http://www.theatlantic.com/politics/archive/2016/09/donald-trump-and-the-politics -of-fear/498116/ (accessed October 17, 2016).

64. Bauman, in discussion with the author.

65. Donald Trump, "Donald J. Trump Statement on Preventing Muslim Immi-gration," Donald J. Trump for President, December 7, 2015, https://www.donaldjtrump .com/press-releases/donald-j.-trump-statement-on-preventing-muslim-immigration (accessed July 30, 2016).

66. Ibid.

67. Ibid.

68. Ibid.

69. Ibid.

70. Ibid.

71. Lynne Hybels, "About Refugees: A Preacher, a Professor, a Rock Star & Me," Lynne Hybels (blog), April 29, 2016, https://www.lynnehybels.com/hope-for-refugees/ (accessed July 19, 2016).

72. Russell Moore, in discussion with the author, March 26, 2016.

73. Ibid.

74. Ibid.

75. Ibid.

76. Ibid.

77. Ibid.

78. Leith Anderson and Galen Carey, *Faith in the Voting Booth: Practical Wisdom for Voting Well* (Grand Rapids: Zondervan, 2016), p. 14.

79. Bob Smeitana, "Bible Influences Only 1 in 10 Evangelicals on Immigration Reform: Christians Are Divided over Whether Immigrants Are Drain on Resources or an Opportunity to Share Jesus," *Christianity Today*, March 11, 2015, http://www .christianitytoday.com/gleanings/2015/march/bible-influences-only-1-in-10-evangelicals -views-on-immigra.html (accessed October 17, 2016).

80. Anderson and Carey, *Faith in the Voting Booth*.

81. Brandon Darby, "Thousands of Illegal Immigrants Bused across US into Cities," *Breitbart News*, June 30, 2014, http://www.breitbart.com/texas/2014/06/30/thousands-of -illegal-immigrants-bused-across-us/ (accessed December 7, 2016).

82. Matt Hansen and Mark Boster, "Protesters in Murrieta Block Detainee's Buses

in Tense Standoff," *LA Times*, July 1, 2014, http://www.latimes.com/local/lanow/la-me-ln
-immigrants-murrieta-20140701-story.html (accessed July 19, 2016); Daily Mail Reporter
and the Associated Press, "Protesters Block a THIRD Bus Load of Illegal Immigrants
from Being Transferred Further Inland in Confrontational Scenes at Detention Center,
Amid Reports Riot Police Could be Brought in to Deal with Showdown," *Daily Mail*,
July 7, 2014, http://www.dailymail.co.uk/news/article-2683998/Protesters-block-THIRD
-bus-load-illegal-immigrants-transferred-inland-confrontational-scenes-detention-center
-amid-reports-riot-police-brought-deal-showdown.html (accessed July 19, 2016); Marty
Graham, "Anti-Immigration Protesters Block Undocumented Migrants in California,"
Reuters, July 2, 2014, http://www.reuters.com/article/us-usa-immigration-california
-protesters-idUSKBN0F65L720140702 (accessed July 19, 2016).

83. Nathaniel Lubin, "President Obama Welcomes 25 New American Citizens
of the Fourth of July," White House, July 4, 2014, https://www.whitehouse.gov/
blog/2014/07/04/president-obama-welcomes-25-new-american-citizens-fourth-july
(accessed September 20, 2016).

84. Barack Obama, "Remarks by the President at Naturalization Ceremony for
Service Members and Military Spouses," White House, July 4, 2014, https://www
.whitehouse.gov/the-press-office/2014/07/04/remarks-president-naturalization-ceremony
-servicemembers-and-military-sp (accessed July 19, 2016).

85. Russell Moore, "The Road to Jericho and the Border Crisis," Russell Moore,
July 13, 2014, http://www.russellmoore.com/2014/07/13/the-road-to-jericho-and-the
-border-crisis/ (accessed July 19, 2016).

86. Melissa Barnhart, "Illegal Immigrant Children Are 'Created in the Image of
God,' Issue Is Not Just Political, Says Russell Moore after Touring Texas Facilities,"
Christian Post, July 23, 2014, http://www.christianpost.com/news/illegal-immigrant
-children-are-created-in-the-image-of-god-issue-is-not-just-political-says-russell-moore
-after-touring-texas-facilites-123710/ (accessed July 19, 2016).

87. Michael Paulson, "US Religious Leaders Embrace Cause of Immigrant
Children," *New York Times*, July 23, 2014, http://www.nytimes.com/2014/07/24/us/us
-religious-leaders-embrace-cause-of-immigrant-children.html (accessed July 19, 2016).

88. Moore, in discussion with the author.

CHAPTER FOUR: AS SOUTH CAROLINA GOES, SO GOES AMERICA

1. "North Greenville University: Rankings," College Factual, http://www
.collegefactual.com/colleges/north-greenville-university/rankings/ (accessed September
21, 2016).

2. Victor Prieto, in discussion with the author, March 2, 2016.

3. Richard Lapper, "Venezuela and the Rise of Chavez: A Background Discussion Paper," Council on Foreign Relations, November 22, 2005, http://www.cfr.org/venezuela/venezuela-rise-chavez-background-discussion-paper/p9269 (accessed December 10, 2016); Prieto, in discussion with the author, March 2, 2016.

4. Prieto, in discussion with the author.

5. Ibid.

6. Ibid.

7. Ibid.

8. Brenda J. Vander Mey and Ashley W. Harris, "Latino Populations in South Carolina, 1990–2002," *Clemson University*, January 2004, http://www.asph.sc.edu/cli/documents/vandermey%20working%20paper.pdf (accessed September 21, 2016).

9. National Council of La Raza, "Nationwide Growth in the Latino Population Is a Boon for the Country," in *Census 2010: Hispanics in the US 2011* (Washington, DC: National Council of La Raza, 2011).

10. Kripa Cooper-Lewter, "Latino Immigrant Families in South Carolina," Sisters of Charity Foundation of South Carolina, March 2013, http://sistersofcharitysc.com/wp-content/uploads/2014/04/Research-Brief-March-2013.pdf (accessed September 21, 2016).

11. "Toward a More Vibrant and Youthful Nation: Latino Children in the 2010 Census," National Council of La Raza, August 25, 2011, https://issuu.com/nclr/docs/latino_children_in_the_2010_census (accessed December 11, 2016).

12. Donald Schunk and Douglas Woodward, "A Profile of the Diversified South Carolina Economy," University of South Carolina, February 2000, http://moore.sc.edu/UserFiles/moore/Documents/Division%20of%20Research/Schunk&Woodward.pdf (accessed September 21, 2016).

13. Jason Specer, "Spartanburg Takes a Look Back at Landing BMW," *State*, July 13, 2014, http://www.thestate.com/news/business/article13868033.html (accessed September 21, 2016).

14. "BMW's Impact in South Carolina: Two Decades of Economic Development," *University of South Carolina*, December 2014, https://www.bmwusfactory.com/wp-content/uploads/2012/11/BMW-SC-Economic-Impact-2014.pdf (accessed September 21, 2016).

15. Betty Joyce Nash, "When South Carolina Met BMW: Behind the Deal That Brought a Halo Effect and Bavarian Meatloaf to Spartanburg," Federal Reserve Bank of Richmond, 2011, https://www.richmondfed.org/~/media/richmondfedorg/publications/research/region_focus/2011/q2/pdf/feature2.pdf (accessed September 21, 2016).

16. "Unemployment Rate: South Carolina (December 1990)," Gainesville, http://data.gainesville.com/unemployment/south-carolina/1990/december/ (accessed September 10, 2016).

17. Harold Smith, in discussion with the author, March 1, 2016.

18. Ibid.

19. Ibid.

20. Ibid.

21. "Population Demographics for Spartanburg County, South Carolina, in 2016 and 2015," *Suburban Stats*, https://suburbanstats.org/population/south-carolina/how-many -people-live-in-spartanburg-county (accessed September 22, 2016).

22. Chuck Bagwell, in discussion with the author, March 2, 2016.

23. Laura Barbas-Rhoden, in discussion with the author, March 2, 2016.

24. Bagwell, in discussion with the author.

25. Ibid.

26. Jana White, in discussion with the author, March 1, 2016.

27. Ibid.

28. Ibid.

29. Ibid.

30. Ibid.

31. Norma Blanton, in discussion with the author, March 3, 2016.

32. Ibid.

33. "Unauthorized Immigrant Population and Trends for States, Birth Countries and Regions," Pew Research Center, http://www.pewhispanic.org/interactives/unauthorized -trends/ (accessed December 11, 2016).

34. Ibid.

35. Blanton, in discussion with the author.

36. Bagwell, in discussion with the author.

37. Ibid.

38. Ibid.

39. Ibid.

40. Bagwell, in discussion with the author.

41. "Religious Landscape Study: Adults in South Carolina," Pew Research Center, http://www.pewforum.org/religious-landscape-study/state/south-carolina/ (accessed September 10, 2016).

42. Daniel Cox and Robert P. Jones, "The Religion and Politics of South Carolina: A State Portrait from PRRI's American Values Atlas," Public Religion Research Institute, February 15, 2016, http://www.prri.org/spotlight/the-religion-and-politics-of-south -carolina-a-state-portrait-from-prris-american-values-atlas/ (accessed December 11, 2016).

43. Thom Rainer, "2014 Update on the Largest Churches in the Southern Baptist Convention," Thom S. Rainer, July 12, 2014, http://thomrainer.com/2014/07/2014 -update-largest-churches-southern-baptist-convention/ (accessed September 22, 2016).

44. Steve Wise, in discussion with the author, March 1, 2016.

45. "Mission: MPACT," First Baptist Spartanburg, http://www.fbs.org/ministries/missions-mpact/ (accessed September 21, 2016).

46. Margaret N. O'Shea, "The Real 'Peach State' Is South Carolina," *T&D*, June 4, 2012, http://thetandd.com/business/the-real-peach-state-is-south-carolina/article_aacd1698-ab4f-11e1-9a60-001a4bcf887a.html (accessed September 10, 2016).

47. Kimmy LaMee, in discussion with the author, March 1, 2016.

48. Ibid.

49. Ibid.

50. Ibid.

51. Ibid.

52. Ibid.

53. Ibid.

54. Ibid.

55. Wise, in discussion with the author.

56. LaMee, in discussion with the author.

57. Ibid.

58. Ibid.

59. Derrick Smith, in discussion with the author, May 2, 2016.

60. Ibid.

61. Meghan Smith, in discussion with the author, May 2, 2016.

62. "About Us," Numbers USA, 2016, https://www.numbersusa.com/about (accessed September 10, 2016).

63. "S. 744, the Border Security, Economic Opportunity, and Immigration Modernization Act," National Immigration Forum, July 2, 2013, http://immigrationforum.org/blog/s-744-the-border-security-economic-opportunity-and-immigration-modernization-act/ (accessed December 11, 2016).

64. Benjy Sarlin, "Conservative Immigration Reformers Make Their Stand in South Carolina," *Talking Points Memo*, March 13, 2013, http://talkingpointsmemo.com/dc/conservative-immigration-reformers-make-their-stand-in-south-carolina (accessed September 10, 2016).

65. "Who We Are," Evangelical Immigration Table, http://evangelicalimmigrationtable.com/who-we-are/ (accessed December 11, 2016).

66. Tom Strode, "Evangelical Coalition Launches Immigration Ads," *Baptist Press*, March 14, 2013, http://www.bpnews.net/39883/evangelical-coalition-launches-immigration-ads (accessed September 10, 2016).

67. Hal Stevenson and Jim Goodroe, "Faith Commends a Kinder Look at Immigrants in Our Midst," *Post and Courier*, March 12, 2013, http://www.postandcourier.com/article/20130313/PC1002/130319741 (accessed September 21, 2016).

68. Mary Orndorff Troyan, "Spartanburg Baptist Minister Lobbies for Immigration Reform," *State*, June 13, 2013, http://www.thestate.com/living/religion/article14434268 .html (accessed September 21, 2016).

69. David Nakamura, "Evangelical Pastors Step Up Pro-Immigration Campaign," *Washington Post*, August 20, 2013, https://www.washingtonpost.com/news/post-politics/ wp/2013/08/20/evangelical-pastors-step-up-pro-immigration-campaign/ (accessed September 21, 2016).

70. Julia Preston, "GOP Congressman in South Carolina Takes a Risk with a Foray into Immigration," *New York Times*, February 21, 2014, http://www.nytimes.com/ 2014/02/22/us/politics/gop-congressman-in-south-carolina-takes-a-risk-with-a-foray-into -immigration.html?_r=1 (accessed September 21, 2014).

71. Napp Nazworth, "Evangelical Ads Changed Attitudes on Immigration, Study Finds," *Christian Post*, September 5, 2014, http://www.christianpost.com/news/ evangelical-ads-changed-attitudes-on-immigration-study-finds-125907/ (accessed December 11, 2016).

72. "The John Birch Society: Immigration," John Birch Society, http://www.jbs.org/ issues-pages/immigration (accessed December 11, 2016).

73. Richard Fausset, "Refugee Crisis in Syria Raises Fear in South Carolina," *New York Times*, September 25, 2015, http://www.nytimes.com/2015/09/26/us/refugee-crisis -in-syria-raises-fears-in-south-carolina.html (accessed September 21, 2016).

74. Ibid.

75. "Gov. Haley Asks State Department Not to Resettle Syrian Refugees in SC: No Syrian Refugees Have Been Brought to State," WYFF4, November 17, 2015, http://www .wyff4.com/news/sc-not-saying-no-to-refugees/36478326 (accessed September 10, 2016).

76. Tim Smith, "With More Refugees on the Way, Senators Push Restrictions," *Greenville Online*, January 19, 2016, http://www.greenvilleonline.com/story/news/ politics/2016/01/19/senators-begin-hearings-refugee-settlement-sc/78994016/ (accessed September 10, 2016).

77. Andrew Shain, "SC Senate Passes State Registry of Refugees," *State*, March 23, 2016, http://www.thestate.com/news/politics-government/politics-columns-blogs/the -buzz/article67809132.html (accessed September 10, 2016).

78. Alan Cross, "Is Religious Freedom Being Taken/Given Away in South Carolina?" Alan Cross Writes, February 2, 2016, http://alancrosswrites.com/is-religious -liberty-being-takengiven-away-in-south-carolina/ (accessed September 21, 2016).

79. Blanton, in discussion with the author.

80. Ibid.

CHAPTER FIVE: WE ARE ALL AFRAID

1. "The New Political Divide: Farewell, Left Versus Right. The Contest That Matters Now Is Open against Closed," *Economist*, July 30, 2016, http://www.economist.com/news/leaders/21702750-farewell-left-versus-right-contest-matters-now-open-against-closed-new (accessed August 8, 2016).

2. Michael S. Schmidt and Richard Pérez-Peña, "FBI Treating San Bernardino Attacks as Terrorism Case," *New York Times*, December 4, 2015, http://www.nytimes.com/2015/12/05/us/tashfeen-malik-islamic-state.html?_r=0 (accessed August 8, 2016).

3. Stephen Collinson, "Washington's Post-Shooting Ritual: Angry Words and Political Polarization," CNN, December 3, 2015, http://www.cnn.com/2015/12/03/politics/san-bernardino-shooting-2016-election-politics/index.html (accessed August 8, 2016).

4. Barack Obama, "Address to the Nation by the President," White House, December 6, 2015, https://www.whitehouse.gov/the-press-office/2015/12/06/address-nation-president (accessed August 8, 2016).

5. Ibid.

6. Donald Trump, "Donald J. Trump Statement on Preventing Muslim Immigration," Donald J. Trump for President, Inc., December 7, 2015, https://www.donaldjtrump.com/press-releases/donald-j.-trump-statement-on-preventing-muslim-immigration (accessed July 30, 2016).

7. Ben Kamisar, "Trump Calls for 'Shutdown' of Muslims Entering the US," *The Hill*, December 7, 2015, http://thehill.com/blogs/ballot-box/presidential-races/262348-trump-calls-for-shutdown-of-muslims-entering-us (accessed August 8, 2016).

8. Washington Post Staff, "Full Text: Donald Trump Announces a Presidential Bid," *Washington Post*, June 16, 2015, https://www.washingtonpost.com/news/post-politics/wp/2015/06/16/full-text-donald-trump-announces-a-presidential-bid/ (accessed August 3, 2016).

9. Ali Noorani, Facebook post, December 8, 2015, https://www.facebook.com/photo.php?fbid=10153647935870733&set=a.8903410732.32063.680280732&type=3&theater (accessed July 31, 2016).

10. Anthony Cave, "Is ISIS Crossing the US–Mexico border?" PolitiFact Arizona, March 10, 2016, http://www.politifact.com/arizona/statements/2016/mar/10/jeff-dewit/isis-crossing-us-mexico-border/ (accessed December 11, 2016).

11. Carma Hassan and Catherine E. Shoichet, "Arabic-Speaking Student Kicked Off Southwest Flight," CNN, April 18, 2016, http://www.cnn.com/2016/04/17/us/southwest-muslim-passenger-removed/ (accessed August 8, 2016); Ashley Fantz, Steve Almasy, and AnneClaire Stapleton, "Muslim Teen Ahmed Mohamed Creates Clock, Shows Teachers, Gets Arrested," CNN, September 16, 2015, http://www.cnn.com/2015/09/16/us/texas-student-ahmed-muslim-clock-bomb/index.html (accessed August 8, 2016).

12. "Anxiety, Nostalgia, and Mistrust: Findings from the 2015 American Values Survey," Public Religion Research Institute, November 17, 2015, http://www.prri.org/research/survey-anxiety-nostalgia-and-mistrust-findings-from-the-2015-american-values-survey/ (accessed July 31, 2016).

13. Besheer Mohamed, "A New Estimate of the US Muslim Population," Pew Research Center, January 6, 2016, http://www.pewresearch.org/fact-tank/2016/01/06/a-new-estimate-of-the-u-s-muslim-population/ (accessed August 8, 2016).

14. Stephen Piggot, "Is Breitbart.com Becoming the Media Arm of the 'Alt-Right'?" Southern Poverty Law Center, April 28, 2016, https://www.splcenter.org/hatewatch/2016/04/28/breitbartcom-becoming-media-arm-alt-right (accessed December 11, 2016); Thomas D. Williams, "Muslim Population in US to Double by 2050, Study Shows," *Breitbart News*, December 10, 2015, http://www.breitbart.com/big-government/2015/12/10/muslim-population-u-s-double-2050-study-shows/ (accessed August 8, 2016).

15. "The Future of World Religions: Population Growth Projections, 2010–2050," Pew Research Center, April 2, 2015, http://www.pewforum.org/2015/04/02/religious-projections-2010-2050/ (accessed August 8, 2016).

16. "New PRRI/Brookings Survey: Even before Orlando Shootings, Americans' Concerns Over Terrorism up Nearly 20 Points," Public Religion Research Institute, June 23, 2016, http://www.prri.org/press-release/new-prribrookings-survey-even-orlando-shootings-americans-concerns-terrorism-nearly-20-points/ (accessed July 31, 2016).

17. Ibid.

18. Ibid.

19. Matthew Yglesias, "New Poll: Voter Worries about Immigration Mostly Aren't about the Economy," *Vox*, July 6, 2016, http://www.vox.com/2016/7/6/12098622/immigration-worries-economy-security (accessed July 30, 2016).

20. Ibid.

21. Ibid.

22. Gregory Rodriguez, in discussion with the author, December 7, 2015.

23. Eric Lichtblau, "US Hate Crimes Surge 6%, Fueled by Attacks on Muslims," *New York Times*, November 14, 2016, http://www.nytimes.com/2016/11/15/us/politics/fbi-hate-crimes-muslims.html?_r=0 (accessed December 11, 2016).

24. Jelani Cobb, "Post-Election, Liberals Invoke States' Rights," *New Yorker*, November 28, 2016, http://www.newyorker.com/magazine/2016/11/28/post-election-liberals-invoke-states-rights (accessed December 11, 2016).

25. Martin Bashir and Max Culhane, "'America's Toughest Sheriff' Unapologetic about Tactics, Inmate Treatment," ABC News, December 14, 2009, http://abcnews.go.com/Nightline/sheriff-joe-arpaio-unapologetic-tactics-illegal-immigrant-crackdowns/story?id=9219341 (accessed December 12, 2016); Eddi Trevizo and Derek Cooley, "Inmates Marched to Segregated Area of Tent City," *Arizona Republic*, February 4, 2009,

http://archive.azcentral.com/community/phoenix/articles/2009/02/04/20090204abrk
-inmatesmarch0204-ON.html (accessed December 12, 2016).

26. "WorldNetDaily," Southern Poverty Law Center, https://www.splcenter.org/
fighting-hate/extremist-files/group/worldnetdaily (accessed December 12, 2016); Leo
Hohmann, "Exploding Muslim Immigration Overwhelms FBI," WorldNetDaily, July 17,
2015, http://www.wnd.com/2015/07/exploding-muslim-immigration-overwhelms-fbi/
(accessed December 12, 2016).

27. Richard C. Longworth, *Caught in the Middle: America's Heartland in the Age of
Globalism*, 1st ed. (New York: Bloomsbury USA, December 26, 2007).

28. Richard Longworth, in discussion with the author, February 2, 2016.

29. Ibid.

30. Ibid.

31. Greg Zoeller, in discussion with the author, February 21, 2016.

32. Ibid.

33. Ibid.

34. Ibid.

35. Ibid.

36. Ibid.

37. "Office of the Indiana Attorney General," State of Indiana, http://www.in.gov/
attorneygeneral/ (accessed December 11, 2016).

38. "Featured Indiana Compact Signatories," The Indiana Compact, http://www
.indianacompact.com/supporters/featured/ (accessed August 1, 2016).

39. "Religious Composition of Adults in Indiana," Pew Research Forum, 2016, http://
www.pewforum.org/religious-landscape-study/state/indiana/ (accessed August 1, 2016).

40. Zoeller, in discussion with the author.

41. Ibid.

42. Associated Press, "Federal Judge Blocks New Indiana Immigration Law," Fox
News, June 24, 2011, http://www.foxnews.com/politics/2011/06/24/federal-judge-blocks-new
-indiana-immigration-law.html (accessed December 11, 2016); "Indiana Backs Off Defense of
New Immigration Law," *Associated Press*, July 31, 2012, http://www.ibj.com/articles/35840-
indiana-backs-off-defense-of-new-immigration-law (accessed December 12, 2016).

43. Gardiner Harris, David E. Sanger, and David M. Herszenhorn, "Obama Increased
Number of Syrian Refugees for US Resettlement to 10,000," *New York Times*, September
10, 2015, http://www.nytimes.com/2015/09/11/world/middleeast/obama-directs
-administration-to-accept-10000-syrian-refugees.html?_r=0 (accessed August 19, 2016).

44. Michael C. Bender, "Jeb Bush Splits with Republicans over Syrian Refugees,"
Bloomberg, November 17, 2015, http://www.bloomberg.com/politics/articles/2015-11-17/
bush-splits-with-republicans-over-syrian-refugees (accessed August 12, 2016).

45. Hunter Walker, "Donald Trump Has Big Plans for 'Radical Islamic' Terrorists,

2016 and 'That Communist' Bernie Sanders," *Yahoo News*, November 19, 2016, https://www.yahoo.com/news/donald-trump-has-big-plans-1303117537878070.html (accessed August 12, 2016).

46. "Syria Regional Refugee Response," United Nations High Commission for Refugees, September 18, 2016, http://data.unhcr.org/syrianrefugees/regional.php#_ga =1.24682622.594277177.1444958423 (accessed September 24, 2016).

47. Phillip Connor, "Nearly Half of Refugees Entering the US This Year Are Muslim," Pew Research Center, October 5, 2016, http://www.pewresearch.org/fact -tank/2016/08/16/nearly-half-of-refugees-entering-the-u-s-this-year-are-muslim/ (accessed August 20, 2016).

48. "Home," Refugee Council USA, http://www.rcusa.org/home (accessed August 9, 2016).

49. Ken Meyer, "Two Former Homeland Security Secretaries Wrote President Obama on Safely Welcoming Syrian Refugees," White House, November 19, 2015, https://www.whitehouse.gov/blog/2015/11/19/two-former-homeland-security-secretaries -wrote-president-obama-safely-welcoming (accessed August 16, 2016); Jeh C. Johnson, "Remarks by Secretary of Homeland Security Jeh C. Johnson at the World Refugee Day Naturalization Ceremony–As Delivered," Department of Homeland Security, June 20, 2016, https://www.dhs.gov/news/2016/06/20/remarks-secretary-homeland-security-jeh-c -johnson-world-refugee-day-naturalization (accessed August 13, 2016).

50. Michele Keleman, "Fact Check: Donald Trump and Syrian Refugees," NPR, June 15, 2016, http://www.npr.org/sections/parallels/2016/06/15/482184991/fact-check -donald-trump-and-syrian-refugees (accessed August 19, 2016).

51. Ishaan Tharoor, "Were Syrian Refugees Involved in the Paris Attacks? What We Know and Don't Know," *Washington Post*, November 17, 2015, https://www .washingtonpost.com/news/worldviews/wp/2015/11/17/were-syrian-refugees-involved-in -the-paris-attacks-what-we-know-and-dont-know/ (accessed August 9, 2016).

52. Patrick Healy and Julie Bosman, "GOP Governors Vow to Close Doors to Syrian Refugees," *New York Times*, November 16, 2015, http://www.nytimes.com/2015/11/17/ us/politics/gop-governors-vow-to-close-doors-to-syrian-refugees.html?_r=0 (accessed August 9, 2016).

53. Matt Adams, "Gov. Pence Suspends Resettlement of Syrian Refugees to Indiana following Paris Terror Attacks," Fox59, November 16, 2015, http://fox59.com/ 2015/11/16/pence-suspends-resettlement-of-syrian-refugees-following-paris-terror -attacks/ (accessed December 13, 2016).

54. Liz Robbins, "11th-Hour Detour Puts Family in Connecticut as Indiana Bars Syrian Refugees," *New York Times*, November 17, 2015, http://www.nytimes.com/ 2015/11/18/nyregion/11th-hour-detour-puts-family-in-connecticut-as-indiana-bars-syrian -refugees.html (accessed August 9, 2016).

55. Katie Zezima, "Mike Pence Wants to Keep Syrian Refugees out of Indiana. They're Coming Anyway," *Washington Post*, August 28, 2016, https://www.washingtonpost.com/politics/mike-pence-wants-to-keep-syrian-refugees-out-of-indiana-theyre-coming-anyway/2016/08/28/2847f4dc-6576-11e6-8b27-bb8ba39497a2_story.html?utm_term=.07a8f997787e (accessed December 11, 2016).

56. Zoeller, in discussion with the author.

57. Kendall Downing, "Governor Pence and ACLU Spar over Resettlement of Syrian Refugees in Indiana," Fox59, November 24, 2015, http://fox59.com/2015/11/24/governor-pence-and-aclu-spar-over-resettlement-of-syrian-refugees-in-indiana/ (accessed August 1, 2016).

58. "Welcome to Exodus Refugee," Exodus Refugee, https://exodusrefugee.org/index.html (accessed August 1, 2016).

59. "Exodus Refugee Immigration v. Mike Pence et al.," ACLU, 2016, http://www.aclu-in.org/issues/equality/immigrant-rights/370-exodus-refugee-immigration-v-mike-pence-et-al (accessed August 13, 2016).

60. Downing, "Governor Pence and ACLU Spar."

61. Joseph W. Tobin, "Statement from the Archbishop Joseph W. Tobin Regarding the Resettlement of a Family of Refugees from Syria," Archdiocese of Indianapolis, December 8, 2015, http://www.archindy.org/archbishop/syria-2015.html (accessed August 1, 2016).

62. Ibid.

63. Zoeller, in discussion with the author.

64. Stephanie Wang, "Court to Hear Appeal on Indiana's Syrian Refugee Ban," *IndyStar*, September 13, 2016, http://www.indystar.com/story/news/politics/2016/09/13/court-hear-appeal-indianas-syrian-refugee-ban/90255588/ (accessed September 19, 2016).

65. Alexander McCall, "Zoeller to Attend Meetings with Refugee Families, Pence Declines," WBAA, December 11, 2015, http://wbaa.org/post/zoeller-attend-meeting-refugee-families-pence-declines (accessed August 1, 2016).

66. Greg Zoeller, "Facing Fears Is Hoosier Heritage," *Pharos-Tribune*, December 19, 2015, http://www.pharostribune.com/opinion/columns/article_95f674a2-7f90-543f-80c5-468814df22f5.html (accessed December 11, 2016).

67. Zoeller, in discussion with the author.

68. Ibid.

69. "Demographics at a Glance," City of Fresno, http://www.fresno.gov/Discover Fresno/Demographics/Default.htm (accessed August 1, 2016).

70. "Fresno County Ag," Fresno County Farm Bureau, http://www.fcfb.org/Fresno-Ag/Fresno-Ag.php (accessed August 1, 2016).

71. Eric McGhee, "California's Political Geography," Public Policy Institute of California, February 2012, http://www.ppic.org/main/publication_quick.asp?i=1007 (accessed December 11, 2016).

72. Margaret Mims, in discussion with the author, February 6, 2016.

73. Ibid.

74. Ibid.

75. Ibid.

76. "Fresno Sheriff-Coroner Margaret Mims," Fresno Country Sherriff's Office, http://www.fresnosheriff.org/admin/sheriff.html (accessed August 1, 2016).

77. Mims, in discussion with the author.

78. Ibid.

79. Ibid.

80. "QuickFacts: United States," US Census, 2015, http://www.census.gov/ quickfacts/table/PST045215/00 (accessed August 13, 2016).

81. Mims, in discussion with the author.

82. "Punjabi Community Finds Home in Central California," California Report, August 3, 2012, http://audio.californiareport.org/archive/R201208031630/c (accessed August 2, 2016).

83. Ibid.

84. Rory Appleton, "Two Arrested in Brutal Attack on Sikh Man: It's a Hate Crime, Police Say," *Fresno Bee*, March 29, 2016, http://www.fresnobee.com/news/local/crime/ article68858142.html (accessed August 2, 2016).

85. Mims, in discussion with the author.

86. Eric Lichtblau, "Crimes against Muslim Americans and Mosques Rise Sharply," *New York Times*, December 17, 2015, http://www.nytimes.com/2015/12/18/us/politics/ crimes-against-muslim-americans-and-mosques-rise-sharply.html?smid=tw-nytimes &smtyp=cur&_r=0 (accessed August 2, 2016); Susan Milligan. "Sikhs Become a Casualty of Anti-Muslim Actions," *US News & World Report*, December 31, 2015, http:// www.usnews.com/news/articles/2015-12-31/sikhs-become-a-casualty-of-anti-muslim -actions (accessed August 2, 2016).

87. Ibid.

88. South Asian Americans Leading Together, "Under Suspicion, Under Attack," report by Sameera Hafiz and Suman Raghunathan, 2014, http://saalt.org/wp-content/ uploads/2014/09/SAALT_report_full_links.pdf (accessed August 12, 2016).

89. Mims, in discussion with the author.

90. Ibid.

91. Ibid.

92. Ibid.

93. "QuickFacts: Lake County, Illinois," US Census, https://www.census.gov/ quickfacts/table/PST045215/17097 (accessed August 13, 2016).

94. "Immigrant Policy Project," National Conference of State Legislatures, http:// www.ncsl.org/research/immigration/summary-of-the-sensenbrenner-immigration-bill.aspx (accessed August 3, 2016).

95. Gabe Gonzalez, in discussion with the author, August 4, 2016.

96. Curran, in discussion with the author.

97. Cal Skinner, "Lake County Sheriff Mark Curran Switching to Republican Party," McHenry County Blog, December 13, 2008, http://mchenrycountyblog.com/2008/12/13/lake-county-sheriff-mark-curran-switching-to-republican-party-2/ (accessed August 3, 2016).

98. Ibid.

99. Curran, in discussion with the author.

100. Kenneth L. Woodward, "Cardinal Francis George: Chicago's Accidental Archbishop," *Chicago Tribune*, April 20, 2015, http://www.chicagotribune.com/news/opinion/commentary/ct-cardinal-francis-george-chicago-vatican-pope-francis-perspec-0414-20150420-story.html (accessed August 3, 2016).

101. Ibid.

102. Ibid.

103. "Lake County Sheriff Goes against the Grain: Fellow Republicans Skeptical of Ideas for Immigration Reform, But Opponent Likes Them," *Daily Herald*, March 12, 2010, http://www.dailyherald.com/article/20100312/news/303129849/ (accessed August 3, 2016).

104. Ibid.

105. Curran, in discussion with the author.

106. Greisa Martinez, in discussion with the author, November 8, 2016.

107. Ibid.

108. Chico Harlan and Jerry Markon, "What It Will Take for President Trump to Deport Millions and Build a Wall," *Washington Post,* November 9, 2016, https://www.washingtonpost.com/news/wonk/wp/2016/11/09/what-it-will-take-for-president-trump-to-deport-millions-and-build-the-wall/?utm_term=.4a67284041e6 (accessed December 12, 2016).

109. Khizr Khan, "Address to the DNC," *The Independent*, July 29, 2016, http://www.independent.co.uk/news/world/americas/dnc-2016-khizr-khan-donald-trump-read-full-transcript-father-muslim-soldier-a7161616.html (accessed August 3, 2016).

110. Ibid.

111. Ibid.

112. Ibid.

113. Ibid.

CHAPTER SIX: IDENTITY, INTEGRATION, INFLUENCE

1. "Impremedia: Who We Are," impreMedia, http://www.impremedia.com (accessed August 13, 2016); Elisa Shearer, "Hispanic News Media, Fact Sheet," Pew Research Center, June 15, 2016, http://www.journalism.org/2016/06/15/hispanic-media-fact-sheet/ (accessed August 25, 2016).

2. Jens Manuel Krogstad and Mark Hugo Lopez, "Hispanic Population Reaches Record 55 Million, But Growth Has Cooled," Pew Research Center, June 25, 2015, http://www.pewresearch.org/fact-tank/2015/06/25/u-s-hispanic-population-growth-surge-cools/ (accessed August 27, 2016).

3. Katherine Vargas, in discussion with the author, August 17, 2016.

4. Doris Meissner, in discussion with the author, August 17, 2016.

5. Betsy Cooper et al., "How Americans View Immigrants, and What They Want from Immigration Reform: Findings from the 2015 American Values Atlas," PRRI, March 29, 2016, http://www.prri.org/research/survey-americans-view-immigrants-want -immigration-reform-findings-2015-american-values-atlas/ (accessed August 28, 2016).

6. James Sterling Young, "Interview with Edward M. Kennedy," Edward M. Kennedy Oral History Project, April 3, 2007, http://web1.millercenter.org/poh/transcripts/ ohp_2007_0403_kennedy.pdf (accessed August 11, 2016).

7. Ibid.

8. Lyndon B. Johnson, "Remarks at the Signing of the Immigration Bill, Liberty Island, New York," LBJ Presidential Library, October 3, 1965, http://www.lbjlib.utexas .edu/johnson/archives.hom/speeches.hom/651003.asp (accessed August 11, 2016).

9. Ibid.

10. David S. FitzGerald and David Cook-Martin, "The Geopolitical Origins of the US Immigration Act of 1965," Migration Policy Institute, February 5, 2015, http:// www.migrationpolicy.org/article/geopolitical-origins-us-immigration-act-1965 (accessed August 11, 2016).

11. Tom Gjelten, "The Immigration Act That Inadvertently Changed America," *Atlantic*, October 2, 2015, http://www.theatlantic.com/politics/archive/2015/10/ immigration-act-1965/408409/ (accessed August 11, 2016).

12. George Gao, "15 Striking Facts from 2015," Pew Research Center, December 22, 2015, http://www.pewresearch.org/fact-tank/2015/12/22/15-striking-findings -from-2015/ (accessed August 26, 2016).

13. Gjelten, "Immigration Act."

14. Ibid.

15. D'Vera Cohn, "Future Immigration Will Change the Face of America by 2065," Pew Research Center, October 5, 2015, http://www.pewresearch.org/fact-tank/ 2015/10/05/future-immigration-will-change-the-face-of-america-by-2065/ (accessed August 11, 2016).

16. Anna Brown, "Key Takeaways on US Immigration: Past, Present and Future," Pew Research Center, September 28, 2015, http://www.pewresearch.org/fact-tank/2015/09/28/ key-takeaways-on-u-s-immigration-past-present-and-future/ (accessed August 11, 2016).

17. Francine Medeiros, "La Opinión, A Mexican Exile Newspaper: A Content Analysis of Its First Years, 1926–1929," *Aztlan* 11:1 (1980): 68–75.

18. Nathan Olivarez-Giles, "La Opinión Publisher Named CEO of the Paper's Parent, ImpreMedia: Monica C. Lozano Will Head the Nation's Largest Spanish-Language Newspaper Company and Keep Her Current Post. She Plans to Beef up Digital Content," *Los Angeles Times*, May 26, 2010, http://articles.latimes.com/2010/may/26/business/la-fi-lozano-20100526 (accessed August 14, 2016).

19. Monica Lozano, in discussion with the author, May 20, 2016.

20. Ibid.

21. Ibid.

22. "QuickFacts: California," US Census, http://www.census.gov/quickfacts/table/PST045215/06 (accessed August 28, 2016).

23. "Demographic Profile of Hispanics in California, 2014," Pew Research Center, http://www.pewhispanic.org/states/state/ca/ (accessed August 28, 2016); Alejandra Lopez, "Demographics of California Counties: A Comparison of 1980, 1990, and 2000 Census Data," Stanford University, June 2002, http://citeseerx.ist.psu.edu/viewdoc/download?doi=10.1.1.397.6699&rep=rep1&type=pdf (accessed August 28, 2016).

24. Jie Zong and Jeanne Batalova, "Central American Immigrants in the United States," Migration Policy Institute, September 2, 2015, http://www.migrationpolicy.org/article/central-american-immigrants-united-states (accessed August 28, 2016).

25. Ibid.

26. Lozano, in discussion with the author.

27. Ibid.

28. MarketingCharts Staff, "Latinos Aspiring to a More 'Ambicultural' Identity," MarketingCharts, February 22, 2013, http://www.marketingcharts.com/traditional/latinos-aspiring-to-a-more-ambicultural-identity-27221/ (accessed August 21, 2016).

29. Michael Hoeffer, Nancy Rytina, and Bryan Baker, "Estimates of the Unauthorized Immigrant Population Residing in the United States: January 2011," Department of Homeland Security, March 2012, https://www.dhs.gov/xlibrary/assets/statistics/publications/ois_ill_pe_2011.pdf (accessed August 28, 2016).

30. Robert Pear, "President Signs Landmark Bill on Immigration," *New York Times*, November 7, 1986, http://www.nytimes.com/1986/11/07/us/president-signs-landmark-bill-on-immigration.html (accessed August 14, 2016).

31. "Special Section Offers Guidance on Amnesty," *Los Angeles Times*, March 13, 1989, http://articles.latimes.com/1989-03-13/news/mn-455_1_special-section (accessed August 14, 2016).

32. "Times Mirror Buys 50% of La Opinión," *Los Angeles Times*, August 30, 1990, http://articles.latimes.com/1990-08-30/news/ti-681_1_la-opinion (accessed August 14, 2016).

33. "Cecilia Muñoz," *White House*, https://www.whitehouse.gov/blog/author/cecilia-muñoz (accessed August 15, 2016).

34. Larry M. Eig, "California's Proposition 187: A Brief Overview," Congressional Review Service, http://www.congressionalresearch.com/97-543/document.php (accessed December 12, 2016).

35. B. Drummond Ayres, "The 1994 Campaign; In Race for California Chief No Candidate Is Favorite," *New York Times*, September 19, 1994, http://www.nytimes .com/1994/09/19/us/the-1994-campaign-in-race-for-california-chief-no-candidate-is -favorite.html?pagewanted=all (accessed August 28, 2016).

36. Cecilia Muñoz, in discussion with the author, July 26, 2016.

37. "Prop. 187 Approved in California," *Migration News* 1, no. 11 (December 1994), https://migration.ucdavis.edu/mn/more.php?id=492 (accessed August 28, 2016).

38. Lozano, in discussion with the author.

39. Ibid.

40. Muñoz, in discussion with the author.

41. Ibid.

42. Gustavo Adolfo Cubias, "Latino Political Power in California," (senior thesis, Claremont McKenna College, April 23, 2011), http://scholarship.claremont.edu/cgi/ viewcontent.cgi?article=1128&context=cmc_theses (accessed September 12, 2016).

43. "Legislators by Generation," National Conference of State Legislatures, http:// www.ncsl.org/research/about-state-legislatures/who-we-elect-an-interactive-graphic.aspx (Accessed September 12, 2016); Ibid.

44. Lozano, in discussion with the author.

45. Robert D. Putnam, *Bowling Alone: The Collapse and Revival of American Community*, 1st ed. (New York: Touchstone Books by Simon & Schuster, 2001).

46. Robert D. Putnam, "E Pluribus Unum: Diversity and Community in the 21st Century: The 2006 Johan Skytte Prize Lecture," *Scandinavian Political Studies* 30, no. 2 (June 2007), pp. 137–74.

47. Ibid.

48. Michael Jones, "The Downside of Diversity: A Harvard Political Scientist Finds That Diversity Hurts Civic Life. What Happens When a Liberal Scholar Unearths an Inconvenient Truth?" *Boston Globe*, August 5, 2007, http://archive.boston.com/ news/globe/ideas/articles/2007/08/05/the_downside_of_diversity/ (accessed August 12, 2016).

49. Putnam, "E Pluribus Unum," pp. 139, 164.

50. Derek Thompson, "Donald Trump and the Twilight of White America: Racial Resentment and Economic Anxiety Are Not Separate Forces. For Many Trump Supporters, They Are Inextricably Linked," *Atlantic*, May 13, 2016, http://www .theatlantic.com/politics/archive/2016/05/donald-trump-and-the-twilight-of-white -america/482655/ (accessed August 12, 2016).

51. Jonathan T. Rothwell and Pablo Diego-Rosell, "Explaining Nationalist Political

Views: The Case of Donald Trump," *Gallup*, September 4, 2016, http://papers.ssrn.com/
sol3/papers.cfm?abstract_id=2822059 (accessed September 27, 2016).

52. Ibid.

53. Ibid., p. 11.

54. Ibid., p. 8.

55. Ibid., p. 12.

56. Ryan Lizza, "What We Learned about Trump's Supporters This Week," *New Yorker*, August 13, 2016, http://www.newyorker.com/news/daily-comment/what-we -learned-about-trumps-supporters-this-week (accessed August 15, 2016).

57. Ronald Brownstein, "The Nation's Divide Reemerges," *Los Angeles Times*, November 9, 2006, http://articles.latimes.com/2006/nov/09/nation/na-assess9 (accessed September 15, 2016).

58. Ronald Brownstein, "Culture Is Replacing Class as the Key Political Divide: On Both Sides of the Atlantic—in the United Kingdom and the United States—Political Parties Are Realigning and Voters' Allegiances Are Shifting," *Atlantic*, June 30, 2016, http://www.theatlantic.com/politics/archive/2016/06/britain-united-states/489410/ (accessed September 15, 2016).

59. Ronald Brownstein, "The Parties Invert: White Working-Class Voters Defect from the Democrats, as White College-Educated Voters Abandon the Republicans—a Reversal a Clinton-Trump Race Could Cement," *Atlantic*, May 23, 2016, http://www .theatlantic.com/politics/archive/2016/05/an-election-in-negative/483905/ (accessed September 15, 2016).

60. Ross Douthat and Reihan Salam, "A Cure for Trumpism: The Case for a Conservative Politics That Stresses the National Interest Abroad and National Solidarity at Home," *New York Times*, July 15, 2016, http://www.nytimes.com/2016/07/17/opinion/ sunday/a-cure-for-trumpism.html?_r=0#story-continues-3 (accessed August 16, 2016).

61. Ibid.

62. Laura Reston, "Immigrants Don't Drain Welfare. They Fund It," *New Republic*, September 3, 2015, https://newrepublic.com/article/122714/immigrants-dont-drain -welfare-they-fund-it (accessed December 12, 2016).

63. Steven A. Camarota, "Welfare Use by Immigrant and Native Households," Center for Immigration Studies, September 2015, http://cis.org/Welfare-Use-Immigrant -Native-Households (accessed December 12, 2016).

64. Leighton Ku and Brian Bruen, "Poor Immigrants Use Public Benefits at a Lower Rate Than Poor Native-Born Citizens," Cato Institute Economic Development Bulletin no. 17, March 4, 2013, http://object.cato.org/sites/cato.org/files/pubs/pdf/edb17.pdf (accessed August 28, 2016).

65. Ibid.

66. Lisa Christensen Gee, Matthew Gardner, and Meg Wiehe, "Undocumented Immigrants' State & Local Tax Contributions," The Institute on Taxation & Economic

Policy, February 2016, http://www.itep.org/pdf/immigration2016.pdf (accessed December 12, 2016).

67. "Economic Report of the President: Transmitted to The Congress March 2013," together with the Annual Report of the Council of Economic Advisers, https://www .whitehouse.gov/sites/default/files/docs/erp2013/full_2013_economic_report_of_the _president.pdf (accessed December 12, 2016).

68. Frederick Treyz, Corey Stottlemyer, and Rod Motamedi, "Key Components of Immigration Reform," REMI, July 17, 2013, http://www.remi.com/download/key -components-of-immigration-reform-2 (accessed August 26, 2016).

69. Douthat and Salam, "A Cure for Trumpism."

70. Putnam, "E Pluribus Unum."

71. Jolie Lee, "Coca-Cola Super Bowl Ad: Can You Believe This Reaction?" *USA Today*, February 4, 2014, http://www.usatoday.com/story/news/nation-now/2014/02/03/ coca-cola-ad-super-bowl-racism/5177463/ (accessed September 15, 2016).

72. Lozano, in discussion with the author.

73. Ibid.

74. Ibid.

75. Ibid.

76. "Wells Fargo to Accept Matricula Consular Card as Identification for New Account Openings," news release, Consulate General of Mexico, November 7, 2001, http://www.estradausa.com/mr/wellsmr110701.htm (accessed August 22, 2016).

77. Ibid.

78. "Wells Fargo ATMS Now Bilingual," ATM Marketplace, February 26, 2003, http://www.atmmarketplace.com/news/wells-fargo-audio-atms-now-bilingual/ (accessed August 22, 2016).

79. Ibid.

80. Richard L Zweigenhaft, "Diversity Among CEOs and Corporate Directors: Has the Heyday Come and Gone?" University of California at Santa Cruz, August 12, 2013, http://www2.ucsc.edu/whorulesamerica/power/diversity_among_ceos.html (accessed September 15, 2016).

81. Ibid.

82. Muñoz, in discussion with the author.

83. Juliet Eilperin, "Obama Has Vastly Changed the Federal Bureaucracy," *Washington Post*, September 20, 2015, https://www.washingtonpost.com/politics/obama-has -vastly-changed-the-face-of-the-federal-bureaucracy/2015/09/20/73ef803a-5631-11e5 -abe9-27d53f250b11_story.html?utm_term=.16d55f39d882 (accessed December 13, 2016).

84. Muñoz, in discussion with the author.

85. Lozano, in discussion with the author.

86. Ibid.

CHAPTER SEVEN: THE NEW TEXAS

1. Mustafa Tameez, in discussion with the author, March 30, 2016.

2. Ibid.

3. John Williams, "Ground Effort Put Brown over Top," Free Republic, December 3, 2001, http://www.freerepublic.com/focus/fr/582570/posts (accessed September 28, 2016).

4. Jim Yardley, "In Houston, a 'Nonpartisan' Race Is Anything But," *New York Times*, November 30, 2001, http://www.nytimes.com/2001/11/30/us/in-houston-a -nonpartisan-race-is-anything-but.html?_r=0 (accessed September 28, 2016).

5. Ibid.

6. Kristen Mack, "Mack on Politics: Campaign Manager Builds on Successes," *Houston Chronicle*, November 5, 2004, http://www.chron.com/news/article/Mack-on -Politics-Campaign-manager-builds-on-1966283.php (accessed September 28, 2016).

7. Jim Yardley, "Democrat in Houston Wins with Some National Help," *New York Times*, December 3, 2001, http://www.nytimes.com/2001/12/03/us/democrat-in-houston -wins-with-some-national-help.html (accessed September 28, 2016).

8. "Immigrant Policy Project," National Conference of State Legislatures, http:// www.ncsl.org/research/immigration/summary-of-the-sensenbrenner-immigration-bill.aspx (accessed August 3, 2016).

9. Tameez, in discussion with the author.

10. Michael O. Emerson, Jenifer Bratter, Junia Howell, P. Wilner Jeanty, and Mike Clin, "Houston Region Grows More Racially/Ethnically Diverse, with Small Declines in Segregation. A Joint Report Analyzing Census Data from 1990, 2000, and 2010," Kinder Institute for Urban Research & the Hobby Center for the Study of Texas, https://kinder.rice.edu/uploadedFiles/Urban_Research_Center/Media/ Houston%20Region%20Grows%20More%20Ethnically%20Diverse%202-13.pdf (accessed December 13, 2016).

11. Tameez, in discussion with the author.

12. Adrian Garcia, in discussion with the author, March 31, 2016.

13. Ibid.

14. "Houston City Council District H—Runoff," Our Campaigns, December 6, 2003, http://www.ourcampaigns.com/RaceDetail.html?RaceID=777354 (accessed September 28, 2016).

15. "About Houston: Facts and Figures," City of Houston, 2016, http://www .houstontx.gov/abouthouston/houstonfacts.html (accessed October 25, 2016).

16. "Voting Age Population by Race/Ethnicity," City of Houston Planning & Development Department, October 28, 2012, http://www.houstontx.gov/planning/ Demographics/docs_pdfs/CD/council_dist_vote_age_pop.pdf (accessed September 8, 2016); "Harris County Voter Registration Figures," Texas Secretary of State, http:// www.sos.state.tx.us/elections/historical/harris.shtml (accessed September 7, 2016);

"QuickFacts: Harris County," US Census, https://www.census.gov/quickfacts/table/PST045215/00 (accessed September 28, 2016).

17. Garcia, in discussion with the author.

18. "Cumulative Report—Official," Harris County General and Special Elections, November 14, 2008, http://www.harrisvotes.com/HISTORY/110408/Cumulative/cumulative.pdf (accessed September 8, 2016).

19. Alan Bernstein, "Dems Baffled by Low Voter Turnout in Harris County: Small Increase in Votes Cast on Election Day," *Houston Chronicle*, November 6, 2008, http://www.chron.com/news/houston-texas/article/Dems-baffled-by-low-voter-turnout-in-Harris-County-1771830.php (accessed September 8, 2016).

20. Muzaffar Chishti and Claire Bergeron, "ICE to Expand New Immigration Enforcement Program in Local Jails," Migration Policy Institute, June 15, 2009, http://www.migrationpolicy.org/article/ice-expand-new-immigration-enforcement-program-local-jails (accessed December 13, 2016).

21. "Houston Sheriffs Round up Thousands of Illegals," *Washington Times*, November 12, 2009, http://www.washingtontimes.com/news/2009/nov/12/team-of-8-deputies-quietly-rounds-up-illegals/ (accessed September 28, 2016).

22. Garcia, in discussion with the author.

23. Ibid.

24. Ibid.

25. Ibid.

26. Theodore Schleifer, "Sources: Adrian Garcia to Run for Houston Mayor," *Houston Chronicle*, May 5, 2015, http://www.chron.com/news/houston-texas/houston/article/Sources-Adrian-Garcia-to-run-for-Houston-mayor-6140978.php (accessed September 28, 2016).

27. "City of Houston Anti-Discrimination HERO Veto Referendum, Proposition 1 (November 2015)," Ballotpedia, https://ballotpedia.org/City_of_Houston_Anti-Discrimination_HERO_Veto_Referendum,_Proposition_1_(November_2015) (accessed September 28, 2016).

28. "Houston Mayor Candidates Adrian Garcia, Sylvester Turner Tied in New Poll," ABC 13, October 7, 2015, http://abc13.com/politics/houston-mayor-candidates-adrian-garcia-sylvester-turner-tied-in-new-poll/1021324/ (accessed September 28, 2016).

29. Ibid.

30. Rebecca Elliott, "Anti-HERO Wave, Campaign Missteps Cited in Garcia's Fall," *Houston Chronicle*, November 4, 2015, http://www.houstonchronicle.com/politics/election/local/article/Anti-HERO-wave-campaign-missteps-cited-in-6611563.php (accessed September 28, 2016).

31. Mike Morris and Rebecca Elliott, "In Close Race, Houston Elects Democratic Mayor Sylvester Turner," *Governing*, December 14, 2015, http://www

.governing.com/topics/elections/tns-houston-mayoral-race-results.html (accessed September 28, 2016).

32. "Municipal Elections in Houston, Texas (2015)," Ballotpedia, https://ballotpedia .org/Municipal_elections_in_Houston,_Texas_(2015) (accessed June 28, 2016).

33. Garcia, in discussion with author.

34. Emily Deruy, "Old Friends Face Off in a Primary with Race at Its Center: Houston Democrats Gene Green and Adrian Garcia Are Asking Latino Voters to Choose between an Incumbent Ally and a Hispanic Challenger," *Atlantic*, February 26, 2016, http://www.theatlantic.com/politics/archive/2016/02/old-friends-face-off-in-a-primary -that-puts-race-at-its-center/471126/ (accessed September 26, 2016).

35. Garcia, in discussion with author.

36. Ibid.

37. "Introduction to Sugar Land, Texas," CityTownInfo, 2016, http://www .citytowninfo.com/places/texas/sugar-land (accessed September 28, 2016).

38. "Welcome to Sugar Land," City of Sugar Land Economic Development, http:// www.sugarlandecodev.com/home.aspx (accessed October 25, 2016).

39. Corrie Maclaggan, "What Ethnic Diversity Looks Like: Fort Bend," *New York Times*, November 23, 2013, http://www.nytimes.com/2013/11/24/us/what-ethnic -diversity-looks-like-fort-bend.html?_r=4& (accessed September 28, 2016).

40. KP George, in discussion with the author, March 30, 2016.

41. "Sugar Land, Texas Population: Census 2010 and 2000 Interactive Map, Demographics, Statistics, Quick Facts," Census Viewer, http://censusviewer.com/city/TX/ Sugar%20Land (accessed June 26, 2016).

42. Ibid.

43. Harish Jajoo, in discussion with the author, March 31, 2016.

44. Ibid.

45. Ibid.

46. Ibid.

47. "Cumulative Sugar Land District 4," Fort Bend County, June 17, 2011, http://fort bendcountytx.gov/modules/showdocument.aspx?documentid=6266 (accessed July 8, 2016).

48. Jajoo, in discussion with the author.

49. Scott Delhommer, "Q&A with Vy Nguyen," *Sugar Land Sun*, August 10, 2014, http://www.yourhoustonnews.com/sugar_land/news/q-a-with-vy-nguyen/article _cd61944d-d52e-5204-9afb-ea7bb0c4c7ec.html (accessed September 28, 2016).

50. "District Profile: Texas House District 26," Texas Legislative Council, April 27, 2016, http://www.fyi.legis.state.tx.us/fyiwebdocs/pdf/house/dist26/profile.pdf (accessed July 8, 2016).

51. Vy Nguyen, in discussion with the author, March 30, 2016.

52. Ibid.

53. Ibid.

54. Ibid.

55. Ibid.

56. "QuickFacts, Sugar Land, Texas," US Census Bureau, http://www.census.gov/quickfacts/table/PST045215/4870808 (accessed December 13, 2016).

57. "QuickFacts, Pasadena City, Texas," US Census Bureau, http://www.census.gov/quickfacts/table/PST045215/4856000,4870808 (accessed December 13, 2016).

58. Ornaldo Ybarra, in discussion with the author, March 31, 2016.

59. Ibid.

60. Ibid.

61. "QuickFacts, Pasadena City, Texas," US Census Bureau, http://www.census.gov/quickfacts/table/RHI705210/4856000,00#flag-js-X (accessed December 13, 2016).

62. Lori Rodriguez, "Pasadena's Culture Shifts with Latino Majority: Pasadena's Culture Shifts with Growing Latino Majority in Just a Few Decades, a Growing Latino Majority Has Reshaped the Home of Urban Cowboy," *Houston Chronicle*, March 25, 2007, http://www.chron.com/neighborhood/pasadena-news/article/Pasadena-s-culture-shifts-with-Latino-majority-1658322.php (accessed September 26, 2016).

63. Ybarra, in discussion with the author.

64. Lori Rodriguez, "Pasadena's Culture Shifts with Latino Majority: Pasadena's Culture Shifts with Growing Latino Majority in Just a Few Decades, a Growing Latino Majority Has Reshaped the Home of Urban Cowboy," *Houston Chronicle*, March 25, 2007, http://www.chron.com/neighborhood/pasadena-news/article/Pasadena-s-culture-shifts-with-Latino-majority-1658322.php (accessed September 26, 2016).

65. "Unemployment Rate—Not Seasonally Adjusted," Google Public Data from US Bureau of Labor Statistics, https://www.google.com/publicdata/explore?ds=z1ebjpgk 2654c1_&met_y=unemployment_rate&idim=city:CT4856000000000:CT4835000000000 :CT0656000000000&fdim_y=seasonality:U&hl=en&dl=en (accessed December 13, 2016).

66. Ybarra, in discussion with the author.

67. Ibid.

68. Carol Christian, "Winds of Change on Pasadena City Council," *Houston Chronicle*, June 16, 2009, http://blog.chron.com/eastharris/2009/06/winds-of-change-on-pasadena-city-council/ (accessed September 28, 2016).

69. Ybarra, in discussion with the author.

70. Ibid.

71. "President Lyndon B. Johnson's Remarks on the Signing of the Voting Rights Act (August 6, 1965)," transcript, University of Virginia Miller Center, http://millercenter.org/president/speeches/speech-4034 (accessed September 29, 2016).

72. "History of the Voting Rights Act," Leadership Conference on Civil and Human

Rights, 2016, http://www.civilrights.org/voting-rights/vra/history.html?referrer=https://
www.google.com/ (accessed September 29, 2016).

73. Ibid.

74. Amy Howe, "Court to Return to Constitutionality of Voting Rights Act: In Plain
English," *SCOTUSBlog*, February 25, 2013, http://www.scotusblog.com/2013/02/court
-to-return-to-constitutionality-of-voting-rights-act-in-plain-english/ (accessed September
28, 2016).

75. Sahil Kapur, "Justice Ginsberg Slams Supreme Court's 'Hubris' in Fiery Dissent
on Voting Rights Act," *Talking Points Memo*, June 25, 2013, http://talkingpointsmemo
.com/dc/justice-ginsburg-slams-supreme-court-s-hubris-in-fiery-dissent-on-voting
-rights-act (accessed September 28, 2016).

76. Cindy Horswell, "Pasadena Mayor's Plans Draw Fans, Detractors," *Houston
Chronicle*, September 7, 2013, http://www.houstonchronicle.com/news/politics/houston/
article/Pasadena-mayor-s-plans-draw-fans-detractors-4795561.php (accessed October 30,
2016).

77. Cindy Horswell, "Pasadena Voters to Face Redistricting Measure," *Houston
Chronicle*, October 30, 2013, http://www.houstonchronicle.com/news/politics/houston/
article/Pasadena-voters-to-face-redistricting-measure-4941044.php (accessed September
28, 2016).

78. Ibid.

79. James A. Baker III Institute for Public Policy, "An Analysis of Voter Support
for City of Pasadena Proposition 1: November 2013," Chron (blog), November 27, 2013,
http://blog.chron.com/bakerblog/2013/11/an-analysis-of-voter-support-for-city-of
-pasadena-proposition-1-november-2013/ (accessed October 25, 2016).

80. Resha Thomas, in discussion with the author, June 3, 2016.

81. Ybarra, in discussion with the author.

82. Jim Rutenberg, "The New Attack on Hispanic Voting Rights," *New York Times*,
December 17, 2015, http://www.nytimes.com/2015/12/20/magazine/block-the-vote
.html?_r=3 (accessed September 28, 2016).

83. Oscar del Toro, in discussion with the author, March 31, 2016.

84. Ibid.

85. "2015 Pasadena City Council Election: Final Unofficial Returns," *City of
Pasadena, Texas*, May 9, 2015, http://www.ci.pasadena.tx.us/default.aspx?name
=election2015 (accessed September 28, 2016).

86. del Toro, in discussion with the author.

87. Ibid.

88. Michael Lipka and Benjamin Wormald, "How Religious is Your State?" Pew
Research Center, February 29, 2016, http://www.pewresearch.org/fact-tank/2016/02/29/
how-religious-is-your-state/?state=alabama (accessed September 26, 2016).

89. Thom S. Rainer, "2014 Update on the Largest Churches in the Southern Baptist Convention," Thom S. Rainer, July 12, 2014, http://thomrainer.com/2014/07/2014-update -largest-churches-southern-baptist-convention/ (accessed September 28, 2016).

90. David Fleming, in discussion with the author, March 30, 2016.

91. Ibid.

92. Craig Hlavaty, "Megachurches Study Reveals Interesting Stats about Where Some of Us Worship Weekly," *Houston Chronicle*, December 13, 2015, http://www.chron .com/life/houston-belief/article/Megachurches-study-reveals-interesting-stats-6683587 .php (accessed September 28, 2016).

93. Fleming, in discussion with the author.

94. Bob Smeitana, "Bible Influences Only 1 in 10 Evangelicals on Immigration Reform: Christians Are Divided over Whether Immigrants Are Drain on Resources or an Opportunity to Share Jesus," *Christianity Today*, March 11, 2015, http://www .christianitytoday.com/gleanings/2015/march/bible-influences-only-1-in-10-evangelicals -views-on-immigra.html (accessed October 17, 2016).

95. Jim Avila and Serena Marshall, "What Would Jesus Do? Evangelists Launch Immigration Ad Campaign," ABC News, April 3, 2013, http://abcnews.go.com/Politics/ OTUS/jesus-evangelists-launch-immigration-ad-campaign/story?id=18865476 (accessed September 28, 2016).

96. Fleming, in discussion with the author.

97. Ibid.

98. Ibid.

99. Ibid.

100. Ibid.

101. Ibid.

102. Ibid.

103. Ibid.

104. Ibid.

105. Ibid.

106. Tameez, in discussion with the author.

107. Ibid.

CHAPTER EIGHT: MY WORKFORCE IS MY FAMILY

1. "QuickFacts: Pasco City, Washington," US Census, http://www.census.gov/ quickfacts/table/PST045215/5353545 (accessed September 13, 2016).

2. "About Broetje Orchards," First Fruits, 2016, http://www.firstfruits.com.

3. Ralph Broetje, in discussion with the author, March 17, 2016.

4. James N. Gregory, "Toward a History of Farm Workers in Washington State,"

Seattle Civil Rights & Labor History Project, 2009, http://depts.washington.edu/civilr/ farmwk_ch1.htm (accessed September 13, 2016).

5. Ibid.

6. Cheryl Broetje, in discussion with the author, March 17, 2016.

7. Ibid.

8. Ibid.

9. "Facts about Farmworkers," American Immigration Council, May 13, 2009, https://www.americanimmigrationcouncil.org/research/facts-about-farmworkers (December 14, 2016).

10. Lou Dobbs, in discussion with the author, February 25, 2016.

11. Jeffrey Sparshott, "Does Immigration Suppress Wages? It's Not So Simple," *Wall Street Journal*, June 1, 2015, http://blogs.wsj.com/economics/2015/06/01/does -immigration-suppress-wages-its-not-so-simple/ (accessed September 15, 2016).

12. "Immigration's Long-Term Impacts on Overall Wages and Employment of Native-Born US Workers Very Small, Although Low-Skilled Workers May Be Affected, New Report Finds; Impacts on Economic Growth Positive, While Effects on Government Budgets Mixed," news release, National Academies of Sciences, Engineering, Medicine, September 21, 2016, http://www8.nationalacademies.org/onpinews/newsitem.aspx ?RecordID=23550 (accessed September 29, 2016).

13. Dobbs, in discussion with the author.

14. Ibid.

15. John Steinbeck, *America and Americans and Selected Nonfiction*, ed. Jackson J. Benson and Susan Shillinglaw (repr.; New York: Penguin Classics, 2003), p. 5.

16. "Ag and Food Sectors in the Economy," US Department of Agriculture, Last updated October 14, 2016, http://www.ers.usda.gov/data-products/ag-and-food-statistics-charting -the-essentials/ag-and-food-sectors-and-the-economy.aspx (accessed September 15, 2016).

17. "No Longer Home Grown," New American Economy, March 18, 2014, http://www .renewoureconomy.org/research/no-longer-home-grown/ (accessed September 15, 2016).

18. Craig Regelbrugge, in discussion with the author, September 7, 2016.

19. Ibid.

20. Julianne Hing, "Alabama Gov. Signs One of the Nation's Harshest Anti-Immigrant Laws: Advocates Warn That the State Is Taking a Major Step Backwards in Its Long History with Civil Rights Struggles," Colorlines, June 7, 2011, http://www .colorlines.com/articles/alabama-gov-signs-one-nations-harshest-anti-immigrant-laws (accessed September 17, 2016).

21. "State Omnibus Immigration Legislation and Legal Challenges," National Conference of State Legislatures, August 27, 2012, http://www.ncsl.org/research/ immigration/omnibus-immigration-legislation.aspx (accessed September 5, 2016).

22. Ibid.

23. Diane McWhorter, "The Strange Career of Juan Crow," *New York Times*, June 16, 2012, http://www.nytimes.com/2012/06/17/opinion/sunday/no-sweet-home-alabama .html (accessed December 14, 2016).

24. "QuickFacts: Alabama," US Census, http://www.census.gov/quickfacts/table/ PST045215/01 (accessed September 13, 2016).

25. Benjy Sarlin, "How America's Harshest Immigration Law Failed," MSNBC, May 9, 2014, http://www.msnbc.com/msnbc/undocumented-workers-immigration -alabama (accessed August 24, 2016).

26. "Alabama's HB 56: The Harshest State-Level, Anti-Immigrant Measure to Date," National Immigration Law Center, September 6, 2011, http://mrzine.monthly review.org/2011/nilc090611.html (accessed September 15, 2016).

27. Alexander Trowbridge and Mackenzie Weinger, "Brooks: Ala. Immigration Law Working," *Politico*, October 6, 2011, http://www.politico.com/story/2011/10/brooks-ala -immigration-law-working-065351#ixzz4KMZXljOE (accessed September 6, 2016).

28. "Plyler v. Doe: Summary of a Fourteenth Amendment Landmark Case," United States Courts, http://www.uscourts.gov/educational-resources/educational-activities/ access-education-rule-law (accessed December 14, 2016).

29. Daniel Trotta and Tom Bassing, "In Alabama, Strict Immigration Laws Sows Discord," *Reuters*, May 30, 2012, http://www.reuters.com/article/us-usa-immigration -alabama-idUSBRE84T16P20120530 (accessed September 5, 2016).

30. "Alabama Economy," Netstate, last updated February 25, 2016, http://www .netstate.com/economy/al_economy.htm (accessed September 13, 2016).

31. Dawn Kent Azok, "20 Years of Mercedes-Benz: Automaker Marks Anniversary in Alabama Amid New Challenges, Controversy," AL.com, September 29, 2013, http:// www.al.com/business/index.ssf/2013/09/post_73.html (accessed August 24, 2016).

32. Verna Gates, "Alabama Immigration Crackdown Nabs Mercedes Executive," *Reuters*, November 22, 2011, http://www.reuters.com/article/us-immigration-alabama -mercedes-idUSTRE7AL0DT20111122 (accessed August 24, 2016).

33. Ibid.

34. "Beason Gets Angry Earful from Farmers over Immigration Law," WBRC, 2011, http://www.wbrc.com/story/15604891/beason-gets-angry-earful-from-farmers-over -immigration-law (accessed August 24, 2016).

35. Trotta and Bassing, "In Alabama, Strict Immigration Laws."

36. Sarlin. "How America's Harshest Immigration Law.""

37. Ibid.

38. "The Man Who Put Intel Inside: Andy Grove, Who Died on March 21st, Was at the Heart of the Computer Revolution," *Economist*, March 26, 2016, http://www .economist.com/news/business/21695361-mr-grove-who-died-march-21st-was-heart -computer-revolution-andy-grove (accessed September 7, 2016).

39. Eva Grove, in discussion with the author, September 8, 2016.

40. Ibid.

41. Ibid.

42. Ibid.

43. Ibid.

44. "Silicon Valley - Making the World a Better Place (supercut)," Vimeo video, 0:48, posted by "cthulberg," 2014, https://vimeo.com/98720197 (accessed September 30, 2016).

45. Mary Mederios Kent, "More US Scientists and Engineers Are Foreign-Born," PRB, January 2011, http://www.prb.org/Publications/Articles/2011/usforeignbornstem .aspx (accessed September 7, 2016).

46. Jeanne Batalova, "H-1B Temporary Skilled Worker Program," Migration Policy Institute, October 7, 2010, http://www.migrationpolicy.org/article/h-1b-temporary-skilled -worker-program (accessed December 14, 2016).

47. David S. Broder, "For Gates, a Visa Charge," *Washington Post*, March 19, 2006, http://www.washingtonpost.com/wp-dyn/content/article/2006/03/17/AR2006031701798 .html (accessed August 30, 2016).

48. Jessica E. Lessin and Miriam Jordan, "Laurene Powell Jobs Goes Public to Promote Dream Act," *Wall Street Journal*, May 16, 2013, http://www.wsj.com/articles/ SB10001424127887323582904578487263583009532 (accessed September 7, 2016).

49. Laurene Powell Jobs, "Immigrants Fuel Innovation. Let's Not Waste Their Potential," *Wired*, October 16, 2016, https://www.wired.com/2016/10/immigrants-fuel -innovation-lets-not-waste-potential/ (accessed October 24, 2016).

50. Mark Zuckerberg, "Immigrants Are the Key to a Knowledge Economy," *Washington Post*, April 10, 2013, https://www.washingtonpost.com/opinions/mark -zuckerberg-immigrants-are-the-key-to-a-knowledge-economy/2013/04/10/aba05554 -a20b-11e2-82bc-511538ae90a4_story.html?utm_term=.98cc00e65ca8 (accessed September 7, 2016).

51. Steve Case, in discussion with the author, March 29, 2016.

52. Ibid.

53. Ibid.

54. Ibid.

55. Ibid.

56. Ibid.

57. Ibid.

58. Tom Nassif and Brad Smith, "Immigration Reform a Necessary Strategy for US Economy," *Sacramento Bee*, March 16, 2014, http://www.sacbee.com/opinion/california -forum/article2593119.html#! (accessed September 4, 2016).

59. Dolores Monet, "Ready-to-Wear: A Short History of the Garment Industry,"

Bellatory, March 3, 2016, https://bellatory.com/fashion-industry/Ready-to-Wear-A-Short-History-of-the-Garment-Industry (accessed September 15, 2016).

60. "Databases, Tables, & Calculators by Subject: Employment, Hours, and Earnings from the Current Employment Statistics Survey (National): All Employees, Thousands, Apparel, Seasonally Adjusted," Bureau of Labor Statistics, http://data.bls.gov/timeseries/CES3231500001?amp%253bdata_tool=XGtable&output_view=data&include_graphs=true (accessed December 14, 2016).

61. Marty Bailey, in discussion with the author, August 14, 2016.

62. Ibid.

63. Ibid.

64. Ibid.

65. Charles Fishman, "Same Place, Different World," *Fast Company*, June 30, 2000, https://www.fastcompany.com/40937/same-place-different-world (accessed September 2, 2016).

66. Ibid.

67. Ibid.

68. Bailey, in discussion with the author.

69. Ibid.

70. Ibid.

71. Ibid.

72. Ibid.

73. Julia Preston, "Immigration Crackdown with Firings, Not Raids," *New York Times*, September 29, 2009, http://www.nytimes.com/2009/09/30/us/30factory.html?_r=0 (accessed September 13, 2016).

74. Bailey, in discussion with the author.

75. "A Framework for Effective Immigration Worksite Employer Enforcement," American Immigration Council, January 5, 2011, https://www.americanimmigration council.org/research/framework-effective-immigration-worksite-employer-enforcement (accessed September 4, 2016).

76. "I-9, Employment Eligibility Verification," United States Citizenship and Immigration Services, https://www.uscis.gov/i-9 (accessed December 14, 2016).

77. Bailey, in discussion with the author.

78. Preston, "Immigration Crackdown with Firings."

79. Bailey, in discussion with the author.

80. Preston, "Immigration Crackdown with Firings."

81. Bailey, in discussion with the author.

82. Shannon Dininney, "Pasco's Rising Hispanic Tide," *Seattle Times*, July 29, 2007, http://www.seattletimes.com/seattle-news/pascos-rising-hispanic-tide/ (Accessed September 16, 2016).

83. "Horizon Initiative: Chambers 2025: Eight Influences Shaping the Next Decade for Chambers of Commerce," Association of Chamber of Commerce Executives, 2015, http://www.acce.org/clientuploads/ce_mag/Chamber_2025_Digital.pdf (accessed September 16, 2016).

84. Ibid., p. 18.

85. Lori Mattson, in discussion with the author, April 7, 2016.

86. Ibid.

87. "The Homes Broetje Orchards Built Near Prescott," *Tri-City Herald*, May 4, 2013, http://www.tri-cityherald.com/news/local/article32123112.html (accessed September 16, 2016).

88. Cheryl Broetje, in discussion with the author.

89. Ibid.

90. Ralph Broetje, in discussion with the author.

CHAPTER NINE: MAKING THE FUTURE

1. Richard C. Longworth, *Caught in the Middle: America's Heartland in the Age of Globalism*, 1st ed. (New York: Bloomsbury USA, December 26, 2007).

2. Richard Longworth, in discussion with the author, February 2, 2016.

3. Ibid.

4. Robert Jones, in discussion with the author, August 11, 2016.

5. Ibid.

6. Jonathan Haidt, *The Righteous Mind: Why Good People Are Divided by Politics and Religion* (repr.; Vintage, February 12, 2013).

7. Ibid., p. 333.

8. "NBC News/Wall Street Journal Survey, Study #16804, September 16–19, 2016," *Wall Street Journal*, September 2016, http://www.wsj.com/public/resources/documents/16804NBCWSJSeptemberPoll9212016.pdf (accessed September 30, 2016), p. 18.

9. Ibid.

10. "As Election Nears, Voters Divided over Democracy and 'Respect,'" Pew Research Center, October 27, 2016, http://www.people-press.org/2016/10/27/6-views-of-domestic-issues-race-immigration-health-care-abortion-supreme-court/ (accessed October 30, 2016).

11. Michael Lind, "This Is What the Future of American Politics Looks Like: This Year, We're Seeing the End of a Partisan Realignment, and the Beginning of a Policy One—and US Politics Is about to Change Big-Time," *Politico*, May 22, 2016, http://www.politico.com/magazine/story/2016/05/2016-election-realignment-partisan-political-party-policy-democrats-republicans-politics-213909 (accessed September 25, 2016).

12. Ibid.

13. Jeffry Bartash, "A Changing America: US More Diverse Than Ever, Millennials Exceed Boomers," *MarketWatch*, June 25, 2015, http://www.marketwatch.com/story/a -changing-america-us-more-diverse-than-ever-millennials-exceed-boomers-2015-06-25 (accessed December 14, 2016).

14. Jonathan Haidt, "When and Why Nationalism Beats Globalism: And How Moral Psychology Can Help Explain and Reduce Tensions between the Two," *American Interest*, July 10, 2016, http://www.the-american-interest.com/2016/07/10/when-and-why -nationalism-beats-globalism/ (accessed September 23, 2016).

15. Ibid.

16. "Pew Religious Landscape Study," Pew Research Center, Religion & Public Life, http://www.pewforum.org/religious-landscape-study/ (accessed September 23, 2016).

17. Brian A. Reaves, "Census of State and Local Law Enforcement Agencies, 2008," bulletin, US Department of Justice, Office of Justice Programs, Bureau of Justice Statistics, July 2011, http://www.bjs.gov/content/pub/pdf/csllea08.pdf (accessed September 23, 2016).

18. "US Foreign-Born Population Trends," Pew Research Center, Hispanic Trends, September 28, 2015, http://www.pewhispanic.org/2015/09/28/chapter-5-u-s-foreign-born -population-trends/ (accessed September 23, 2016).

19. Adrian Walker, "For Immigrants, a Sigh of Relief," *Boston Globe*, June 16, 2012, https://www.bostonglobe.com/metro/2012/06/16/for-immigrants-sigh-relief/ AGRuRHSuc2o4xP80grxQYL/story.html (accessed September 22, 2016).

20. David Montgomery, "Rep. Luis Gutierrez Fights to Put Human Face on the Immigration Reform Struggle," *Washington Post*, May 8, 2009, http://www.washington post.com/wp-dyn/content/article/2009/05/07/AR2009050704170.html (accessed September 23, 2016).

21. "Pelosi Tells Illegal Immigrants That Work Site Raids Are Un-American," Fox News, March 18, 2009, http://www.foxnews.com/politics/2009/03/18/pelosi-tells-illegal -immigrants-work-site-raids-american.html (accessed September 23, 2016).

22. Brenda Gazzar, "Immigration Reform Activist Robert Gittelson of Tarzana Dead at 54," *Los Angeles Daily News*, August 16, 2014, http://www.dailynews.com/article/LA/ 20140816/NEWS/140819569 (accessed September 24, 2016).

23. Luis Gutierrez, in discussion with the author, March 22, 2016.

24. Ibid.

25. Serena Marshall, "Obama Has Deported More People Than Any Other President," ABC News, August 29, 2016, http://abcnews.go.com/Politics/obamas -deportation-policy-numbers/story?id=41715661 (accessed December 14, 2016).

26. Gutierrez, in discussion with the author.

27. Daniel Stid, "Is Transpartisanship the New Bipartisanship?" Hewlett Foundation

Blog, May 21, 2014, http://www.hewlett.org/blog/posts/transpartisanship-new -bipartisanship (accessed September 22, 2016).

28. Ibid.

29. Robert Jones, in discussion with the author, August 11, 2016.

30. Deepak Barghava, in discussion with the author, October 26, 2016.

31. Ibid.

32. Ibid.

33. Adrian Carrasquillo, "Are You Ready for the Big Debate Immigration Clash between Trump and Clinton?" *BuzzFeed News*, September 21, 2016, https://www .buzzfeed.com/adriancarrasquillo/are-you-ready-for-the-big-debate-immigration-clash -between-t?utm_term=.nbz1pPMZZ#.vjlm7EoWW (accessed September 22, 2016).

34. Jens Manuel Krogstad, Jeffrey S. Passel, and D'Vera Cohn, "5 Facts about Illegal Immigration in the US," Pew Research Center, November 3, 2016, http://www .pewresearch.org/fact-tank/2016/11/03/5-facts-about-illegal-immigration-in-the-u-s/ (accessed December 14, 2016).

35. Ronald Brownstein, "The Growing Gap between Town and Country: As Trump-Like Views Gain Strength in Rural Areas Internationally, Diverse Urban Centers Push for Acceptance," *Atlantic*, September 22, 2016, http://www.theatlantic.com/international/ archive/2016/09/global-cities-need-immigrants/501059/ (accessed September 22, 2016).

36. Emily Yahr, "Read George W. Bush's Speech at the African American Museum, 13 Years after Signing the Bill to Build It," *Washington Post*, September 24, 2016, https:// www.washingtonpost.com/news/arts-and-entertainment/wp/2016/09/24/read-george-w -bushs-speech-at-the-african-american-museum-13-years-after-signing-the-bill-to- build-it/ (accessed September 28, 2016).

ABOUT THE AUTHOR

A li Noorani is an innovative political strategist and coalition builder. Applying these skills to the contentious issue of immigration, since 2008 Ali has served as executive director of the National Immigration Forum, one of the nation's premiere advocacy organizations, promoting the value of immigrants and immigration.

Born and raised in California as the son of Pakistani immigrants, Ali quickly learned how to forge alliances among people of wide-ranging backgrounds, an experience that has served him well. Though he is based in Washington, DC, Ozy.com wrote, "[Ali] is not your typical Beltway ambassador." His approach and relationships are deeply bipartisan, as he works outside the usual political silos to test new strategies.

To address the social and cultural tensions underneath America's intense immigration debate, Ali strives to meet people where they are, but not leave them there. As Dr. Russell Moore, president of the Ethics & Religious Liberty Commission of the Southern Baptist Convention said, "[Ali] genuinely tries to understand where people are coming from." This makes for days that cross the entire political spectrum as he looks to find new points of consensus.

Ali's writing has appeared in the pages of the *Washington Post*, on CNN.com, in the *Houston Chronicle*, and in the *Miami Herald*, among other publications. His television-news appearances include CNN, Fox News, MSNBC, and PBS *NewsHour*. Humble and affable, Ali has spoken to audiences across the country.

Ali is a graduate of the University of California at Berkeley, and he has a master's degree in public health from Boston University. He is a lifetime member of the Council on Foreign Relations.

While *There Goes the Neighborhood* is Ali's first book, he hopes this provides an on-ramp to a career in fashion writing. Given his dubious sartorial taste, he is deeply misinformed.

INDEX